'Cadjan – Kiduhu'

'Cadjan – Kiduhu'

Global Perspectives on Youth Work

Edited by

Brian Belton

SENSE PUBLISHERS
ROTTERDAM / BOSTON / TAIPEI

A C.I.P. record for this book is available from the Library of Congress.

ISBN 978-94-6209-765-0 (paperback)
ISBN 978-94-6209-766-7 (hardback)
ISBN 978-94-6209-767-4 (e-book)

Published by: Sense Publishers,
P.O. Box 21858, 3001 AW Rotterdam, The Netherlands
https://www.sensepublishers.com/

Printed on acid-free paper

TABLE OF CONTENTS

PRACTICE

FOREWORD

When Brian first asked me to write a foreword to this book, I was slightly apprehensive – had I become so removed from youth work practice to be able to do the book justice? It didn't take long to connect back into the breadth of issues and challenges that I have faced and experienced over the years as a volunteer, part-time youth worker, full-time youth worker; youth work trainer, youth officer and service director.

I worked with Brian many years ago in Islington and had the professional privilege to be his youth officer. My overriding memory of Brian was a worker who thought deeply about his work and 'challenged' those around him in relation to what they were looking for and how he could facilitate it. It was a period where 'personal empowerment' of young people was being strongly espoused, but only the most skilled staff could make real. Brian challenged the young people in his project and his approach and thoughts about the work challenged me also and made me a better officer, thinking through far more about what we were trying to achieve and why.

And so to this book; Brian has brought together a set of writings which maintain this approach, connecting with the reader and provoking thought, reflection and challenge, whilst celebrating the contribution of great youth work and youth workers.

The book draws experiences from across the world and is a book for our times. These experiences will resonate with readers describing not just the 'youth work journey' but, critically, the cultural context of the work in different areas. Understanding better the position of young people in different cultural contexts and traditions is essential to delivering services today – the world is a much smaller place with mobility rarely experienced before. Services across the UK are working with a great diversity of cultures, languages and traditions and how we develop services that are young people-focused, understanding both history and current context, is at the heart of what our youth services should be about.

Nearly 30 years ago, I was a specialist youth officer for recruitment and training of black and ethnic minority workers for the ILEA and I can recall my initial well-meaning, but somewhat naïve, approaches to engaging different communities about their perceptions of youth work and how we could encourage young people to consider this as a legitimate career and achieve a 'more representative workforce'. I soon realised both the importance and limitations of working through 'community leaders' and recognised how direct engagement with young people was key to supporting their aspirations. Although good progress was made, the approach would founder today. This book illustrates a variety of political and historical contexts and experiences faced by youth workers and young people and helps to challenge thinking and assumptions, requiring more inclusive approaches and challenging the mainstream to change and adapt. Therefore, the concept of a 'representative workforce' needs refining. Yes, we need a more diverse workforce but the idea that the workforce can accurately reflect the experiences of its population is not sustainable as a fixed goal. The diversity and mobility of the population requires a diverse workforce able to work effectively and empathetically with any young people that 'walk through or are outside the door'. Our workers need to represent a diversity of learning and experience rather than a formulaic representation as in previous times – this is now the day job.

The book explores and describes the heart of youth work practice – the nature of relationships and engagement between youth worker and young people and how these develop in the wider social and political context. Youth workers have high community profile but little status in our education hierarchies – all status is hard earned, based on the quality of their relationships and evidence of the difference they make.

So to the evidence, this is described in relation to demonstrating the need for funding but it is not just about that. Our most skilled youth workers have a strong instinct and insight on what makes a difference but they can no longer afford to assert this without evidence – we are in an acutely difficult time financially and need to get wise to the most efficient ways of recording impact. Reference is made to statistics and 'the numbers game'. Statistics don't provide answers but they do help to ask questions. We need to combine the qualitative with the quantitative and use this to help make balanced judgements about our work and decisions about priorities and resources. It is just as much about how youth workers decide to use their time as how decisions are made by funders. It is neither a science nor an art but a combination of the two.

This book describes and emphasises the importance of work being directly led by young people. Successfully engaging young people in co-production – planning and delivering services – should be our first reference point when funding youth work, thus breaking traditional funding arrangements, where adult-led organisations that had funding for many years have 'hung on for dear life' and are now seeing the world pass them by.

Helping young people to find a voice and engage in the democratic decision-making processes is explored here and these are essential challenges to youth workers and decision makers. Even the most effective of engagement systems has to reflect on whether young people are being 'incorporated' in adult decision-making. Providing the 'facts and figures'; the evidence which points in a clear direction – the 'Wednesbury Reasonable' principle that local authorities have to demonstrate when decisions are challenged – can be constructed in ways which make it difficult for young people to disagree with the adult conclusions. Although consensus is no bad thing, sometimes some 'less logical' youthful rebellion is needed – it may be less comfortable but provides an edge to decision making – '*We don't care about the logic, your statutory duties; the financial implications; the conflicting priorities – we just want good youth provision*'.

This book explores the role of youth worker in 'supporting learning' and the attempts to support its legitimacy by describing it as 'informal education'. But what is the link between what youth workers do and 'formal education'? Youth workers aren't on the same 'firm ground' as teachers who have the school or classroom with clear institutional structures and norms; a hierarchy of support; a national curriculum; subject expertise etc. But that firm ground can also limit and stifle so the great teachers work within those structures and bring to the classroom those key characteristics inherent in the best youth work: reflection; discernment; trust; and relationships that enthuse and challenge young people to think laterally, grow intellectually and emotionally. To do this, they need to take risks – things that youth workers have to do to survive any day. So it is as much understanding how 'formal educators' can learn from the so-called 'informal educators' and how young people have learning opportunities from both. Reference is made to youth workers leaving the profession and moving on to becoming teachers or social workers. Whilst regrettable in some ways, it's a reflection of the economic realities of pursuing a full-time career in a profession under severe pressure financially. But whichever course youth workers take, the qualities they take with them can only enhance their chosen direction.

This book describes the changing demands on youth workers in times of austerity – are they becoming more 'agents of the state' or, indeed, have they always been? This is tricky ground – youth workers do not have the luxury of statutory structures and funding. They have to show resilience and flexibility to move with the 'prevailing political priorities' with the knowledge that these change and shift, whilst holding onto the underlying nature of their relationships with young people. This is particularly important as youth work resources are steered more towards targeted youth work. As eloquently described in a number of contexts in the book, we need to shift our thinking about youth workers from working with young people who are 'the problem' with deficits, to working with young people who are 'the future' with potential – that is the investment required.

So, what is this skill that youth workers bring – is it just a survival tactic or more a *'conscious pragmatism'* that combines their analysis of the social and political context, their core values and making a practical difference in real life situations? The book sets out a huge diversity of work described as youth work but, critically, the underlying characteristics of 'what holds it together'. Brian provides some very practical definitions and describes those core values in the context of political and economic reality.

This is what Brian brought to his youth work practice – not just 'academic navel gazing' ending up in corners of contradiction and unable to move; rather a 'heads-up, eyes open' reflective, cerebral and practical understanding of the work, thus enabling young people and those around him to think and choose different paths with confidence.

I recommend this book to challenge you to do the same.

Thanos Morphitis O.B.E.
Director of Strategy and Commissioning for Islington Children's Services

BRIAN BELTON

INTRODUCTION

'Cadjan' is a Sinhala word, which refers to palm leaves matted or plaited together to form a thatch or roof of many small dwellings and other buildings in Sri Lanka. This is where 'Nest', the charity that will benefit from the royalties of this book, is located (please see details below). 'Kiduhu' is the Tamil equivalent. This title for our book was chosen because it exemplifies the nature of the pages that follow. Writers, practitioners and scholars from all over the planet, have put together their ideas, perspectives and hopes for and about work with young people, either in their context or from their context. From this weaving together of relatively heterogeneous elements, the hope is that you, the reader, will get the impression of something of the homogenous whole that youth work might be understood to be. We, like youth work, are no one thing, but collectively, perhaps like youth work internationally, we have a common purpose that connects and joins us. We hope you will identify and perhaps become part of this on or after reading what we have offered.

CORE RELATION

The point of this book is not to show or say what youth work is. Given the range of voices, approaches, views and functions of the contributors how could we claim that youth work might be one, or any single, consistent or constant something over or between contexts, throughout time? In places we do try to give a general idea of the mutable shape and motivation of practice. For instance, in the first chapter I do offer a 'place to stand' (for now, for a moment), but the hope is that this will be developed and altered rather than adhered to in any regimented way; such ossification of youth work would be a contradiction in terms and practice – ours is an evolutionary project – if youth work is anything, unfailingly it is a 'growth business'. Although it is understandable, if one is confined to any one context, to believe it is or has definitively been this or that fundamentally or primarily. Part of the rationale that has bloomed out of the joint creation of this book is to present different practice and theoretical milieus. This might go some way to promoting the understanding that to lock down youth work in notional stasis, or bolt it into a 'carceral archipelago' of a conventional or acceptable trajectory would be the antithesis of practice, which would effectively destroy it as youth work. For all this, not a few writers have effectively touted to achieve just this, or perhaps identified (put a flag in) what they see (or want to be) the 'core' of youth work practice.

xi

But youth work isn't an apple. A global and historical perspective of youth work clearly shows it to be a relentlessly developing range of responses to a persistently moving, growing and shifting range of phenomena, issues and directions presented by and to societies and the young people of and in those societies. Here we present a set of responses in the face of and from within that shifting field that can generically be called 'youth work; we do this in this time, from many places and a diversity of identity, but we all identify what we have presented and ourselves professionally and/or academically with what we agree to be youth work.

This said, looking for or trying to cobble together a central theory or fulcrum of practice is a draw; there is security in being able to say 'that is this' – but security is not the goal – curiosity, discovery and learning are chancy pursuits, that's what makes them exciting. The hope for security is an anathema in this adventure. However, there is the illusion of status in being 'at the core'; one can identify oneself as an 'expert', part of an elite or priesthood of sorts, inhabiting the 'inner sanctum' of professional knowledge. One can see this as being attractive to the insecure; the first task of any group that craves protection is to set up a cabal, cult or clique; a freemasonry of 'fellows'. But the cult or closed shop the expert inhabits is a contradiction in terms of intellectual activity and logically also with regard to inclusionary practice.

Some years ago I was speaking at a YMCA conference, part of which was devoted to 'identifying the core' of the movement. I think I upset a few colleagues by pointing out that the identification of an 'included' group (those who are at or in tune with the core) excludes others (if everyone is at the core there is no core of course). I'm not sure how a Christian or an 'association', or any supposedly open or inclusionary faith, discipline or organisation can rationally go about erecting barriers that effectively create a peripheral population or marginal groups (the 'excluded'). One popular response was variations on 'We'll lose all the Christian's'. Well, God moves in mysterious (unexpected) ways (which doesn't feel very secure does it; what'll she do next? God knows!)

When I was a boy my grandmother told me that when she was a girl, as a Gypsy, she and her family were not allowed in the Church when it was full; they were the ones that had to stand outside to listen to the sermons etc. One day, it was pouring with rain and she was soaking. She told me she asked God, 'Why don't they let us in the Church?' She said God replied to her, saying, 'Don't worry about it; they won't let me in either'.

The search for central principles, set in stone, to create a 'community of practice' is redolent of the above. The moment one sets the parameters of a community a distinct group of the included are recognised, but at the same time this identifies those excluded from (not of) that community. The higher the walls, the less permeable the boundaries of any given community, the more difficult it is for people or knowledge of others or the world to get in or out. This is why the more impermeable a community is (the more 'specialist' it becomes) the more it turns into the locale of prejudice and discrimination ('we' are like this, so we are 'in', they are like 'that' so they are 'out'). I would hope we might think of youth work, its development and practice, more in the vein of an idealised incarnation of the Islamic concept of 'Ummah'; encompassing the potential of the inclusion of all.

ACCIDENTAL INTERNATIONAL PRACTITIONER

What I have found, as an accidental international practitioner, is what makes youth work exciting and dynamic is that belongs to nobody because it belongs to everybody. Youth work is not what one person says it is, youth work is what all youth workers do. I love this about youth work; it is defiant in the face of categorisation – it makes fools of the academically pompous and those who believe in their own power over the shape and direction of general practice. You might not agree with this, this time next year I might not agree with it, but in the words of Eldridge Cleaver, former Head of the International Section of the Black Panther Party, 'Too much agreement kills the chat'.

It is in the spirit of the above ideas that this book is presented. It was thought important that the editorial hand should pass lightly over the contributions. This allows free play to individual styles in order that particular ideas and descriptions of situations are put over as much as possible (given that most of the material has been written in a second language). We have attempted to bring together a mix of responses from academic enquiry, to musing on the nature of practice and overviews of the development and delivery of youth work; theory, rhetoric, explanation and polemic (amongst other considerations) inhabit the streets and alleyways of this work, as does joy, scepticism and curiosity. Think Brueghel's 'Children's Games' and/or the 'Conviviality' of Illich; his 'eutrapelia' ('graceful playfulness').

While there has been a subtle attempt to suggest order, the reader looking for continuity of structure might be forearmed in the knowledge that there has been an attempt not to impose a particular regime of presentation. However, while this might, reading individual chapters, appear to be much the same in terms of content, taking the book as a whole one might come to a quite different conclusion. One of the things youth workers find out pretty swiftly at the start of their careers is that people are inherently pattern makers; be there no form, we find an order. This might be understood as the 'ground floor' of 'world making'.

CHAPTERS

The book has been divided into three sections; Theory, Organisation and Practice. This division is not definitive, as many of chapters overlap in terms of focus and ideas. However, we have chosen to gather the chapters under these headings for the casual use and convenience of the reader.

The section on 'Theory' tends to be made up of material expressing (in the main) outlooks and ideas about practice, consideration of current understanding and delivery but also the potential for development and adaptation of the same.

The material clustered under the heading 'Organisation' concentrates on how work is organised in various national and regional environments, its contextual character and direction. However, as you will see from the opening chapter of this part of the book, to write about context can and does evoke aspects of response similar to those made in the first part of the book.

The final part of the book, 'Practice' leans toward a focus to the experience of face-to-face work. This provides something of a collective voice from the point of delivery of practice, although once more, the reader will gather this is not a total or ridged demarcation. Many, perhaps all of us, would agree that such an ambition, to divorce practice from the development of theory and the context of delivery, is not possible in an intellectual sense or perhaps desirable from any perspective; implementation of practice in the development of theory.

THEORY

In *Professionalising Youth Work: A Global Perspective – Criteria for Professional Youth Work; Its Principles and Values* Brian Belton provides an overview and development of more than five years work in conjunction of the Commonwealth Youth Programme in the South East Asian context. The task was to define youth work as a professional practice.

The chapter is the product and advancement of debate, deliberation and research in Malaysia, Bangladesh and Sri Lanka. Most of the conclusions presented by Brian were also informed by responses from the Maldives, India and Pakistan, incorporating views from across youth work and related sectors, calling on hundreds of professionals, volunteers, academics, NGO representatives, state officials and other stake holders. The collaboration resulted in policy developments across the region, and the start of a professional association in Sri Lanka.

Professionalism here is not characterised by salary, personal status or employment. The aim of this collaborative enterprise was to raise the consciousness of the skills, attitudes and knowledge needed to provide best practice, in order to establish youth work standards requisite to particular contexts and to some extent across contexts. Professionalism, in terms of this chapter might be thought of as an ethical and moral imperative, protective of young people, but also a means to raise, maintain and continually improve delivery of services.

The original findings, first framed in 2012, have been reviewed and built on via subsequent experience, new information and the continued sharing of perspectives. Language has thus been adapted; trajectory modified and content reviewed and elaborated on to provide a starting place for thinking about the nature and purpose of youth work over a global horizon. The ambition is not to say 'this is all things to all people' but to offer something to all people, to use, adapt, build on, deploy or reject. It is our starting place, a base camp from which a journey might start.

Hip Hop is Dead! Youth work in a state of decline? This is the question Curtis Worrell addresses, highlighting the comparisons between the development and direction of youth work and hip-hop culture. Deploying revealing metaphor, phraseology and descriptive simile, Curtis sets out a position that helps expand on and illuminate the character of a unique youth movement/culture. However, in the process of making his analysis he provides a critical perspective of the past, future and current youth work, all the time allowing his own practice and client experience to guide and temper his position.

The chapter exposes how the history of youth work is often viewed through a 'rose-tinted magnifying glass', that sometimes feels like a sort of reverse crystal ball, looking back to a days when the state was (supposedly) some sort of benign supplier of 'good things' for young people for the sake of it (ostensibly being concerned with embedding a largely unelaborated social, group and individual morality). It goes on to provide a reorientation of this illusion, facilitating the reader's understanding that youth work is not, and has hardly been, since its inception as a national, non-secular service, with codified practice and qualification, undertaken for its own sake or for detached ethical reasons, allied to a cross societal and cultural shared idea of the 'common good'.

Implicating an aspect of popular culture, which is also for Curtis an abiding interest and a passion (as it is for many youth workers and young people) the work offers both a personal and a social interpretation, so heightening potential and actual insight.

Dana Fusco looks at *The Social Architecture of Youth Work Practice*, articulating the relational space for transformative work with young people, a space that good practitioners seem to know well, more by intuitive action than word. The model builds from the everyday lived experiences of youth workers, and others who work with young people, as well as from intellectual discourses in youth work and youth studies, and its cousin fields around the world. In this chapter, the author asks: *What is the space that youth work practice occupies? How is it created and why? Finally, what are the challenges to creating this social architecture today and what can be done so that transformative spaces with and by young people remain possible?*

Hans Skott-Myhre, *Building a New Common: Youth Work and the Question of Transitional Institutions of Care*, argues that the youth work is a field of endeavour founded on care. The question of how to care, who receives care, how to deliver care, and what is care, however, is neither simple nor uncontested. For many, if not most of us, caring and care are synonymous. However, caring about someone and caring for him or her are not necessarily directly related. Both the affective relation of caring for someone and the practices associated with that sense of caring are both quite complicated.

In youth work, both the feeling of caring and the practices associated with and generated by such feelings are often conceived of as acts and affects centered within and between individuals. That is to say that I, as an individual feel a sense of caring within myself for another individual and, on the basis of those feelings, interact with the other in a caring manner.

Brian Belton in *Compassion and the 'Colonial Mentality'* states that:

> The worst thing about youth facilities is that they are 'youth' facilities. As a youth, the last place I or anyone I knew wanted to go was a place designed for 'youth'.

He goes on to ask how much room there is to make what there is for youth what youth want, arguing that it is not surprising that as a society, with the colonisation era being historically a comparatively recent period, wherein most of our institutions (education, health, law etc) were formed, the echo of the culture of colonisation and its controlling ethos continues to resonate; we are quite used to other people setting our social agenda. Within this atmosphere over recent years there has been an on-going discussion across what are broadly referred to as the 'caring professions' about the place of compassion in practice, but at what point does compassion become a form of patronisation; is there something colonial about the ambition to 'share suffering' (the meaning of the word 'compassion')?

In this chapter Brian echoes the position of Richard Sennett (2003) questioning what he sees as degrading forms of compassion that effectively undermine respect for those in need. He argues that mutual respect can create connections across the potential segregations of inequality that are made more profound by effectively seeing some people as relatively pitiful, reliant on the bountiful compassion of those of us who imagine ourselves to be deep wells of this unconditional sentiment.

ORGANISATION

Leadership Training for Youth: A Response to Youth Rebellion? by Harini Amarasuriya examines youth involvement and state responses to three armed insurrections and looks at the way in which the involvement of youth in these uprisings shaped state-led youth development and youth work initiatives.

Hanrini argues that the conceptualisation of 'youth problems' has facilitated an approach to working with young people that locates the source of these 'difficulties' in the personalities and characters of young people, while dismissing and ignoring many of the structural problems of contemporary Sri Lankan society.

For Hanrini this approach glosses over the many structural inequalities in Sri Lankan society, which have affected the life chances and aspirations of youth, while emphasising individual vulnerabilities (it is a perspective that blindly assumes deficit). The reader might question how much the 'rehabilitation' of troublesome youth in Sri Lanka mirrors western responses to young people in terms of ambitions to train, initiate change and educate (for instance, how much might the ethos and purpose of the three week long 'Leadership Attitude and Positive Thinking Development Training' in Sri Lanka resemble the likes of the National Citizenship Service (NCS) in the English context?).

This chapter exemplifies how youth work and forms of so called 'non-formal' education can made to serve the purposes of indoctrination and control. It demonstrates how youth work can be used in attempts to pacify and disempower young people by way of deficit models, responding to understandable reactions and behaviour as if it were unreasoned. In the process this deflects attention away from social issues, defining social unrest as the consequence of a psychological malaise, so effectively justifying programmes of 'treatment' for youth, rather than addressing the social causes of rebellion and collective anguish in the face of state injustice.

In *Current Issues in Youth Work Training in the Major English-Speaking Countries,* Jennifer Brooker puts forward the idea that in essence contemporary youth work today is the same the world over; we work with young people, sometimes during very difficult times in their lives, helping them to become the best versions of who they are. Providing guidance and support in the form of activities, challenges and/or opportunities, in both formal and informal settings, youth workers work within the space where young people find themselves, whether through design or circumstance.

Historically social intervention with young people outside the school context was either educationally or fitness focused. It was provided by well-meaning, untrained individuals or Christian-based organisations such as the YMCA and the Boys and Girls Brigades from the first half of the Nineteenth Century onwards. Formal pre-service training for youth workers began during the Second World War in the United Kingdom and Australia in response to world events. However it was initiated by two very different sectors of the community, education in the United Kingdom and sport and recreation in Australia. In Canada and the United States youth work began within the social welfare system after World War Two, based on a Therapeutic Care model, similar, yet different, to that of Europe at the time.

Today youth work has morphed considerably from the work with young people of almost two hundred years ago. The targeted approach is built around two predominant frameworks in operation globally: positive youth development and therapeutic care. The only consistency to be found in training is its primary focus – training workers to work with young people.

Training and current global frameworks for youth work are not universal and as a result youth workers, who perhaps ought to be able to travel the world to work in their chosen field wherever they find themselves, are usually not recognised as such unless they are in their homeland of training.

This chapter will compare pre-service training for youth workers in various national contexts, looking at the similarities and differences. Jen also considers the impact of this situation on practitioners.

In *Youth Policies in the Nordic Countries,* Helena Helve presents the 'Nordic model', comparing and contrasting the youth policies of Denmark, Finland, Iceland, Norway, Sweden and three areas with home rule; the Faroe Islands, Greenland and the Åland Islands.

Although there are differences in culture, politics and language, the Nordic countries have many ties based on common history. Close to a quarter of a century after the fall of the Soviet Union (1991) the Nordic countries have also built up close connections to Baltic countries Latvia, Lithuania and especially Estonia.

Nordic Youth cooperation is discussed, including Nordic youth policy and youth research organisations. Helena argues that the Nordic youth policy cooperation in future should create the conditions that are able to reflect the differences and similarities in the development of Nordic countries and strengthen and connect youth across the Nordic borders, promoting cross-national cooperation in education, employment, social entrepreneurship and political participation.

The Development and Implementation of Youth Policy in Malta, by Miriam Teuma tells how up until the 1990s, there was no youth policy in Malta although there were education policies, health policies and other related policies that impacted on and influenced the lives of young people.

Prior to the development of distinct youth policy in the 1990s youth work in Malta was almost exclusively the province of the Catholic Church and its voluntary organisations, such as the Society of Christian Doctrine, Catholic Action and the Salesians, together with the British presence, which included organisations such as the Malta Scout Association. However, this tended to be at once paternalistic and directional. It was to a large extent premised on what was deemed 'character forming' in light of Christian morals and mores.

In this chapter Miriam provides an insight into the development of a youth service, the will and organisation that has provided a service contextualised by a modern state in the context of the European Union.

Emina Bužinkić's *Brief on Youth in Contemporary Croatian Society* makes the point that sociologically and politically speaking, Croatian youth have a history of being caught up in political, social and economic crisis, conflict and transitions that need to be understood and considered in terms of the supply and delivery of youth work. The legacy of this experience is deep social trauma and insecurity. This is presents challenges to young people and has a range of effects on the quality of everyday life. Croatian society since its independence has been obliged to deal with huge social differences, economic instability and lack of opportunities and prospects for young people. Emina looks at the development and potential future of youth work from this background.

PRACTICE

Indra Kerha, referring directly to her practice experience, presents a critical deconstruction of some of the assumptions, practice ethics and aims that hold back our work in terms its professional profile and purpose. In *Demanding Lives, Difficult Paths* she confronts the clumsy dichotomies inherent in the contradictory tasks practice at times presents us with. Subtly questioning deficit/colonial models of practice, Indra challenges the over-reliance of reflection as the 'royal road' to developing our response to the challenges and joys of our work. This will of course not win everybody over, particularly those stuck in the groove of the reflection mantras that ring around our work. However her enquiry and spirit of disputation stays true to the best traditions of the best of youth work as well as the professional commitment to scrutinise practice.

Turning the tables in the 'change' debate, Indra looks at our own need to change (respond) to the various and changing needs of your clients. She leads the reader to question, whether in the last analysis it is a moot point how much anyone can change the position or predisposition of another person; sometimes professionals succeed in getting people to look as if they have changed, but as Indra indicates, there is no way of knowing if what we perceived to be change is in fact an alteration in personal trajectory, an act, or a figment of our own imagination secured by our need to see what we wish to see.

Indra helps the reader to understand that it is likely that the only change we can be close to being sure of, or might be in control of, are the changes we make in our own approach, attitudes and responses. This is probably as true for our clients as it is for ourselves. But perhaps it is only our egos that allow us to believe that the root of change in others lies in our activity.

Pilgrim. Barnaul, Russia is a short reflection on the nature and impact of practice on both youth workers and young people. Sofya Gileva reflects on how informal learning, through creative activity, small group work, and the provision of testing situations can ignite debate and discussion, that can amount to life enhancing/changing experiences. She relates to how the sharing feelings and the values of things of importance can be a means to understanding of the self and others.

The German YMCA in Tension between Institutionalisation and Movement, written by Günter Lücking reflects on how the traditions of a particular realm of youth work can underpin but also retard development of practice and delivery. He ponders how we can draw on past practice and meld the best of this with the wants and needs of contemporary youth to provide appropriate and fulfilling services.

Anna Mirga writes about *Youth Engagement in the Gitano Associative movement in Catalonia and Emerging "Youthscapes".* According to Anna, ethnic mobilisation is a process in which groups organise around aspects of ethnic identity for collective reasons. This differs from political mobilisation in that it invokes elements of ethnic identity, but shares much the same processes which become vehicles conveying representation and collective action.

For Anna, the organisations of civil society (especially as NGOs) have taken much of the initiative for the ethnic mobilisation of Roma/Gitano communities. This means of effecting Roma rights can be seen as failure of political integration of Roma/Gitano representatives in formal politics but can also be understood through the deliberative democracy discourse and the means for strengthening of democratic functioning of the State.

The political representation through NGOs rather than through mainstream politics, as a form of civic participation, has become common not only among the Gitano population but the wider Spanish society. The role of young people has been significant and as such they have been recognised as a major force in social movements.

Following these considerations this chapter looks at how these developments might translate into the reality of the Gitano ethnic mobilisation, and more specifically questions the role of Gitano young people in the ethnic mobilisation.

NEST SRI LANKA

As stated above, any proceeds from this book will be donated to Nest, Sri Lanka. In 1984 Sally Hulugalle started Nest with a friend, Kamini de Soysa.

Nest works to strengthen families and individuals to cope when a crisis occurs so that their kith and kin may remain in their home and not be abandoned to institutionalisation. The organisation also trains Health Workers to live and work within the community. This work started after Sally and Kamini visited the long stay unit of the mental hospital Mulleriyawa where they found over a thousand women virtually incarcerated for life, and subject to enormous suffering.

The Aims and Objectives of Nest

- To promote happiness (in families, individuals and the environment).
- To lift the yoke of labelling, institutionalisation and stigmatisation.
- To promote understanding in the areas of mental health and wellbeing.
- To promote justice and freedom.
- To help women, children, families and individuals to cope within their communities.
- To encourage development in public services and the environment.

Nest relies on public, individual and programme funding/donations to do the work of the organisation. It is non-profit making and does not charge for its services.

Nest promotes the wellbeing of those who are marginalised for reasons such as being considered mentally ill or infected with the HIV virus. Nest uncompromisingly supports and champions the rights of those who are victimised, including women and children and others vulnerable to abuse or exploitation.

Training

Community Health Workers take part in an on-going training programme at the Gladys School of Community Health Work and Development, which is situated adjacent to Kåre House (Gampaha District). All trainees receive free accommodation, transport and food on duty. Trainees are posted to different parts of Sri Lanka where Nest works.

The Nest Community Health Centre

The Ududumbara (Kandy district) and Kåre House Centres are run in such a way that families and individuals can stay overnight for specialist clinics and appointments. Community members can drop in at any time. Education for Health is promoted through information and discussions; Workshops on Mental Health and HIV and AIDS issues; Awareness Programmes; Library; classes on basic livelihood skills and Computers; Home and Organic Gardening; First Aid; Language and Cookery classes are available. Nest Centres are like any other house on the road and Community Health Workers live and work from them. They travel by foot, motorcycle, trishaw and public Bus. A playgroup for children under five years of age is provided.

Promotion of Well Being

Nest gives priority to the promotion of mental wellbeing and one of the principal means of achieving it is by its facilitation of the return of those institutionalised to their homes and communities, and working to minimise the stigma attached to such illnesses.

Another feature special to Nest is that it does not go to a community with a plan already drawn up. Nest approaches the community with an open mind and has a framework inspired by its mission statement within which it will operate;

– To enable individuals to establish necessary community links in order to access services and support.
– To strengthen local services in order to strengthen communities' coping systems.
– To influence national and local policy in order to ensure that communities are provided with effective and respectful services.

The Gladys School of Community Health Work and Development was born of a desire to extend the frontiers of community work and development, including the much neglected aspect of improving mental wellbeing.

You can find out more about (and make a further donation to) Nest on http://www.nestsrilanka.org/

ABOUT THE AUTHORS

Harini Amarasuriya is currently a senior lecturer at the Department of Social Studies, Open University of Sri Lanka. She completed her PhD in Social Anthropology from the University of Edinburgh. Her dissertation work explored the nexus between the state, development policy and practice within the bureaucracy in Sri Lanka. She is active in the development sector as a researcher and practitioner and worked for several years as a child protection and psychosocial practitioner prior to joining the Open University, Sri Lanka.

Harini's research interests include children and youth issues, globalisation and development, micro-politics and the state. Her recent publications include: *NGOs, The State and 'Cultural Values: Imagining the Global in Sri Lanka,* (2012) with Jonathan Spencer, *Early Marriage and Statutory Rape in Selected Districts in Sri Lanka,* (2012) with Savitri Goonesekere, *Discrimination and Social Exclusion of Youth in Sri Lanka,* 2010 and *Why Aren't We Empowered Uet? Assumptions and Silences Surrounding Women, Gender and Development in Sri Lanka* (2010) with Asha Abeysekera.

Brian Belton PhD comes from an East London Gypsy family and entered youth work in the early 1970s docklands area where he was born and brought up. While working in youth work related situations around the world, including Israel, the Falkland Islands, Germany, the USA, Thailand, Hong Kong, Zambia, South Africa, China and Canada, Brian's interest in identity and ethnicity flourished and today he is an activist and researcher of Roma issues in Europe and an internationally recognised authority on Gypsy Ethnicity, having written widely on that subject, delivering papers most recently in the USA, Austria, Greece, Sweden and Slovenia as well as around the UK. In 2013 he started a three-year research programme focusing on the social exclusion of Roma with partners in Spain, Germany and Turkey.

Currently, a Senior Lecture at the YMCA George Williams College, traditionally one of the biggest trainers of youth and community workers in the UK, Brian has just completed involvement with developing professional practice in youth work across South Asia (working in situ in Bangladesh, Sri Lanka and Malaysia). He recently organised and delivered youth work training in Iceland, which drew participants from 15 European countries (speaking 13 different languages). At the time of writing he is involved in developing partnerships developing detached and outreach youth work with practitioners in Holland, Romania, England and Malta.

Having written close to 80 books and numerous articles and learned papers, spoken regularly at conferences, on radio and TV, throughout the UK and beyond, Brian is a recognised and respected academic and writer in the field of professional youth and community work and informal education.

Jennifer Brooker (MYHEM, MEd, ND) has been an educator for almost 30 years, working in various communities throughout Australia and around the world, at all levels of education. Currently the Youth Work Coordinator at the Royal Melbourne Institute of Technology (RMIT) University, Melbourne, she is the time of writing undertaking research focused around improving youth work training in Australia, the focus of her PhD study, which is a comparative and historic study of youth work in Australia, Canada, New Zealand, the United Kingdom and the United States. This will be extended to mapping youth work training offered around the world and the creation of an international youth work passport.

Jen coordinates various youth work qualifications for both student and industry groups. She has also been involved in various youth projects around the world with numerous partners.

Emina Bužinkić. Emina lives and works in Zagreb, Croatia and occasionally in Morocco. She is employed at 'Documenta – Centre for Dealing with the Past' as a Programme Coordinator. She is also coordinator of activities related to the advocacy of reparations of civilian war victims and monitoring of war crime trials.

Since 2002 Emina has been involved in the work of the Croatian Youth Network, formally as President and Secretary General. She is Project Co-ordinator at the Centre for Peace Studies. For the last eight years she has been participating in the work of the Governmental Council for the Civil Society Development and the Governmental Youth Council. She is a member of the National Committee for Human Rights and Democratic Citizenship Education. Over the last three years Emina has been a member of the Council of the President of the Republic of Croatia for Social Justice.

Active in the field of human rights, Emina has been engaged in advocating civic education and also implementing training for young people in peace building and dealing with the past and human rights issues and is Director of the Educational Programme Youth Studies in Croatia. Her many publications include *Dealing with the Past – Handbook for Civil Society Organisations* and *Civilian War Victims in Croatia.*

Emina has MA in Political Science (public policy, management and development) from the University of Zagreb and has completed a number of non-formal educational programmes such as Peace Studies and the Academy for Political Development as well as vocational education in the study of Arabic language and political culture of North African countries.

Dana Fusco is a professor at the City University of New York, York College (Jamaica, NY, USA). She has over 20 years of experience in the fields of youth work and education. For the past several years, her focus has been on professional education and building the discipline of youth work.

In 2012–2013, Dana served as the Howland Endowed Chair at the University of Minnesota where she studied youth work education. She has authored dozens of articles on youth work and the recent volume, Advancing Youth Work: Current Trends, Critical Question. Dana has worked with young people in a variety of school and community settings, and continues to practice youth work in the contexts in which she lives, works, and plays. You can follow Dana on Twitter (@YouthWorkAdv) or on Facebook (AdvancingYouthWork).

Sofya Gileva: YMCA. The 'alma mater'. An autobiographical essay would be simply boring, so I decided to tell you about the highlight of my life. The YMCA. I got acquainted with YMCA five years ago, when I got to work in the YMCA camp, which is situated in my native city. Everything was different to what I was used to before – people were different, the way they talked, argued, explained, lived, even smiled. It was strangely attractive, because the atmosphere they built around them was inviting and worth living in. The main thing what appealed to me was that they cared. By then I have seen a lot of indifference in my life.

Then I got to know what YMCA was. It is the 'Young Man's Christian Association', which started in 1844. Christian might have sounded weird to my atheistic ear, but I did not care. At the beginning it was hard to understand what the YMCA does and how it functions, because I was overloaded with history. The first summer with YMCA brought me to a very important meeting held in Barnaul. There I was told one defining phrase, which I have been using for five years to tell what YMCA is about:

> YMCA is aimed at making the world a better place. Locally it does what the community needs, doing camps or planting corn, either one is necessary and helps people to improve their life.

No more is needed to tell about the activity of the YMCA.

My first travelling experience started in 2010. I went to Germany for Youth Workers Teen Camp. The tears come to my eyes when I am thinking about it. To my mind, no one outside the YMCA could ever experience atmosphere like this. That is when I understood the value of the 'C word' ('Christian') in YMCA. It is when you understand that means we are all brothers and sisters, it is when you see people say the Lord's Prayer simultaneously in more than 10 different languages and you are thrilled, it is when people you have never known before are happy to see you, it is when you get to know people from different countries and when you see them again in two, three, four years – it feels like family. And most importantly it is when you understand you can change the world.

After that, I took a leave from the Y and went to live in Germany for a year. It was an unforgettable experience, but let us come back to my YMCA story. Later on, I started travelling even more; I have been to three events in half a year – I have been to Germany, Czech Republic, Iceland and Poland, and I can say that what I am involved in is a huge diverse movement, one which aims for the empowerment of young people, who can make the world a better place. For the first time in my life I felt empowered, I felt like I can make a difference, I felt like I can do something significant.

The YMCA is my "alma mater", my university gave me academic knowledge, but the YMCA gave me experience, cleared out my vision, taught me values, and filled me with ambitions, because it has been giving me opportunities and space to grow. Looking back I am proud to say I learned loads; I am a changed person; I am, every day, a better person than I was yesterday. I am self-developing every hour of my life; I am the change YMCA wants to see in people. And after all, it is essential that I continue this change. My train has gained speed and it ain't halting, I am on top of my life, making a change every day and every hour. I am 22. Can you imagine what's coming in the future?

Helena Helve PhD is Professor Emerita from the School of Social Sciences and Humanities at Tampere University and Adjunct Professor of Sociology and Comparative Religion at Helsinki University, Finland. She has been professor for the M.A. European Youth Studies Curriculum Development Project (2009–2011) and the Nordic Youth Research Coordinator (1998–2003), Vice president of EASR (2000–2007), President of the ISA RC 34 Youth Sociology (2002–2006) and President of the Finnish Youth Research Society (1992–2005).

Helena has directed several international and national research projects. Her publications include: *Social Inclusion of Youth on the Margins of Society: Policy Review of Research Results* (with D. Kutsar, 2012); and coedited books *Youth and Work Transitions in Changing Landscapes* (with K. Evans, 2013); *Youth and Social Capital* (with J. Bynner, 2007) and *Contemporary Youth Research: Local Expressions and Global Connections* (with G. Holm, 2005).

Indra Khera was born in 1984 in West London to a Panjabi human rights activist and an Australian hippy. She began her career in youth work in 2005 as a volunteer with New Horizon Youth Centre in Kings Cross, London and went on to work as a Housing Support Officer with young mothers. Additionally, she facilitated music production and DJ workshops at numerous youth clubs and later secured a job with Raw Sounds where she worked with young people and adults experiencing mental health problems.

Indra conducted music sessions within in-patient settings, including acute, intensive care, early intervention and medium secure forensic units, as well as various recording studios throughout London. In 2012, she graduated with first-class honours in BA Youth & Community Development at Canterbury (YMCA George Williams College). It was here that she was inspired by key thinkers such as Fanon, Foucault and R.D. Laing who furthered her understanding of the oppressive dynamics prevalent in the psychiatric field.

She is currently manager at Raw Sounds, mother to a young son, and is completing her MSc in Mental Health Research and Population Studies at the Institute of Psychiatry, Kings College. Whilst she is critical of research methods that are reductionist and disempowering to survivors of psychiatry, she hopes to conduct effective, collaborative and meaningful user-led research with young people experiencing psychosis.

Günter Lücking was born in 1955. He is married to Monika, they have three grown up children. Günter studied Youth and Community Work at the YMCA College Kassel. He completed a study with Gep Frankfurt in public relations and communication management/consultancy. He has worked with local YMCA executive staff at Portsmouth, Waiblingen and Bünde and was the TEN SING professional in the CVJM-Westbund region from 1994 to 2004.

Since 2005 Günter is CVJM-Bundessekretär/YMCA-secretary for the regions of Ostwestfalen-Lippe, Bentheim and Münsterland. He has been active in the programme of the European YMCA and TEN SING Festivals over the last 20 years. Among others he has launched the European YMCA Youth worker camps.

Anna Mirga is PhD candidate in Social and Cultural Anthropology at the Universitat Autònoma de Barcelona (UAB, Spain). She holds an MA in European Integration from UAB and an MA in Comparative Studies of Civilizations from the Jagiellonian University in Cracow (UJ, Poland).

Anna is a Roma rights activist, co-founder of the Roma Educational Association "Harangos" (Poland) and the Roma Youth Association "Ternikalo XXI" (Spain). Both organisations are associated to the European Roma Youth Network 'TernYpe'. She is co-author of the recently published study 'Lost in Action? Evaluating the six years of the Comprehensive Plan for the Gitano Population in Catalonia', coordinated by the Federation of Roma Associations in Catalonia (FAGIC) and EMIGRA Research Group (Universitat Autònoma de Barcelona, Spain) and financed by the Open Society Foundations.

Currently Anna is an Open Society Foundations Roma Initiatives Fellow, conducting a comparative study of Roma associative movements in various countries of Latin America and Europe.

Thanos Morphitis was born and brought up in the London Borough of Islington where he went to school and attended local play and youth centres. He started volunteering in his early teens and started part-time play centre work at 16. He studied Social Policy and Administration at university, going on to become a qualified youth worker, working in the voluntary sector for 10 years. This led on to a series of posts within the Inner London Education Authority (ILEA) as Specialist Youth Officer for Recruitment and Training of Black and Ethnic Minority Youth Workers and then as Deputy Senior Youth Officer for Islington, before moving on to the role of Assistant Chief Education Officer for the Borough following the abolition of the ILEA in 1990.

Thanos leads on the financial strategy and commissioning for schools; early years services; health services for children; play and youth services; services for disabled children; CAMHS; youth safety and crime; and family and parenting support in the London Borough Islington. He plays a lead role in the children's trust, chairing several of borough-wide strategy boards and leading a number of strategic reviews. Prior to this Thanos was Assistant Director for CEA@Islington, the Council's education partner, taking responsibility for strategy and service delivery across a wide range of services including special educational needs, school admissions and exclusions together with responsibility for special schools, Pupil Referral Units and oversight of a number of mainstream schools in the borough. Previously, he was Deputy Director of Education (also in Islington) and in addition to the above responsibilities, led on the establishment of one of the first fully integrated Early Years Services nationally. Currently he is Director of Strategy and Commissioning for Islington Children's Services. Thanos was awarded an OBE in 2014 for services to children and families.

Miriam Teuma has an M.Ed in Educational Leadership from the University of Sheffield and been a lecturer in Youth and Community Studies at the University of Malta for the past ten years. She is a founding member and President of the Maltese Association of Youth Workers.

Miriam has extensive experience at European Union, Council of Europe and international level on youth related issues and is a member of the Council of Europe's Steering Committee for Youth (CDEJ). She is also a board member of ERYICA (European Youth Information and Counselling Agency). She has worked with the European Knowledge Centre for Youth Policy, SALTO and the EurMed Youth Platform.

In December 2010, Miriam was appointed as the first Chief Executive of Agenzija Zghazagh, the National Youth Agency of Malta. As Chief Executive she has implemented a range of initiatives including a youth information and counselling service and an extensive youth empowerment programme as well as youth training centres, youth cafes and youth hubs.

Hans Skott-Myhre is an associate professor in the Child and Youth Studies Department at Brock University. He is cross-appointed to the graduate programme in Popular Culture as well as being core faculty for the Inter-disciplinary Ph.D. in Humanities and adjunct faculty in the Child and Youth Care programme at the University of Victoria.

Hans spent twenty-five years as a youth worker and family therapist working primarily with runaway and homeless youth before retiring into academia. His research interests include radical and political approaches to youth/adult relations, subcultures, critical disability studies and anti-psychiatry, post-capitalist subjectivity, post-Marxist politics, undoing whiteness, and political readings of popular culture.

He is the author of *Youth Subcultures as Creative Force: Creating New Spaces for Radical Youth Work* and co-author with Chris Richardson of *Habitus of the Hood* as well as co-author with Kiaras Gharabaghi and Mark Krueger of the forthcoming book *With Children*.

Curtis Worrell was raised in a small town in the South of England on a council estate by his Bajan mother.

Whilst attending school, Curtis was placed in an Inclusion Unit due to his unacceptable behaviour. This was located on the same site as a youth centre called Junction 6. It was this place that gave him his first experience of youth work and he began attending the youth club to use their music studio facilities. Whilst attending, Curtis began to engage in services, and was able to be part of trips to Africa, exploring Edinburgh and social engagements that most young people from council estates did not have the opportunity to access.

Drifting away from the youth club as he got older, Curtis struggled to find a job or a course that satisfied him until a family friend suggested he got in touch with his youth worker from Junction 6. Curtis went to meet his previous worker at the youth club and whilst waiting for her to become available, he met some young people there. Curtis was then invited to attend a post-session discussion with the youth workers and some of the young people.

It was from this visit back to Junction 6 that Curtis began volunteering his services and pursuing a career working with young people. Whilst employed with Junction 6, Curtis embarked on National Vocational Qualification (NVQ) training. He realised that his inquisitive nature could enhance his studies and decided to qualify as a professional youth worker. At the time of writing he is now close to gaining is professional degree in this field.

Curtis is the product of youth work, having interviewed his first line manager as a young person back when he was 13-years-old. He is passionate about working with young people.

THEORY

BRIAN BELTON

PROFESSIONALIZING YOUTH WORK: A GLOBAL PERSPECTIVE

Criteria for Professional Youth Work; Its Principles and Values

This chapter is a development of work that first appeared under the auspices of the Commonwealth Secretariat and the Commonwealth Youth Programme Asia Centre (India) in 2012. This was a mid-point of a project, working together with colleagues in India, Pakistan, Malaysia, Maldives, Sri Lanka and Bangladesh to develop professional practice in these contexts and begin the process of building professional associations for youth workers.

What follows reflects the joint learning at the conclusion of the project, brining together ideas and findings, in particular from conferences in Sri Lanka, Malaysia and Bangladesh that have led to policy and practice developments in those countries.

PROFESSIONALISING YOUTH WORK

On a global level it is hard to argue that it is not part of the mission of peoples and governments, from an earliest possible point, to establish within populations the advantages and values associated with the promotion of equity, human rights and good governance. Throughout the world these qualities are fostered by youth work. Broadly stated this has historically involved adults working with and alongside young people, taking responsibility for their actions and dealing with the consequences of the same. This might be understood as the foundation of adult attitudes that youth workers have traditionally presented as a model for young people to evoke responsible, human and ethical conduct, as a means to improve their lives and society.

The field of youth work (variously labelled and in a range of forms) has been integral to participatory nation building. This is particularly present in the context of the dynamic role youth workers can play in addressing young people's welfare and rights in a responsive manner and by providing an interface between young people and decision-making processes at all levels. Throughout the world youth workers have taken socially important steps in professionalising youth work, which have included (and continue to encompass) a vast range of educational and training initiatives in the field. This has also seen the creation of complementary programmes to strengthen mechanisms and procedures, professionalising youth work in terms of developing competency and ethical practice in youth work.

B. Belton (ed.), 'Cadjan – Kiduhu': Global Perspectives on Youth Work, 3–21.

Now, globally, governments and NGOs continue to consolidate these processes. It is hoped that this document chapter might add to this process, by helping advance a responsive approach to the requirements of young people and their expectations. At the same time, what follows will seek to reflect the principles and purpose of youth work, while adhering to and promoting Human Rights conventions. This stance looks to strengthen practice/components to continue the professionalisation of youth work throughout the world. Professionalisation does not equate only, or necessarily to a salaried occupation but an attitude and response to practice.

TOWARDS BUILDING A CONCEPT OF YOUTH WORK

Youth work can be generally defined as a profession practiced by those working with young people in a range of settings. Youth workers, worldwide, can be found working in clubs and detached (street based) settings, within social/welfare services, sports/leisure provision, schools and, over the last decade or so in museums, arts facilities, libraries, hospitals, leisure and sports centres, children's homes and young offenders institutions.

The focus of youth work is on (but not limited to):

1. *The social learning of young people.*

   This is not usually simply forms of instruction, but includes a range of approaches, mostly developing learning opportunities out of everyday experience. This may consist of leisure and social pursuits, but also calls on more formal methods when appropriate.

2. *The wellbeing of young people.*

   This includes attention to and working with young people, their parents, guardians and carers to understand, relate to and make use of their rights, promoting and having concern for young people's welfare, while extending appropriate professional care.

The above, although for purposes of analysis separated into two discreet areas, might be usefully understood as complimentary foci; one confirms and enacts the other. The overall aim of youth work is to enhance the life experience of young people and their contribution to society as active, involved, useful and valued citizens.

The central purpose of youth work could be defined as *working with young people to play an assertive and constructive role in the strengthening and regeneration of their immediate communities and wider society.* This said youth work is not a specialism as such. Historically and socially its function has been to adapt and change according to social, economic and political needs and exigencies. Indeed, in places like the UK where there has been an ongoing pressure for youth work to become 'informal education' or latterly identify a 'core' competence or function, such as 'social pedagogy', the move towards specialisation threatens to effectively deskill youth workers whilst transforming them into mobile class room assistants, homework tutors or surrogate remedial teachers.

In a number of global regions youth workers can be found working directly for the government or local government, often involved in community development and community learning situations, capacity building, providing forms of accredited and non-accredited learning. However, in Europe for example, youth workers are increasingly deployed by voluntary organisations (although via a range of funding arrangements, including direct and indirect state resources) in issue-related work (drugs, sexual health, homelessness, parenting etc.). Many such organisations, particularly faith based groups, will concentrate more on less directive and informal practice, although most youth work will be set within formal institutions and include forms of guidance and instruction from time to time. Like a good teacher a skilled youth worker will blur the rather false dichotomy of informal and formal learning.

Youth workers can and are involved in education; they are employed to operate in formal institutions like schools, colleges and universities and can, in such situations, be thought of as wholly involved in the external structures that are education. However, their work is nearly always more inclined to working with young people that the latter might be motivated or inspired to learn; learning being an internal, psychological event or events. On a consistent basis this might be thought of as the 'getting of wisdom'. While schools and other related institutions might almost invariably be tasked with delivering education, they are not always, for everyone, unfailingly places of learning. In different places and different times they are and have been (wholly or partly, consciously or inadvertently) sites of indoctrination, propaganda or dominated by forms of memorisation and the pressure to conform.

In Africa, Asia, South and Central America youth workers are likely to be working for non-governmental organisations in sport, arts, social welfare and health fields. Substantial numbers will be involved in contexts similar to their counterparts elsewhere in the government/statutory sector, as youth service officers or youth volunteers within Youth Ministries, other Ministries and Departments.

Globally, youth work is a very diverse profession in terms of social tasks and employment situations. In recent years, with transnational economic and political changes, what youth workers do worldwide is becoming more similar. The demise of the national youth services internationally, alongside cuts in State funding of welfare and capacity building services, is likely to give rise to a growth in the role of voluntary and faith organisations in youth work.

VALUES AND PRINCIPLES

Generally speaking youth work's initiatives to professionalise reflect the values and principles enshrined in the ethos of Human Rights, which affirm the promotion of international understanding and a shared belief in:

- The liberty of the individual
- Equal rights for all regardless of race, colour, creed or political belief
- The inalienable right of the individual to participate by means of free and democratic political processes in framing the society in which they live.

World-wide, youth workers have risen above all forms of colonial domination and racial oppression and have been consistently committed to the principles of human dignity and equality via the promotion of self-determination, overcoming poverty, international cooperation, association based on consultation, and the continuing exchange of knowledge and views on professional, cultural, economic, legal and political issues.

All this has been framed with the intent to foster and extend multi-national association in order to expand human understanding and contribute to the enrichment of life for all.

The values of youth work further emphasise the anti-colonial values effectively recognising:

- Human rights as the foundation of democracy and development
- Equality of all human beings, regardless of gender, race, colour, creed or political belief
- Self empowerment, pursued through education, self and joint freedom of expression and participation
- Equity and/or fairness in the relationships between nations and generations, protection of vulnerable groups within a non-deficit/asset conscious approach.
- Democracy – facilitating the opportunity for to express their opinions and promote participation in decision-making
- Social and personal development based on principles of sustainability
- Diversity of views and perspectives in both national and international forums
- Dialogue and co-operation, building common ground and consensus
- Peace, without which the above values are unobtainable.

This list, in terms of language and trajectory, has and continues to evolve and change with circumstances and over contexts. For it not to do so would be self-contradictory. However, it is certain that in recent decades youth work has acted to facilitate and provide forums tasked with essentially decolonising initiatives via the continued focus, in spirit and action, on the principles and values that underpin humane practice. This has strengthened and continues to seek to maximise the contribution of youth in peace building, democracy and development worldwide.

TRANSLATING PRINCIPLES TO PRACTICE

Values have little impact if we fail to act on them. Youth work, in its most effective incarnations, critiques and confirms, extends, develops and alters the above goals. This said, the above ambitions provide a strong foundation for the development of professional youth work. Setting out expectations for professional practice and can also provide the academic standards for professional qualifications as well as criteria for training at a more practical level.

Governments and voluntary organisations can promote the professionalization of youth work by the delivery of quality services, through three main principles of work with young people ('FEC'):

- *Facilitating:* creating the conditions in which young people can act on their own behalf, and on their own terms, rather than relying on other people, in particular professionals, to do things for them.
- *Endowing:* putting democratic principles into action in the fullest sense, so that young people can play a constructive part/role in decision-making that affects them at different levels of society.
- *Confirming:* operating in accordance with value systems that give a sense of purpose and meaning to how young people use their skills and knowledge.

Many regions and institutions have developed generic core competencies of youth work. These competencies can be built into the way that youth workers undertake their practice with young people, professional peers and with organizations/institutions that are duty bearers, in fulfilling the rights of young people. FEC is intended to elucidate the same in a compact way.

Putting the emphasis on the youth worker's role in facilitating, endowing and confirming demonstrates the commitment to 'expediate' rather than set up a 'welfaring' or entirely educative model of service delivery; to expediate (from the Latin) means to 'set loose' or 'freeing the feet'. This expansively equates to a laboratory practice. Although the youth worker is not unconcerned about the welfare or education of the young people they work with, as their well-being and understanding of the world is central to being active and useful citizens. The professional role of the youth worker, therefore, involves balancing core values with the personal and collective potential of those they work with and amongst with political and economic realism.

BUILDING A PROFESSIONAL YOUTH WORK SECTOR

The professionalisation of any service is a process rather than an exact science. Professional youth work, in any national situation needs to be shaped by and evolve out of cultural and social contexts; each country may have different sets of institutions, processes, procedures and criteria to make professionalization possible. It is hoped that the ideas presented in this chapter will not be taken as merely a plan to be implemented, but as part of this book offering something of a beginning to an ongoing dialogue that will, by response and adaptation, result in professional youth work customised to the context of respective countries and cultures. The vision is not conformity to one model of professional practice, but a diversity of interpretations adhering to a set of shared values and principles that may develop and adapt over time and place. Youth work, by its character and aims, is a bespoke practice. Hence by definition it does not need to be tied to forms of pedagogical intervention (for instance) although it might inculcate the same. Indeed to make youth work any one thing for all time and everywhere is to effectively kill the essence youth work as a responsive and flexible form of practice.

INTRODUCTION TO YOUTH WORK

Youth work involves relating to and taking a level of responsibility for other people's children and the life direction of young people and therefore is fundamentally concerned and primarily focused on *care*. However, this care needs to be expressed in a suitably professional manner, which includes an appropriate level of detachment; youth workers are not 'big brothers/sisters' neither are they 'friends' (although they might be 'friendly'), nor is the youth worker's role a parenting one (in most contexts youth workers are not legally considered, because they are youth workers, to be in 'loco parentis' – they do not legally take the place of the parent). Consequently a professional detachment needs to be developed in terms of care. I will return to this issue later in this chapter.

Given the cultural and national differences in legal requirements, age groupings and social expectations connected with the care of young people across countries and cultures, this care role needs to be set within the parameters of Universal Rights. This framework can complement and underpin existing national legislation, practice, ethical and care standards/requirements. This means that youth workers not only need a working knowledge of childhood and Human Rights, but also the ability to interpret this knowledge and the associated principles into practice (see *A Rights Based Approach* below).

Youth work premised on the values and principles of universal Human Rights conventions needs to achieve a number of outcomes in terms of the delivery of practice and social development. These outcomes include creating opportunities for young people to develop their individual and inter-relational capacities for personal and social benefit. This is understood as 'a good thing' in itself; it has both social and learning benefits. This process serves young people in terms of becoming more aware of themselves, but at the same time they provide part of the means to make themselves understood by others, to be a valuable resource with regard to the life of their neighbourhood, district or nation and the betterment of wider global society. This, being achieved within a framework of equality and democratic principles, requires the professional youth worker to be cognisant of care principles, human rights considerations and more generally a 'social and political educator' (see *Social and Political Education* below).

Worldwide, youth work has traditionally been seen as a sort of secondary or 'para-profession' in relation to occupations like teaching and social work; it has been understood as something of a luxury rather than a necessity. While youth work does have distinct skill sets and is informed by a range of theory and practice, claiming guiding principles and values, these do change over time, context and sometimes, even from person to person. Writers, academics and practitioners have reasoned this is because youth work is 'no one thing', but a combination of roles. However, others, looking to give the practice a greater level of integrity, purpose and perhaps status, have looked to provide youth work with a more definite grounding. This has, in some places, led to attempts to label or rename youth workers as 'youth support workers', 'youth development workers' or 'informal' and/or 'community' educators. But these titles have proved to be transitory and provide no clearer indication of the professional role. In fact they seem to give rise to evermore vague time, place and culture specific definitions of and justifications for practice.

There is very little critical literature relating to youth work. Most of what is written promotes and rationalises models of practice, which are, in the main, based on heresy and stories, romantic and/or unconventional political views, guesses and assumptions. Such material often results in workers preaching homespun morality. This echoes the colonial/missionary era, which was underpinned by forms of instruction and domination. We need to move away from this by avoiding simplistically telling youth workers how to operate "on" young people. If we are to be of service to young people we are going to need to understand ourselves more as servers (servants) than authority figures; we exist professionally to work with or serve young people, to develop their influence and authority rather than merely extend our authority over them.

At the same time, young people are portrayed as a group (as the colonial 'native' was) to be personally or socially lacking (in deficit); deficient in terms of education, morality or even the civilising effects that can only be accessed with the aid of the 'informal educator', 'social pedagogue' or 'youth development worker'. As sections of this book confirm, youth, as a population group, are commonly depicted by way of assumptions, developed out of social fears, not unusually inflamed by the media, about declining personal standards and/or moral degeneracy. The whole age group is frequently portrayed as in need of 'support', 'help', being beset by vaguely described psychological problems such as 'lacking self esteem' and 'attention deficit'. As such young people are contradictorily represented, sometimes at the same time, as both a threatening 'enemy within', the seed of moral and social degeneracy, and as a relatively incapable or infirmed group, in need of extensive adult and professional patronage; they are taken to be both 'weak and vulnerable' as well as 'intimidating and powerful'.

It is this strange duality of response that translates to a social view of young people as being 'pathological' relative to 'responsible adults' and as such this invites a model of intervention that smacks (reeks) of a treatment (deficit) model; the overriding aim of much of the work with young people is correctional in ethos, being applied to individuals or groups understood and responded to as 'non-conformist' or 'disaffected' (abnormal). This project or effort to 'normalise' is understandably not that popular with young people. Hence places or programmes earmarked as 'youth facilities' tend not to be called upon by the majority of young people for any significant length of time.

Logical analysis of this suggests that this deficit model of practice relies on convincing workers and young people that they (young people) have innate insufficiencies and that there is something inherently impaired in the condition of youth. Apart from being inherently unattractive (repellent) this perspective is covertly oppressive. In effect its basis is rooted in what Franz Fanon, a psychiatrist, philosopher, activist and writer who worked in the North African context, saw as the propagation of a 'colonial mentality'; this dismal outlook implies that some population groups have 'inborn' inadequacies that need to be treated or compensated for by way of forms of social discipline or reformation. South African anti-apartheid activist Steve Biko saw that convincing people that this lack was real was a means of the continuance of coercive domination. As he remarked; *The most potent weapon of the oppressor is the mind of the oppressed.* Echoing this is Bob Marley's plea, repeating Marcus Garvey's counsel to; *Emancipate yourselves from mental slavery* recognising that *none but ourselves can free our minds.*

This being the case, a new concept of youth work is required that rejects such deficit models and promotes instead, one that is diametrically opposite – a model which lays emphasis on young people as personifying the vibrant hope and potential of any society; a model based on Human Rights and a recognition that the individual is confirmed in their humanity by their contribution in and to their community, their nation and the world.

ARTICULATING PRACTICE

Youth work, globally, needs to adopt a distinctly anti-colonial philosophy in keeping with the principles and mandates of Human Rights, creating a strand of homogeny in practice that diversity can inform and develop. The ethos and rationale articulated in humane principles lays the foundation for this new vision that regards young people as stakeholders in society. It also places a positive emphasis on youth, seeing this stage of life as a well of human resource with enormous potential; it understands young people to be the custodians of all possible futures and the section of society that can preserve the best of the past.

Although the strength of youth work lies in its ability to be responsive in terms of conditions, demands and environments, providing bespoke services over a wide horizon of practice delivery, it is also held back from developing as a profession because it is unable to clearly and succinctly articulate precisely what it aims to do and how it intends to do it. This does not imply youth work is intrinsically complex, but it does indicate that following contemporary western models of practice is problematical. On the one hand, western states have looked to youth work to respond in pragmatic ways to demands driven by socio-economic necessity, developing a comparatively cheap, relatively flexible work force. On the other hand, historically and culturally, youth work has been shaped by moral, spiritual and political motivations, aimed at producing a more ethical and/or questioning population. This is what Indian scholar and author Shehzad Ahmed has described as 'Education versus Idealism'[1]. In this situation the State looks to youth work to respond to regional, national and/or global conditions (largely economic), however at the same time youth workers focus on aims, primarily driven by personal values/feelings/points of view and/or often poorly informed political/social objectives. As such, youth workers have sometimes found themselves in conflict with management and State policy.

Youth work internationally, as part of its initiatives to professionalise, has consistently aimed to propose a model of practice that avoids the replication of this antagonistic situation. This involves building a pragmatic vision of practice that harmonises broadly-based professional ethical concerns, State policy and the requirements of young people. This needs to be undertaken by encompassing models of care, development and education that to some extent arise from and are relevant to the post-colonial context.

As such, this chapter is informed by the anti-colonial/anti-oppressive attitude and values as exemplified by the likes of Julius Nyerere, Mahatma Ghandi and Nawal Sadaawi. Their principles are incorporated in the philosophy of Ubuntu (see Box 1 below) and similar ideologies and theories.

Box 1

Nyerere's ideas of *Ujamaa* (1968)

1) The advancement of social, economic, and political equality through the enactment of basic democratic practice; challenging all forms of discrimination and prejudice
2) Villagisation – looking to make the best use of and developing local resources
3) The encouragement of self-reliance within a framework of interdependence – promoting a consciousness of how individuals are reliant on groups, while groups are dependent on the cooperation of individual members

Gandhi, *My Views on Education* (1970)

1) The focus of practice being on the development of the whole person
2) Look to draw out the best qualities of people
3) The development of the personality/culture being as important as forms of academic learning and acquisition of skill
4) Practice to aim to be self supporting

Ubuntu[2]

1) Listening to and affirming others with the help of processes that create trust, fairness, shared understanding and dignity and harmony in relationships
2) Consciousness is about the desire to build a caring, sustainable and just response to the community (village, city, nation or global family)
3) Emphasis on our common humanity and the ethical call to embody our communal responsiveness in the world, offering an alternative way to re-create a world that works for all.
4) Learning how to live together with respect, care, dignity and justice and to re-organise resources accordingly

---

5) Sharing ideas and resources and making basic services, such as food, housing and access to health and education accessible and visible to all.

The political underpinning of Ujamaa and the attitudinal disposition of Ubuntu confirm and mirror the values and conduct of social learning.

Nawal El Saadawi (2010)

1) Encourage thinking (use of the brain) rather than instruction following
2) Promoted understanding that education is not separate from politics
3) Develop a comprehension that we need to advance from old-fashioned ways; need for intellectual renewal
4) Advocate independent thought; doubt is the servant of knowledge. Truth will withstand all tests. Doubt is the first step towards knowledge
5) Work to discover personal creativity from inside; we are all born creative

Care

Youth work provides care in a context, which requires an appropriate level of professional detachment. Box 2 below throws light on the character of professional care.

Box 2: Nursing as Professional Care

Nursing perhaps provides the clearest examples of 'caring detachment'. For instance, my father passed away a couple of years ago. My family and I rushed, from all over London, to his bedside at the East End hospital where he died. My mother was already with my dad, understandably very upset after close to 60 years of being with him, which added to the general grief we were all experiencing. However, the nurses did not gather around my father's deathbed, crying and attempting to share in our feelings of loss and relative helplessness. One went and made tea, two others started to look after my father's body, disconnecting life support systems, cleaning him up a little, doing what needed to be done professionally.

All the time they were reassuring us, as individuals, as a group and as a family; they were attentive and respectful, without being intrusive or pretending they were 'one of us'. Collectively the activity of the nurses was thoughtful, showing that they knew what they were doing; they provided a strong scaffold of professional behaviour at a time when my family and I were exposed and vulnerable emotionally and needed their surety and sensitive but sensible and at points quite firm, support. The nurses never lost their focus; they were not family members; they were not there to mourn, but to extend the necessary and appropriate care expected of professional nurses (carers). The level to which they succeeded in doing this, without intrusion, was a measure of their professionalism. As we, my family and I, were free to fall apart, they 'kept it together' so, eventually, we could re-group and effectively pull ourselves together and deal with the situation.

This is managing care; it is a concern for the welfare and wellbeing of others, but it is tempered by appropriate objectivity and thoughtfully sensitive detachment. This is not disinterest, but neither is it presumptuous. This level of professional detachment is what your workers must try to mirror in their work.

Nursing versus Youth Work

A young person, Nural, approached a youth worker, Farah, asking to talk to her in private. After they found a suitable place to chat, Nurul told Farah that she wanted to go swimming with her friends, an activity that Farah had arranged, but that she couldn't swim, and was embarrassed about this becoming known to everyone else. At this point Nurul became quite emotional, saying she was unhappy about being 'left out' and being seen as 'stupid'.

Here, Farah had several courses of action open to her; she was called upon to make a professional judgement:

1. She could have told Nurul not to be so silly/emotional and that her friends would probably understand
2. She could have put her arms round Nurul and told her no matter what her friends thought she (Farah) would always like her
3. She could have promised to teach Nurul to swim herself
4. She could have found a class, run by a qualified swimming teacher, that Nurul might attend
5. She could spend more time with Nurul, working with her to explore her feelings and finding out what she might want to do about the situation

Just by starting to consider options Farah showed professional care, however how she proceeded would demonstrate her ability in terms of extending appropriate professional care.

1. Farah might want to explore Nurul's emotional response further. Was her response typical of her, was it 'over the top' and if so why might that be? How can Farah be sure that Nurul's fears about the reaction of her friends are just related to swimming?
2. Can Farah really commit to 'always liking' Nurul? What does 'liking' entail? Does Farah understand 'liking' in the same way as Nurul?
3. Does Farah have the time/skill to teach Nurul to swim safely?
4. Should Nurul's parents be involved in any decisions about going to

> classes? How can Farah be sure that Nurul or her family might be able to meet the cost of swimming lessons?
>
> For a youth worker, extending professional care is often not quite as straightforward as it might be for a nurse. However, appropriate care is a constant consideration in the role of the youth worker.

It is probably a mistake to think of ourselves, as professionals, as having 'relationships' with young people. Our work is 'associative'; we have a professional association with our clients (young people). Unlike lawyers or politicians, we do not 'represent' our clients; we work *with* them (as a service) in order that they might *represent themselves to what they judge to be their best advantage/interests* (as individuals and as a group). We are not nurses, psychiatrists, psychologists or doctors, so we are not looking to 'cure' or 'treat' people. We are not teachers, so we are not *centrally* concerned with forms of instruction, although our work might, from time to time encompass mentoring, leading or guiding, and we want young people to become more knowledgeable, aware and ultimately wise. We are not counsellors, therapists or social workers, but this does not preclude us from making referrals to such professionals if we think this might be suitable or necessary (not to do so might be understood as being unprofessional). We are not police officers, however we should be aware enough to know at what point we need to involve the police in our work. An understanding of all this is encompassed in having the ability to extend appropriate care.

SOCIAL AND POLITICAL EDUCATION

The approaches outlined in Box 1 might be translated via an understanding of *social learning*. This is the intellectual and personal means to interact and develop in the social context. It is an adaptation of social education as mooted by Davies and Gibson (1967: 12), *any individual's increased consciousness* of themselves, their *values, aptitudes and untapped resources and of the relevance of these to others*. For them social education *enhances the individual's understanding of how to form mutually satisfying relationships*. This involves a search for the means to discover *how to contribute to, as well as take from* associations with others.[3]

The replacement of 'education' with 'learning' represents an understanding that youth work is not reliant on a formal structure – this is what educational essentially is understood to be – delivered via a curriculum by way of the 'educational machines' that are schools, colleges and universities, by people trained in various techniques, procedures and strategies of delivery. The emphasis on learning recognises youth work, in its most effective and humane incarnation, to be a creative process of involving and learning with young people, which can produce the physiological process of learning as a means to advancing understanding, awareness (of self, other and the world) and ultimately social wisdom. Social learning recognises learning not so much as a 'one-way-street' (wherein one teaches while the other learns) but more of a collaborative, mutual and complimentary process that can be engendered more between people (including youth workers and young people). Learning in youth work is a 'two-way street' as the youth worker to be effective needs to be, at times, taught by young people, about their viewpoint, culture or other perspective in order that their practice might be effective. This might be understood to encompass the political underpinning of Ujamaa and the attitudinal disposition of Ubuntu. It is a means to promote not only the interdependence of individuals, groups and communities for the benefit and well-being of all, but promote understanding of 'interdependence'; that each is reliant on all and all is reliant on each.

Social learning also reflects the role of the youth worker, working with groups of people, creating a collective consciousness, working for social change collaboratively with duty bearers to advance positive development at local, national and international levels. As you can see, the active, social and asset focus is quite the antithesis of the individual, psychological, deficit, treatment model. As part of this, a sense of personal and social responsibility can be generated and the motivation for betterment of the self, but also an understanding of how this will contribute to the positive development of society. For an example of this see Box 3 below.

Box 3

A youth worker came into contact with a group of young refugees. She identified that they had a common interest in playing soccer and that they wanted to form a team. The youth worker and the young people started by discussing a name and a motto for the team. This allowed for the group's first self-designed democratic activity; names and mottos were discussed, nominated and voted on.

Thus 'Better World United' (BWU) was born, with the agreement that they existed to 'Play by the rules for the good of all'.

Following this several tasks were identified that were necessary to starting the football team. This included organising training, team selection, arranging matches with other teams and identifying sponsorship to pay for kits and balls.

Within a year BWU were cooperatively organising three teams, sponsored by a local sports shop. Seven of the young people were taking coaching qualifications, while three were involved in training other young people involved in the teams, having gained basic coaching qualifications. The youth worker continued to keep in contact with the young people, but did not need to be actively involved beyond giving the occasional piece of advice when asked. But she also referred other youth workers to them, working on issues such as sexual health and clean water projects. Out of this several of the young people became involved in voluntary youth work themselves.

So, starting from a collective, fairly straightforward desire of a small group of young people, the youth worker had worked with this group to fulfil their wishes, out of which arose a sense of responsibility for each other and others, which in turn provided a range of resources for the wider community/society. In the process the physical, academic, organisational, leadership, innovatory and collaborative skills

---

> of the young people were developed and enhanced. These of course represent a
> pool of qualities/social capital that can be redirected and deployed in other aspects
> of personal, community and national life.

Thus social learning facilitates fundamental political education (democracy, representation, advocacy etc.). First and foremost the professional stance of social and political learning requires practitioners to personify, by way of their practice;

a) *The ability to take and manage responsibility*
b) *Deal with the consequences of action.*

EXPECTATION

Youth work, framed within a professional context of social and political learning and Human Rights, is anchored to a raft of expectations of both practitioner and client. The expectation of the youth worker is that they will have the ability to make professional judgements aligned to the aims, objectives and desired outcomes of their practice. However, we need to have expectations of young people in order that they might detect an interest in/care about their wellbeing and that they might develop the motivation to have expectations of themselves.

In the west, much youth work has failed because of expectations being seen as a burden on young people; that they should be largely left to 'find their own feet' without 'pressure' (as if pressure might be expunged from life). This *laissez-faire* attitude has effectively abandoned many young people in terms of their wider socialisation; largely being left to their own devices, although supported by youth workers to take advantage of rights/entitlements/welfare benefits. However, because of the lack of expectations, many young people, have no real sense of duty (other than to themselves) and have been drawn into pockets of social selfishness, an 'all against all' attitude, which is ideal for the development of cultures of crime and disaffection (that is in some cases generations long). This whole package is a microcosm of a capitalist society at its most abstracting and destructive.

PROFESSIONAL JUDGEMENT

The nature of professional judgement starts with the understanding that youth workers, as practitioners, are not neutral; they are obliged to make judgements. A judgement might be understood as being different from an assumption or an opinion; a judgement is an opinion based on evidence. The more evidence one has, the more secure one's judgement might be said to be. There is of course better and worse evidence, but the difference between the two is a judgement in itself. However, the more an opinion is made without evidence, the more likely it is that it will be prejudiced (a 'pre-judgement') or discriminatory.

So you can see that it is important that youth workers are able to evidence professional judgement by demonstrating how and why they choose to do one thing rather than another. The following youth worker's recording of practice demonstrates this;

16

The group came into the club shouting and, what looked like play fighting, with each other. Others looked a bit intimidated, backing away from the group quite quickly. I chose not to immediately reproach them about their behaviour, as when colleagues had done this before it had seemed to make matters worse. However, I had worked with a group previously that acted in much the same way, and I had noticed that engaging one or two of them in conversation had appeared to help the group acclimatise to the environment relatively straightforwardly. So, recognising Abidin, I commented how she had styled her hair differently and how I thought it looked good ...

The worker, using a range of evidence drawn from her experience of practice, makes a professional judgement; it is a 'professional' judgement because it is based on practice and experience rather than personal bias. Her judgement might have been good, not so good, or even poor (depending, at least partly, on the outcome) but she had nevertheless used judgement because she had drawn on evidence; her action was not based wholly on supposition, feelings and what is sometimes vaguely called 'instinct', but on judgement built on evidence. This enabled her to make what might be considered to be an 'ethical choice' to take one course of action rather than another/others. This is something more than reflection, although reflection and consideration might be part of the process.

Youth workers, committed to social and political learning, working within a Rights framework, are required to make professional judgements, work with young people in order that they might make effective judgements (ones that can be acted on) for the development and betterment of society.

Box 4

In a message delivered to the UN General Assembly Special Session on 8 May 2002, delegates Gabriela Azurduy Arrieta, aged 13, from Bolivia and Audrey Cheynut, a 17-year-old from Monaco, outlined a range of objectives premised on a concept that, a world fit for everyone must be a world fit for young people. It was stated that this requires to be founded on respect for children's rights, which is reliant on;

> *... governments and adults making a real and effective commitment to the principle of children's rights and applying the Convention on the Rights of the Child to all children.*

The overall vision encompassed a range of provision relevant to youth work including:

- The provision of centres and programmes.
- Education for life that goes beyond the academic and includes understanding, human rights, peace, acceptance and active citizenship.
- Active participation – raised awareness and respect among people of all ages about every young person's right to full and meaningful participation.
- Involvement in decision-making and planning.

> The message went on to make a number of points concerning the identity and reputation of young people, asserting:
>
> - They are not the sources of problems, but the resources that are needed to solve problems.
> - They are not expenses but investments.
> - They are not just young people; they are people and citizens of the world.
>
> There was also a commitment by young people to:
>
> - Defend the rights of young people.
> - Treat each other with dignity and respect.
> - To be open and sensitive to difference.
>
> The message was concluded with the statement;
>
> *You call us the* future, *but we are also the present.*

A RIGHTS-BASED APPROACH

A rights-based approach to youth work entails a process of engagement with young people based on human rights. Within this process all rights should apply equally to all and young people are understood to be agents in determining the actions and activity that are best for them as individuals and collectives. The role of 'duty bearers' is understood as being primarily the State with regard to ensuring these rights and this should be recognised and acted on.

The primary document that articulates basic human rights is the Universal Declaration of Human Rights (UDHR). The United Nations Convention on the Rights of the Child (UNCRC) is also an important document for youth work as many young people are legally or socially considered to be children.

The statements by young people in Box 4 demonstrates how they, through effective social and political learning, are able, by the taking and using of their authority as growing citizens, to influence their immediate environment and also have an impact at national and international levels.

Furthermore, at local, regional, national and global levels, the UDHR and the UNCRC can act as a foundation to the underpinning care basis of youth work that might complement and reinforce existing local and national care frameworks/custom and practice. Importantly, this involves transparent practice that proceeds from and is informed by consultancy and negotiation with young people.

Article 19 of the UDHR says,

Everyone has the right to freedom of opinion and expression; this right includes freedom to hold opinions without interference and to seek, receive and impart information and ideas through any media and regardless of frontiers.

Article 12 of the UNCRC states that children should be able to express their views

... freely in all matters affecting the child ...

This is congruent with the attitudes and values encapsulated within the principles and practice of social and political learning. However, to maintain such equivalence human rights cannot be an immutable set of gospel like texts. Human rights, like any other formulation of ideas, precepts and principles are given value and meaning to the extent that those they impact upon have access to the means of elaboration on and/or altering the same. For the rights of young people to be relevant and effective the informed involvement of young people needs to be sought and promoted.

YOUNG PEOPLE'S PARTICIPATION

Central to the social learning response is the acknowledgement (as hinted at above) of the need for the professional *to be able to be taught about the wants and needs of young people by young people*. This is led by an understanding that the motivations, desires and passions of young people will likely be the richest seams of their future accomplishments and social contribution. In this approach, young people take the lead in learning within the social context. It is the job of the youth worker to respond to this in an appropriate and adequate manner. This stance allows the young person to enable and empower themselves – the opposite, to foster the reliance of an 'enabler' or look to other people to empower oneself, is close to the suppositions of the colonial missionary. Such an approach proceeds from the presumption that young people have, in the form of their integrity as human beings, potential, ability, influence, authority and power and as such is counter to colonial assumptions of deficit. Conversely, the professional who sets out to empower or enable others relies on inherently colonial attitudes, as this outlook assumes a lack of power and ability on the part of young people.

As seen in Box 5 below, many pertinent ethical and competency considerations from youth work stem from response of young people.

Box 5

The following is adapted from *Declaration of Learner's Rights and Responsibilities,* which was written by a group of six young people between the ages of 15 and 17. It is quite a formal model that demonstrates young people taking responsibility for their lives and their learning via a rights agenda. The original document was presented at a Rights of the Child Conference in Victoria, British Columbia, Canada and to the Canadian Minister of Education in June 1995. It was again presented to the UN Conference Habitat II, Istanbul Turkey in 1996. The Declaration was also published internationally by UNESCO and many organisations in countries around the world have shared it with their communities. As citizen learners this statement asserted that young people had the right to:

---

1. Allow their own experience and enthusiasm to guide their learning.

2. Choose and direct the nature and conditions of their learning experience. As a learner they take responsibility for the results they create.

3. Perfect the skills to be a conscious, self-confident and resourceful individual.

4. Be respected while taking the responsibility to respect others.

5. Be nurtured and supported by their family and community, while their family and community have the right and responsibility to be their primary resource.

6. Enter into relationships based on mutual choice, collaborative effort, challenge and mutual gain.

7. Be exposed to a diverse array of ideas, experiences, environments, and possibilities. This exposure being their responsibility of themselves, their parents and mentors.

8. To evaluate their learning according to their own sensibilities; also having the responsibility and right to request to be included in the evaluations of their mentors.

9. Co-create decisions that involve and concern them.

10. Openly consider and have the responsibility to respect the ideas of others, whether or not they accept these ideas.

11. Enter a learning organisation, which offers, spiritual, intellectual, emotional, and physical support, and operates in an open and inclusive manner.

12. Equal access to resources, information and funding.

A PRACTICAL DEFINITION FOR YOUTH WORK

The aims of youth work practice need to be measurable and achievable. Vague and indeterminate terms need to be avoided if this is to be made possible. Looking at youth work worldwide, the following definition of its key purpose seems to express much of global practice:

Youth workers engage with young people that they (young people) might work with them (youth workers) to cultivate their (young people's) innate abilities to develop their personal and human potential, in a holistic manner. Working alongside young people youth workers facilitate personal, social advancement and learning. This encompasses the political learning of young people, developing their own voice and capacity to influence, and so take authority/responsibility, within society.

This is entirely compatible with the principles and values of youth work and human rights. Young people are our most important resource and we need to collaborate with them to develop their individual potential in order for them to live fulfilled lives.

At the same time, this formulation of youth work enables the development of appropriate standards of practice by which the quality of youth work can be measured, providing a means to develop, better deliver and achieve desired outcomes.

CONCLUSION

This chapter has offered a paradigm of facilitating, confirming and endowing youth work practice that can be tailored to specific contexts over time, place and culture. Being able to say what youth work is and what it might do is necessary to lay the ground for the instigation of professionalisation of practice, as you cannot professionalise that which you have not defined and agreed on. In short, the above is an attempt to put the horse before the cart as sense might dictate. It might (and I hope it will be) the purpose of writers, academics, practitioners and young people to refine and reach consensus in relation to the character and function of youth work in respective countries, and on this foundation, move on to develop appropriate policies, occupational standards, professional associations, supervisory structures, training and the infrastructure to build a vibrant and consistently evolving/adapting profession as befits situation and context.

NOTES

[1]   Ahmed, *Educational Thinkers of India*, (New Delhi: Anmol Publications).
[2]   See for example Caracciolo and Mungai (2009), Harber and Serf (2004).
[3]   Quote Davies and Gibson.

REFERENCES

Ahmed, S. (2006). *Educational thinkers in India.* New Delhi: Anmol Publications.
Biko, S. (1987). *I write what I like.* Oxford: Heinemann.
Caracciolo, D. M., & Mungai, A. M. (Eds.). (2009). *In the spirit of Ubuntu: Stories of teaching and research.* Rotterdam: Sense Publishers.
Davies, B., & Gibson, A. (1967). *The social education of the adolescent.* London: University of London Press.
el Saadawi, N. (2010). *The essential Nawal El Saadawi.* London: Zed Books.
Fanon, F. (1965). *The wretched of the earth.* London: MacGibbon & Kee.
Fanon, F. (1967). *Black skin white mask.* New York: Grove Press.
Gandhi, M. K. (1970). *My views on education.* Bombay: Bharatiya Vidya Bhavan.
Harber, C., & Serf, J. (2004). *Exploring Ubuntu: Education and development – An introduction to theories and debates.* Birmingham: Development Education Centre.
Marley, B. (1908). *Redemption song.* MYV Networks.
Nyerere, J. (1968). *Ujamaa.* Oxford: Oxford University Press.

CURTIS WORRELL

HIP HOP IS DEAD! YOUTH WORK IN A STATE OF DECLINE?

Synopsis

In 2006 Rapper Nas proclaimed, 'Hip-hop is dead'! This chapter sets to find out whether or not youth work is also in a state of decline. I seek to establish a comparative parallel development between youth work and hip-hop by looking back to the histories of the two phenomena as well as conducting interviews with past colleagues. What I discovered is that the style of youth work that has become my norm, being "informed by political and moral values", as well as having, "belief in equality and respect for the environment" (Belton, 2010: 69), is in decline. However, looking at the historic reasons behind youth work it is evident this style will forever be in the minority and therefore constantly in a state of decline. Using hip-hop's new recruits, such as, J Cole, Kendrick Lamar and Wale, I unearth the catalyst behind the revival of hip-hop and highlight how it can be used to suggest a way forward in youth work.

SHOUT OUTS!

It is customary in hip-hop for a DJ, or Rapper, to give a shout out to the ones that offered support, inspiration and assistance. First and foremost I would like to thank the people who gave up their time to allow me to interview them. Writing this has allowed me to recognise how lucky I am to have been given to opportunity to work alongside some of the best youth workers I have ever witnessed.

A special shout out to Bianca for allowing me to volunteer at J6 and your continued support and so much more.

A special acknowledgement to Vicky for joining in with a chorus of: "you down with IPP, Yeah you know me", when our individual performance plans were due.

Moira I thank you for making education enjoyable, and encouraging me to apply for George Williams.

Thanks to my first study group 'Bristol still rocks' and Sara, thanks for taking the time to swap essays on deadline day and always putting my mind at ease.

Big shout out to my SE study group, for accepting me and challenging my views.

Thanks to Brian for encouraging me to become more critical and supporting my development as a professional youth worker.

And last, but not least, my proofreader TB, for making my words legible-ish.

B. Belton (ed.), 'Cadjan – Kiduhu': Global Perspectives on Youth Work, 23–46.

INTRODUCTION

"Everybody sound the same, commercialise the game
Reminiscin' when it wasn't all business
If it got where it started
So we all gather here for the dearly departed"
(Nas, 2005: 3:10 – 3:20)

Youth work and popular culture is a broad subject, which would be impossible to critically examine in depth within a chapter of this length. I have decided to concentrate on the parallels between youth work and hip-hop, not only because I am a hip-hop fan but also because I feel that they have both followed similar paths.

Hip-hop and other genres, such as punk, were formed by young people feeling discontent with their environment and their status within society, prompting them to use music as a vessel to voice their frustrations. As this chapter has a focus on hip-hop, I aim to bring hip-hop's energy to fruition with the use of metaphors, imagery and the occasional use of profanity. I do this not to alienate but to, 'keep it real', and to share my passion as well as, 'show love', to both hip-hop and youth work.

I met this girl when I was ten years old
And what I loved most she had so much soul.
She was old school,
When I was just a shorty,
Never knew throughout my life
She would be there for me.
(Common, 1994: 0:20 – 0:30)

In 1994, rapper Common Sense (now known as 'Common'[1]) spoke these words on his track entitled *I used to love H.E.R.*[2] This track tells the story of a girl Common met as a young man and fell hopelessly in love with. Over the years, she was led astray by materialistic elements of life and they drifted apart and fell out of love. Common reveals in the last line of the song that the female in question was indeed hip-hop.[3]

Many of the song's lyrics could relate to my own experience of youth work. Youth work opened my eyes to so much of the world and as a young man I found myself bewitched by her passion and the unwavering belief that she held for me. Over the years I have become disenchanted with her but unlike Common, rather than say I used to love her and move on, I aim to fight for this relationship with youth work and cover my ears when she says, 'it's not you it's me, I'm just in a bad place right now'.

My intention is to look at the condition of youth work whilst critically examining the similarities youth work has with hip-hop. I am aware that it is unconventional to draw comparisons between hip-hop and youth work, as I have not been able to find any literature which does this, or that analyses youth work through alternative lenses. Popular culture grows out of youth culture, therefore it follows that youth work is intrinsically linked to youth culture.

The rationale behind focusing on a comparison between these two phenomena was sparked by the Jimmy Hoffa[4] style disappearance of 'real' hip-hop in 2006, which prompted rappers and many people involved in hip-hop to start saying, "Hip Hop is dead" (Nas, 2006). It struck me that there has been similar thoughts that real youth work is disappearing and that it has been replaced by statistically charged and economically motivated work, leading young people and youth workers to suffer as a result. I believe the two disciplines have followed similar developmental paths and both have suffered institutional strangulation, cutting their flow of creativity. In order to prove this suspected link, I will begin by analysing the journeys that both have taken. To do this, I will be taking a particular slant on the history of youth work (all history of course being 'a particular slant').

In order to define what real youth work is to me, I carried out interviews with youth workers who operated the youth club that I attended while growing up. These youth workers took me on residentials, both within and outside of the UK, as well as supporting me in my development as a youth worker. Through these interviews, I hoped to discover where I have inherited my key values from and the fundamentals that inform my practice. I wish to establish an understanding of what I believe youth work is and what I believe to be in decline.

The death of hip-hop in 2006 (like any murder case) prompted an investigation, with rappers playing the role of detective, asking pertinent questions. By using the questions rappers asked about the death of hip-hop and adapting them to youth work, I formulate a list of suspects and cross-examine them to enable me to ascertain the cause for youth work's demise.

The question of whether hip-hop is dead or not was raised eight years ago. Since then, hip-hop has loosened the garrotte from its neck enough to allow creativity to flow once again, leaving hip-hop in possibly the best place it has been since the 1990s.[5] I will be attempting to discover the catalyst behind this revival and if hip-hop's methods can be adapted and applied to youth work so as to ignite its revival and loosen the noose that seems to threaten to cut-off the life-blood of the practice.

THE HISTORY OF YOUTH WORK

Bernard Davies placed the birth of youth work in the 19th century with the, "establishment of a range of philanthropic organisations providing (usually separate) leisure-time facilities for boys and young men and girls and young women" (Davies, 2009: 65). Other historians date youth work's birth back to the late 18th century, placing, "the activities of pioneers such as Robert Raikes and Hannah More as an important forerunner of the work" (Smith, 2014). Smith regards Ragged Schools as the precursors of youth work due to their targets, demonstrated in the 13th annual report of the Ragged School Union held in 1857. This report identified that,

> The surest way of lessening juvenile crime and fitting outcast children for "the battle of life", is to give to the very poorest the opportunity of acquiring a sound Scriptural and Industrial Education. (Ragged School Union, 1857: 4)

The report is similar to the current aims of youth work (if one disregards the scriptural education for young people) and consequently reducing crime amongst the young while preparing them for independence. However, the Ragged Schools were similar to Sunday Schools with a strong focus on religion and held helping the less fortunate as central to its aims. This can be seen in the subtitle of the report:

ESTABLISHED FOR THE SUPPORT OF FREE SCHOOLS
FOR THE DESTITUTE POOR OF LONDON AND ITS SUBURBS.
(Ragged School Union, 1857: 1)

But this movement was a very disciplined, formal and authoritarian compared to anything we would see today. In practice such places, with their beatings and aims, were miles away from the kind of provision that would be recognised as youth work – they were closer to prisons in terms of their mission to reform and general regime

An interesting point made by Davies is that the work after the 19th century, "unlike Raikes and More's initiatives, was not being done to working-class people by their 'betters' but by and for the working class peoples" (Davies, 2009: 65). Smith also points out that the Young Men's Christian Association (YMCA), which was set up in 1844, is considered the first dedicated youth organisation, although it has to be said this was initially premised on reading rooms and the study of the Bible. Smith does go on to talk about more radical youth work like the creation of 'the Espérance' by Emily Pethick and Mary Neal. Pethick, who, "went on to become the treasurer and key organiser with the Pankhurst's of the English Suffrage Union" (Smith, 2014).

However, with the exception of the latter, it is apparent that Smith's historical account is dominated by a religious movement. This is contrary to the youth work that I have been involved in and religion has not been the driving force of the work that I have witnessed. Youth work, as the practice we'd recognise today, undertaken for its own sake (rather than with evangelical or political purpose) was instigated by duties given to local authorities (most widely post Second World War) via the state – this was essentially a secular process – youth work continues to be used by faith and other interests, although not as an end in itself, but as a means to other ends.

A view that holds more familiarity with me is described by Jon Savage. Savage describes the 'Rainbow Corner' (opened in November 1942) as a result of the American GI[6] coming to Britain during the Second World War. Rainbow Corner, "aimed to recreate that staple of American adolescent life, the corner drug store" (Savage, 2008: 418). This demonstrates that Rainbow Corner was not influenced by ragged schools, Sunday schools or The YMCA; Rainbow Corner was a simulation of what the American soldiers had back at home in the United States of America.

GIs shot pool, played pinball or listened to a jukebox stocked with the latest hits. The two dining rooms could seat two thousand men, while the basement snack bar (…) served waffles, hamburgers, doughnuts, coffee and endless Cokes. (Savage, 2008: 418)

The 'mass observation' project enabled this model to be adapted for what we'd recognise as a youth club – a place to 'be'; chiefly concerned with socialising and the fundamental benefits that can arise out of the same.

This recreational hub for young people to hang out in is more in keeping with my own experience of a youth club, as well as public perception of what youth workers do. It appears that public opinion is that most youth workers simply play pool with young people. I have personally experienced this on many occasions.

The influx of American soldiers brought its own problems, such as a rise in crime; "figures for 1944 showed an increase of 50 per cent from 1938", and also, "during the war, one-third of all babies were born illegitimately" (Savage, 2008: 419). Rainbow Corner did have workers but they were not specifically called youth workers. I find it difficult to imagine that the workers were encouraging illegitimate babies and criminal activities as opposed to working with the young people to reduce this issue, like a youth worker would. Sexual expression is an expression of youth; encourage youth expression and sexual expression – unlike the ragged school's repression – will occur. Maybe it's a matter of personal perspective which of these might be preferred, but perhaps most 16-year-olds would probably pass on the ragged school option.

Late in the Second World War, *Picture Post* ran an article about Rainbow Corner and they described it as, "the perfect example of what a club for young people should be", stating that,

> … this US establishment shamed most wartime British efforts to cater to its youth: The Americans have come and created fine centres of recreation for their men. (…) Rainbow Corner should become a shining model for the new voluntary service response for the needs of 'British young people'. (Savage, 2008: 421)

Savage paints a picture closer to my experience of youth work and the journey I have taken; yet it is still very different. I am no closer to defining what youth work is or understanding where it came from. Maybe this confusion concerning the history of youth work is the reason why the phrase itself is so hard to define. Smith's religious historical account of youth work may be down to how his own experiences have influenced his perspective, as it has my own. Or perhaps it is typical of the most common mistake of the amateur historian – to read the present into the past? The earlier 'enclaves' of 'work with the young' (with faith, political and even military ambitions) might be thought of to have about as much in common with youth work at its ethical zenith as a penny-farthing has with a modern racing motorcycle? Rainbow corner might at least be understood as a sort of 1950s BSA TT model.

RESEARCH AND RESULTS

The aim of my research was to gain insight into where I have inherited my own values and perceptions of youth work. In order to substantiate my claim that youth work is in decline and to establish whether others support my claim, I carried out qualitative research, interviewing key members who have inspired my own youth work journey.

The responses from my interviews highlighted that work with young people should aim to work with young people so that they might, "participate in new experiences" (Appendix 2), and, "broaden their horizons". As a young person, I was exposed to new experiences, such as, seeing my first play whilst taking part in a trip provided by my youth club. I was also encouraged to resign from my job to enable me to go on a month's long trip to Africa. Having been given opportunities like these, I learnt to see that expanding the horizons of the young people I work with is important and this is an aim that I continue to work towards.

Another goal that came up often was to 'challenge young people'. This is something of a clichéd catchphrase that gets bounded about in youth work. Bit like 'confront' it feels inappropriately aggressive. Others include being 'non-judgmental' and 'boosting young people's self-esteem'. The overuse of these phrases renders them meaningless. For instance, there is no reliable or expedient way in the course of youth work practice to measure relative self-esteem both prior to, or subsequent to, the worker's intervention. Youth projects have attempted to measure these outcomes through evaluations, which are normally no more than numerical score cards. These are then used to generate statistics, but offer no realistically authentic indication about an individual's feelings. The idea that youth workers should remain non-judgemental is inaccurate and maybe risky as their ability to make professional judgements (be they paid or voluntary) is at times crucial. Although this is situational, and maybe youth workers avoid consciously looking to convert young people to their views, youth workers do need to make judgements in the interest of safeguarding but also about things like 'is this person feeling hurt?' or 'am I helping this person too much?' Consequently it could be deemed unprofessional to actively avoid making judgements, or probably more accurately, pretending we are not making them.

Despite this, I feel similar to one of my interviewees that youth workers, "constantly challenge themselves and therefore can't help but challenge others". While perhaps we might need to see ourselves as more questioning than 'challenging' or; confrontational (one doesn't necessarily want to sound too much like a latter day Mike Tyson) one might hope that this would eventually lead to discovery and understanding – challenge can expect counter challenge and as such a confrontation.

This questioning stance encourages dialogue, which can lead to dialectic and, it is often claimed, the same can result in the building of positive associations with young people, although who decides what is 'positive' and how do we know how positive is sometimes moot points.

My research also uncovered a more passionate sense of the origins of youth than those claimed by Smith or Davies. Bruce spoke to me about how he feels that, "youth work was always seeking to challenge authorities and encouraging young people to do the same". He started Basingstoke's first Lesbian, Gay, Bisexual and Transgender (LGBT) group after noticing a lack of provision for these groups. Although initially management refused to support it, Bruce was able to get the backing of other professionals and run it voluntarily for a year before presenting a report to the head of service and obtaining the support of colleagues in the field.

Che Guevara argued that,

> The arms of the enemy, his ammunition, his habits must be considered; because the principal source of provision for the guerrilla force is precisely in enemy armaments. If there is a possibility of choice, we should prefer the same type as that used by the enemy. (Guevara, 2008: 56)

I have found this to be resonant amongst some youth workers who can take something such as a grant (funding) form, which is meant to be used for encouraging young people back to work, and instead using it to provide a more generic experience for a much wider group of young people.

I started in youth work as a volunteer, inspired in part by my own experiences as a young person and the work I witnessed and benefited from. One example of this is when I witnessed a previous manager of mine, Bianca, facilitating a sexual health session working with the 'naughty' boys from the local school. They were playing a sexual health version of the popular children's game 'Pass-the-Parcel'. I was amazed at how Bianca had turned this sensitive and potentially embarrassing subject into a fun and competitive game.

I know I am not alone when I say that somebody has inspired me to pursue youth work. Bruce said there were several people who inspired him to want to work with young people, one of who was Mike Jones. Jones led the first ever team in the world to kayak the river Dudh Kosi, which runs from the summit of Mount Everest. Bruce was impressed with Jones' ability to work with young people so that they might thrive in demanding and unfamiliar circumstances.

While speaking to my interviewees about how they see current youth work, overall there was a tendency to use relatively emotive phrases such as, "it's a shame", "youth work does not exist", as well as speaking as if youth work has been a victim and its demise a planned attack. I feel that youth work is currently in a critical state. When I say this, I am not referencing all aspects of youth work; I am referring to the passionate, innovative, questioning guerrilla warfare type of youth work (see Belton, 2009: 145-165). This type of youth work is concerned with working with young people to create new opportunities and experiences for young people, rather than generating statistics and moulding young people in to commodities for the labour market to exploit; youth work in the UK having been given the task of readying young people for exploitation, playing a part in providing a relatively skilled, relatively compliant, relatively cheap workforce.

Whilst thinking about the past, it is not uncommon to reflect on it through rose-tinted glasses, or even a rose-tinted magnifying glass. I was therefore pleased that my interviewees did not paint an idealised picture of the past. Amongst the responses was Clare, who hoped,

> That it's not still mostly happening in second-rate rooms with 'five a day' and other public health posters on the wall, with cupboards filled with equipment that no one knows how to use (because Dave who used to work there has left).

Chris echoed Clare's fears adding that, "at its worst it can be a pool table in the corner of a hall amidst a hubbub of chaotic behaviour – little more than a shelter with some semi-responsible adults keeping a watchful eye on young people".

While some youth workers might see the above scenario as a great starting point for a more dimensioned sort of youth work than the 'get 'em doing stuff' school, it is important to take the potentially distorted view of past practice into consideration when discussing the history of youth work. Todd Boyd highlights this when he argues that the, "civil rights generation has come to stand as something sacred" (Boyd, 2002: 9) and the post civil rights generation are seen to have achieved nothing in comparison. They are almost held, "hostage because its members did not have to eat at segregated lunch counters" (ibid., 2003: 9). However, Boyd is not trying to disrespect the civil rights generation. Like myself is grateful for those who 'laid down their life'. However, the fight continues and constantly living in the past, effectively downplaying the achievements of the current generation, can halt a generation from moving forward. I feel that this hostage situation can be related to in both youth work and hip-hop where the past is held up as the golden years and those who have been around for a long time sometimes have a 'been there done that attitude'.

'YO! HIP HOP STARTED OUT IN THE HEART'
(HILL, L 1998: 00:00 – 00:20)

The lyrics 'Hip-hop started out in the Park' have been repeated for generations starting with MC Shan in 1988 and Jay Z some 20 years later. Which is no surprise given its accuracy, in 1970, by a group of people in the Bronx. I have no certainty about this but I do not believe that their aim was to change the world while they stole electricity from streetlights to power their block parties. However, shape the world they did. As hip-hop grew it began to infiltrate the world from water[7] to the White House.[8] Drake once said, "Started from the bottom now we here" (Drake, 2013). The history of this social movement is so expansive and like the roots of a tree, it would be implausible to follow each individual root. The purpose for delving into the history of hip-hop is to draw out the comparisons between it and youth work; I have therefore kept the history brief.

'Hip-hop' has become a noun that describes a genre of music; however it is actually describes a movement or culture. Within hip-hop culture there are many elements, the main four being 'graffiti', 'b-boying' or break dancing, 'DJing' and 'rapping'. KRS One expanded on this with five additional 'elements: beat boxing, fashion, language, street knowledge, and entrepreneurialism' (Hess, 2007: X). My focus will be the rap element of hip-hop, as a comparative to the element of dialogue in youth work.

Amongst many places rap can trace its roots, such as, Girot story telling in West Africa and spoken word jazz. Many of its characteristics can be traced back to a game called, 'The Dozens'. The Dozens is, "a game of exchanging, in contest form ritualized verbal insults, which are usually in rhymed couplets and often profane" (Greene, 2012: 376). A typical dozens verse could be,

> I don't play the dozens, the dozens ain't my game, but the way I fuck your mother is a god damn shame. (Wald, 2012: 3)

It is thought that its name derives from a punishment for slaves whereby they were, "grouped in lots of a 'cheap dozen' for sale to slave owners. For a black to be sold as part of the 'dozens' was the lowest blow possible" (Saloy, 1990). As slaves faced insults on a daily basis, the dozens made light of these insults in a 'sticks and stones', tongue out kind of way. Many anthropologists and sociologists see the dozens as a game, ritual, or rite of passage for young black men. Robin Kelley disagrees with this believing that they have misinterpreted it. Kelley claims:

> Ethnographers seem to be oblivious to the fact that their very presence shaped what they observed. Asking their subject to 'play the dozens' (...) creating a ritual performance for the sake of an audience. (Kelley, 1998: 52)

He argues, "the pleasure of the dozens is not viciousness of the insult but the humour, the creative pun, the outrageous metaphor" (Kelley, 1998: 53). I believe that the characteristics used in the dozens, such as the use of outrageous metaphors, creating humour, the essence of competition and rhyming are prevalent in modern rap music. Given rap's connections with the dozens it would be logical to conclude that hip-hop has hereditary connections with struggle and oppression. This is further confirmed when one learns that the 1970s' Bronx is the birthplace of hip-hop.

The Bronx, in the 1970s, was, amongst other things known as: 'America's worst slum', 'the city of despair', 'ghetto of ghettos', 'the cancer' (Hess, 2007: 1), confirming that hip-hop is the music of the downtrodden. Further evidence that hip-hop spoke for the have-nots, is that the first block parties were only able to take place because DJs illegally plugged in 'their sound systems into the street lights to party' (Hess, 2007: 5).

Block party DJs used the breaks from other musical genres to create their own sound. Hip-hop continues this tradition of sampling and of reworking pre-recorded music; a practice Mark Dery calls the, "musical equivalent of shoplifting" (Dery, 2004: 471). Dery believes for this reason, "Rap by definition, is political music" (Dery, 2004: 471). Hip-Hop music grew out of a harsh dissonant environment, but due to its survival instincts and rebellious mentality, it has been able to adapt and evolve in order to make beautiful music in harmony with the struggles of the people. Hip-hop has also become so prosperous and popular that it is now out selling other genres. It is this prosperous nature that has led a significant number of hip-hoppers to question hip-hop's 'realness', claiming that it has sold out and that it is now an inferior imitation of what it once was. Gloria Clemente, Rosie Perez's character in the film, *'White Men Can't Jump'*, summarises this double-edged sword of success that hip-hop has found itself impaled on. Perez said,

Sometimes when you win, you really lose,
and sometimes when you lose, you really win,
and sometimes when you win or lose, you actually tie,
and sometimes when you tie, you actually win or lose.
Winning or losing is all one organic mechanism
(White Men Can't Jump, 1992)

As perplexing as Perez's monologue is (if everyone loses there are no winners – or losers) hip-hop's success has in some way been its own undoing. It is similar to the 'girl' that Common referred to; as she became more attractive she became corrupted in Common's eyes. The penalty for placing your head above the parapet is that you will either be decapitated or recruited. However, with hip-hop having this much power it is inevitable that it will become corrupted with businesses wanting to make money from it, as well as being able to hold a certain level of control over the public. Hip-hop artists promoting various brands such as 'Timberland' and 'Crystal Champagne' demonstrate this.

Youth work's success of being able to build relationships with young people and encourage them to question their environment has been hijacked in something of the same way. The success of hip-hop is no longer just attracting rappers who want to show off how nice[9] their raps are, or those seeing it as a medium to address injustice. It is now also attracting those who have infiltrated the industry purely for monetary gain. The music that once was referred to as the, "CNN for black people" (Cowen, 1998: 173) has now become the butt of some people's jokes. Comedian David Alan Grier talks about hip-hop in his stand-up routine, saying,

The world lost a luminary recently. Hip-hop. And it drowned from too much [bleep] AND CHAMPAGNE. What the hell happened to you, hip-hop? Artists with names like, terminator x and furious five AND [bleep] WITH ATTITUDE Once preached about social awareness and political enlightenment when did fight the power[10] become WAIT TILL YOU SEE MY [Bleep]?[11] [*Sic*] (Grier, 2010)

Grier highlights the downfall of hip-hop, and how others like Joell Ortiz[12] agree that for a time, hip-hop was seen as a laughing stock.

In the introduction, I made reference to my view that both hip-hop[13] and youth work have followed similar journeys. From examining the literature of both, it is evident they both started with an idea of growing organically in response to needs – the need for education, finding a voice, and escape by way of entertainment. In my experience, youth work had the aim to increase social awareness, to encourage young people to question their environment and to have fun. Some youth workers believe that having your practice, 'informed by political and moral values', as well as having a 'belief in equality and respect for the environment' (Belton, 2010: 69), is *'radical youth work'*. However, I consider this to be the very spirit of youth work, because my formative years were spent working with youth workers who promoted social awareness and questioning. Radical youth work has become my constructed norm. In fairness to Belton (2010) he does make clear that that is kind of what 'radical' means – 'back to foundations'. He makes this point pretty clearly – he is not trying to be 'rebellious', he sees current practice (including the attempted contortions of 'informal education' and 'social pedagogy') largely as the antithesis of what youth work 'is' – just like what might be called 'hip hop', that which has been appropriated by the means of exploitation, can be said to authentically be hip hop.

It seems doubtful that the growth of youth work as we know it stemmed from Ragged Schools, which were really an institutional injection of social conformity and control at the base of society, faith interventions such as 'the Espérance' or even from its affiliation with the political and social struggle of the Suffragettes. However, the obvious similarities with the Rainbow Corner provision, that reflected the need of young people to be provided with something different than what perhaps adult society might collectively approve of, demonstrates the inherent rebellious nature of youth work and those who have facilitated the practice. They have suffered with the rose tinted glasses syndrome of believing that everything was better 'back in the day', but it stands to reason that there must have always been both good and bad examples, as it is not possible for one to exist without the other. As the saying goes 'if something is everything then it is actually nothing'. It is this spirit of being politically motivated, questioning your environment and speaking out, which was once inherent, that is now being considered extrinsic, leaving those who choose that path wearing the label of radicalism, or 'political rapper'.

But maybe we pick our own labels. Seeing what was once 'normal' as being now radical is saying that what is now considered radical was once reactionary. Many in the past managed to fool themselves and not a few may still suffer from the false consciousness that they do not serve political masters of an ideological hue they might not wish to understand they salute at every turn. At least to some extent fibbing about funding bids does not a revolution make. Drawing a salary, using resources for state or organisational ends implicates one; to deny this is to be a fool or a liar – working with it is another option – 'it is as it is, and this is what I do with what it is?'

"THE QUESTION AIN'T WHETHER IT'S DEAD. IT'S MORE LIKE,
WHO KILLED IT AND WHEN"
(BUDDEN, J 2005: 00:14 – 00: 20)

In December 2006, veteran rapper Nas released an album entitled, '*Hip Hop is Dead*'. The album featured a gloomy cover with the photo taken from the perspective of looking out from a grave. Nas is dressed all in black, crouched down at the mouth of the grave with vultures circling above him in the sinister skies, as he drops a single rose into the grave. The cover sets the tone, and confirms that Nas is not in two minds about what he feels about the state of hip-hop. In an interview,

Nas explained his reasons for the controversial title and claimed, "Hip-hop is dead because we as artists no longer have the power" (MusicMP3.RU, 2006).

This album sparked others to question the state of hip-hop. Rapper Joe Budden turned detective on his 16 minute track entitled, *Who Killed Hip-Hop*, where he set about finding the culprit for this crime. He listed a range of suspects from the humble iPod to hip-hop's self-proclaimed king, Jay Z. This track was the catalyst behind my questions to the culprits of the demise of Youth Work.

Budden begins by pointing the finger at the highlighting of record sales, he raps, "It was a few years ago, but I remember the summer. 50 Cent made fans start looking at the numbers" (Budden, 2005, 01:00 – 01:10). In the summer of 2007, rapper 50 Cent made a statement, prior to the release of his *Curtis* album and Kanye West's album *Graduation*. The statement said that if Kanye out sold him he would retire.[13] Competition has always been part of hip-hop, from Kool Moe Dee vs. Busy Bee in 1981 to LL Cool J vs. Canibus in 1997. However, this 50 Cent and Kanye feud was different, as unlike previous rap battles where the winner would be the person with the best lyrics, like in the dozens, instead this time it was all about record sales.

This statistical approach came up during my interviews with youth workers. Bruce felt the source of the demise of youth work is that it is becoming 'statistic led'. He also concurs with Budden[14] claiming, 'to be honest statistics mean very little'. But of course they do mean something, in terms of gaining funding for the work we do.

In the UK (like other contexts) the shift in the emphasis for youth work has been gradually moving from working towards outcomes such as, 'achieve economic well being' and 'enjoy and achieve' (Fraser, 2007: 5), to now working with youth contracts, which have an emphasis on taking NEET (Not in Education, Employment, or Training) young people and turning them into EET (Engaged in Education, Employment, or Training) young people. Along with youth contracts comes Payment By Results (PBR). However, given the character of our society one can't help but want what the alternative to this might be – payment despite results? That latter doesn't feel possible or realistic.

However, when I first heard of PBR it reminded me of the summer I spent cold calling and canvassing for double glazing sales, working on commission. Commission driven environments are notoriously cut throat places, and therefore I was confused as to why it was being introduced to youth work. Within this new scheme a provider can receive payments, 'up to £2,200 per person, depending on how successful they are at helping young people to make a sustainable move into a positive outcome' (Department for Education, 2013). But why would this be surprising given we live in a capitalist society – why would I expect some kind of socialist model to be employed by a capitalist government?

By positive outcome they mean turning young people into commodities for the labour force market. A 17-year-old has around 12,500 working days ahead of them, maybe more if the retirement age keeps on increasing. When I was 17 I was encouraged to quit my job to enable me to go to Mali for four weeks. That helped convince me to become a youth worker – as such this trip had a function. It was a good investment in terms of the maintenance and advancement of capitalism because it made me a potential agent of the same; a person who might help in creating a relatively skilled, relatively compliant, relatively cheap work force.

While there is no way of knowing what effect that trip had on me, when I returned I knew I didn't want to work in retail for another year. – in effect this was part of what transformed me from a worker into a worker who produces workers.

Fran Abrams questions the logic of setting targets like those that pertain widely in youth work. She asks, "… could there not be some flexibility for the voluntary sector just to do what it did best – to form relationships that worked" (Abrams, 2010: 148). But how exactly did they 'work'? The voluntary sector historically has gained most of its funding from the state, its agencies and allies (including big business) – might Abrams believe that somehow the sector was at some point independent of those who funded it? That feels simply naive.

Although Abrams is referring to the voluntary sector, building relationships is what youth workers do best (but that has a rationale to it like every other target). The attention that youth workers now have to pay to results (although results have long been a factor, although perhaps not as overtly as over the last 20 years) I can see only resulting in two possible outcomes:

1) Youth workers conform, which most do, although many talk about 'working within the system' as if they were able to both be part of the system while rebelling against it – at least some of this feels like self delusion once you've heard overt compliance described in this way for the 10,000th time

2) They revert back to the guerrilla tactics.

However, neither of these possible tactics avoid young people being seen as potential commission instead of as individual human beings. The introduction of PBR also confirms Moira's (research respondent) fears that youth workers have been 'wooed by money', leaving them chasing the funding and forgetting the reasons why they become youth workers. But this is not altogether new. Youth workers have always been obliged to 'go for funding', certainly since the 1970s.

Hip-hop has also been seduced by money and many have forgotten why they became rappers; their aim is just to wear their wealth and live an extravagant life, or as rappers refer to it to 'floss'. Jay Z openly admits that he, "… dumbed down for my audience to double my dollars" (Jay Z, 2003: 01:40 – 01:50), and he goes on to say, "If skills sold, truth be told, I'd probably be lyrically Talib Kweli. Truthfully I wanna rhyme like Common Sense. But I did 5 mill" (Jay Z, ibid.). Jay Z is acknowledging that being lyrical does not necessarily bring the money in, so he is opting to simplify his rhymes in order to sell more records. The point that Moira was making is that you don't need lots of money to carry out good youth work and history shows youth work has never got lots of money ever but you do need some money some times.

I feel that at one point in history, to obtain funding for projects was easier with initiatives such as the Youth Opportunities Fund, but that too had political strings attached, as did the 'Manpower Services Commission' and 'Youth Opportunities Programme' before that. But need for funding seems to have made youth workers more dependent on money than their own skills and motivation. This dependency has meant the creativity that used to develop through running sessions with just a stack of old newspaper and some balls made from balloons and rice is lost, and these skills are not passed on.

Budden also listed the temporary nature of rappers in hip-hop as cause for concern; he explains, "Hip-hop is just a stepping stool. Till we find another role we can step into" (Budden, 2005). This was in reference to rappers jumping ship, leaving hip-hop to become actors, fashion designers and nightclub owners. This is being mirrored in youth work as youth workers leave to become social workers and teachers, or setting up commercially oriented training organisations. Of the people I interviewed, not one of them is still practicing youth work. So it seems even those who critique the practice selling out have sold out? 'Things aint wot they used to be' – more Max Bygraves than Gill Scott-Heron? Some have moved into similar sector professions such as teaching, while others no longer work with young people due to the constraints around it.

Prior to embarking on my own professional training I was encouraged to think about what I was doing from my then Head of Service as they believed a Social Work degree would open up more doors for me in the future. There is a belief that social work is somehow a more proficient and adaptable profession. Although one might wonder what a social worker would have to say about that proposal, youth workers have a different set of skills, which are equally as valid as that of social workers, although youth work has always had trouble providing the evidence to back such a claim. The problem that comes with youth workers leaving the profession is its affect on the group; as members leave the group becomes potentially weaker. That said, if the liabilities leave, those that lack the commitment, skill, tenacity or belief, this might result in solidarity between kindred souls. The boat moves faster when it's lighter and those who don't row anyway are effectively passengers.

However, for the most part employed youth workers are not given the choice of staying in professional practice. I worked for one of the youth services that merged with Connexions to become the Integrated Youth Support Services. Once this happened there was a move towards working with targeted groups and careers and as a result many of the youth workers, who did not work exclusively with targeted groups, were made redundant and open access youth provisions were closed.

This also had an impact on voluntary workers but in the UK, as throughout the world, there are hundreds of times more volunteer youth worker than those in employment. Youth work, as a practice, is not reliant on those paid to undertake it; far from it.

In the context of hip hop Budden drew attention to a list of label mergers[15] and YouTube.[16] For him, because YouTube and social networking sites give everybody the facilities to put their music out there, the record companies no longer monitor it, so the quality cannot be guaranteed. I feel that this is a good thing for music as it encourages variety. I am not about to blame YouTube for causing a decline in youth work; however, the British government has given a similar ease of access to young people's services. The National Citizenship Service is the Coalition's initiative started in 2011. The aim is to build, 'skills for work and life', while young people, 'take on new challenges and meet new friends' (GOV.UK, 2014). The programme consists of residentials and young people setting up projects, which are activities that youth work has traditionally carried out. However, in 2012, Serco, a company which has a history of winning military contracts,[17] began pursuing contracts to monitor and tag offenders, as well as becoming one the world leaders in providing custodial services to governments. Now, 'the private sector services firm has won the largest number of regional contracts to deliver the government's National Citizen Service in 2013 and 2014' (Third Sector, 2014). With large organisations, such as, Serco, carrying out so many roles in society my fear is that it won't be long until we are living in a world similar what George Orwell described in *Nineteen-Eighty-Four*.

Having looked at many reasons for the decline of youth work, for example, a focus on measurable outcomes (although it is difficult to see how one can have unmeasurable outcomes) it seems youth work has been suffocated by the seduction of money as well as large private organisations carrying out the work. The work that is on offer looks sterile or clearly ideologically led, but that doesn't mean we have to do it. There are still 'real' rappers out there – they don't have to be defined by their recording contracts.

However, these reasons have a common thread and the thread that has managed to weave its way into the fabric of youth work is more like capitalist stain. With the emphasis being on encouraging young people in to the job market as well as new monetary initiatives such as PBR. This said, it has to be questionable if this has ever been different. From its inception as a generic service in the 1960s youth work has been part-and-parcel of the capitalist system, how could it have ever somehow dodged (not been part of) capitalism, its functions and norms?

The role of youth work has never been what I define youth work to be – encouraging, questioning, giving young people the chance to experience new things and develop their own ideas. My research corroborates my ideals. However, the aims that youth work has been funded for is: to create a, 'relatively flexible, relatively compliant, relatively cheap work force with the aim of making Britain more competitive within the international capitalist labour market' (Belton, 2010: XI). What else could be the case – unless we believe there is some sort of philanthropic strain within the kind of state that kills innocent people with drones to facilitate international capitalism?

Due to the guerrilla tactics youth workers employed in the past, youth workers were able to work under the radar and work towards the alternative aims, which were not total economically driven. But this has not gone unnoticed. In the UK and probably elsewhere, this stealth-like work has caused those who fund the work to place tighter restrictions on youth work. This is substantiated with the 'Department for Education relinquishing responsibility for youth policy in England to the Cabinet Office' (CYPnow, 2013). I see this response as similar to a teacher who moves the troublesome pupil to sit next to them so that they can keep a closer eye. The question is can the pupil still manage to talk to their peers from under this watchful eye.

"YOU CAN REMAIN STUCK IN A BOX. I'MMA BREAK OUT AND THEN HIDE EVERY LOCK"
(LAMAR, K 2012: 2:45 – 2:51)

Hip-hop is now in a state of recovery and is arguably in the best place it has been for the last decade or so. This rejuvenation is due, in part, to the influx of new rappers giving hip-hop a new lease of life and is no longer being detained by the past. Hip-hop, as a youth and/or cultural movement, has matured and been impinged upon by those who wish to change it. As a result the founders of the genre act like the guardians of hip-hop, as pushy over protective parents who wish to direct their child down a certain path, meaning hip-hop has grown up with creativity and defiance for parents. Therefore it was inevitable that new rappers would inherit the rebellious gene. The new wave of rappers have swaggered into hip-hop with a backpack[18] full of energy and ambition surrounded by a youthful air of self assurance, even with a whiff of arrogance. Along with this injection of youthful exuberance, youth work should consider other strategies from hip-hop to ensure its own survival.

Youth work and youth workers have suffered in the same way that hip-hop did, falling victim to looking at the past as the answer. In models put forward by Tuckman (1965), which are used by youth workers, studies that took place over 40 years ago are regurgitated as if they were facts not theories. Ideas like usefulness of 'thinking-in-and-on-action' fall into the same sort of bracket, being overused and they relative usefulness under substantiated – perhaps the likes of this stuff aren't even theories as it is hard to see how they might be proved or disproved in any robust way?

Part of the work that youth workers carry out is about praxis, whereby you read and understand the theory and then try it out, to see how it works, and use some professional judgement instead of merely responding to order. It is easy to fall into the trap of shoe horning theories into practice, as Sherlock Holmes once said, "Insensibly one begins to twist facts to suit theories, instead of theories to suit facts" (Doyle, 2003: 189). For example, seeing a group arguing, and interpreting this as the 'storming phase',[19] believing that how you respond to this is a, "moment of truth from which either optimal functioning or hopeless fragmentation will likely follow" (Behrman, 1998: 154). Instead I urge new youth workers to have a similar self-assurance to that shown by freshmen rappers and believe that their opinions, judgements and ideas are just as valid as Tuckman (indeed one is tempted to say they have to be more valid … at least they were born after 1938!). Concluding that a single intervention is not the making or breaking of a group.

New rappers are not completely dismissive of the past. For example, in 2013, J Cole released a track entitled *Let Nas down* Cole states, "long live the idols, may they never be your rivals" (Cole, 2013). Cole uses the song to explain to Nas and his fans the reasoning behind releasing the pop rap record called *Work out* in 2011. In a talk Cole said that he was so happy with the *Work out* record and that he had learnt the radio game and believed that he 'beat the game' with that record (Mike YI, 2013). On the *Let Nas Down* track Cole is disappointed but unapologetic, believing that Nas should understand as Nas has made radio tracks[20] in the past.

I feel that in order for youth work to be rejuvenated youth workers should be respectful but not obsequious of the work of those who write instructional style youth work books. That said, respect is something earned. while the 'nostalgiaites' disallow entry into the sect of anyone they see as heretical (anyone saying something other than backing up their repetition) it's a moot point how much respect they might warrant.

Youth work could also benefit from learning the game and beating the game philosophy, as shown by Cole returning to the guerrilla roots of the past. Youth work may be constantly given directive polices and initiatives, such as youth contracts, but for the revival of youth work to occur youth workers need to find ways to make these programmes work for young people, or formulate their own programmes. Youth work, like music, is never going to be a one size fits all, as it is about dealing with individuals and individual tastes, as well as dealing with the times and contexts.

As rapping has evolved from 'the dozens', challenging and competition is inherent. This trait has enabled hip-hop to grow and gave breath to its new life. In 2013, rapper Kendrick Lamar featured on a track with rappers Big Sean and Jay Electronica. On the track Lamar said,[21] "I'm Makaveli's offspring, I'm the king of New York,[22] King of the Coast, one hand, I juggle them both" (Lamar, 2013), as prior to this rappers were competing to be the best rapper from either coast. He goes on to say,

> I'm usually homeboys with the same niggas I'm rhymin' with
> But this is hip-hop and them niggas should know what time it is.
> And that goes for Jermaine Cole, Big KRIT, Wale,
> Pusha T, Meek Millz, A$AP Rocky, Drake,
> Big Sean, Jay Electron', Tyler, Mac Miller
> I got love for you all but I'm tryna murder you niggas.
> Trying to make sure your core fans never heard of you niggas.
> They don't wanna hear not one more noun or verb from you niggas.
> What is competition? I'm trying to raise the bar high.
> (Lamar, 2013)

Lamar is not trying to cause beef[23] he is laying down a challenge to other rappers, reminding them that competition is part of rap's make up. I'm not suggesting that youth workers start challenging each other to a rap battle, but in my experience youth workers are not good at self-promotion. There are many great youth projects going on, the problem is that no one hears about what great work they are doing. The surrounding community may see and value the work of a youth provision but it is not appreciated in a wider context. If it were, it would be more difficult to close these projects.

On the other hand, if youth work achieves it is because it takes a political stance, as soon as this is recognised it tends to become a target to be reformed or wiped out – much the same as happened to hip-hop.

I had the pleasure of working in a youth club that had been there for over 30 years and I spoke to older members about their experiences of the club. I am sure that this is not the only youth club with this type of legacy. If youth workers started to share their practice with other youth workers and professions I believe it would bring respect for the profession, enable the transfer of skills, as well as enable front line youth workers to shape youth policy. Add that to the self-policing approach that hip-hop has shown, such as rappers using their songs to discuss the over-use of words such as Nigga and Bitch. Wale uses his Track *Kramer* to talk about the difference between Nigga and Nigger claiming that:

Nigga ain't bad, see, niggas just had
A clever idea to take something they said
Into something we have, something we flipped,
to something with swag, nigga, don't be mad.
(Wale, 2008: 01:58 – 02:08)

Lupe Fiasco has a similar track but this time he refers to the word 'bitch'. On his track *Bad Bitch* he tells a story of the current use of the word and how it is becoming confusing for kids. Lupe has a Freudian view of the word and suggests it is similar to Freud's Madonna/whore complex, whereby, "men love they have no desire and where they desire they cannot love" (Singer, 1987: 32). In Lupe's story the boy and girl have different perceptions of the word claiming, "He thinks disrespectfully, she thinks of that sexually" (Fiasco, 2012).

This is exploration – it is akin to youth work in this respect – it doesn't just shut something down because it is or potentially is offensive – it looks at the world square on which is different to applying sellotape to someone's mouth or just shutting them down.

As a profession that places great importance on the use of dialogue it's surprising that questioning and self-policing are not commonplace in youth work. Much of the time we seem to do little more than focus on 'confronting' and 'challenging', what is taken as unacceptable or against personal or social norms – it tends to often be 'dialogue on my terms'.

Both Lupe and Wale question the over-use of words that are commonplace in hip-hop. Yet it's rare in youth work that youth workers will question accepted norms, such as, working towards boosting self-esteem and the agreement that youth work is almost impossible to measure. We sing ourselves one song but the lyrics belie the actions?

I feel that employing this approach in a youth work setting could be vital to its rejuvenation. As Eldridge Cleaver once said, "Too much agreement kills a chat" (Cleaver, 1968: 31). By replacing the agreement with questioning we could resuscitate the chat and hopefully youth work.

There are countless numbers of reasons for the revival of hip-hop but I feel the largest contributor is that it has regained its political voice on a global scale. Whether it's Palestinian hip-hop group Dam, who rap about poverty and the Israeli-Palestinian conflict, or French Rapper Keny Arkana who comments on the 2005 civil unrest. In the UK we also have politically aware rappers such as Plan B. On his track, *Ill Manors*, Plan B talks about the state of Great Britain. He claims that, "We got an Eco-friendly government, they preserve our natural habitat. Built an entire Olympic village around where we live without pulling down any flats" (B, 2013). Plan B is commenting on how the government is seeking to preserve the conditions in which some people live, in this case the feverish tower blocks of east London. He goes on to ask, "Who closed down the community centre? I kill time there, used to be a member. What will I do now until September?" (B, 2013). Plan B is commentating on the London riots of 2011, suggesting that maybe, if the community centre wasn't closed, the youth would have something to do during the summer. These themes are carried on throughout the album, as part of the hip-hop musical '*Ill Manors*'.

However, this is resonant of social engineering, arguably 'making the world safe for capitalism'. Does the state care about the so-called 'riots' because capitalism doesn't like its investments threatened? Bring in the youth workers to quell the restless young with no stake in capitalism – get them to have a stake in it so preventing them from trying to resist or threaten it?

Becoming politically aware, challenging stereotypes and questioning young people's norms, and the norms of how young people are viewed and referred to, was a feature of the youth work that I experienced when younger. As a young person I felt that I was politically informed from reading the papers and watching the news. It was through attending my local youth club that I gained perspective on politics and began to realise that it did affect my area and me. I have led sessions where young people are telling me about benefits scroungers and how they steal our money. Regardless of my personal view, I feel that youth workers should be giving a more balanced opinion on the political system that they live in. If they don't they are effectively supporting every negative perspective relating to you that's turned out in the media – can we honestly or meaningfully declare our neutrality without betraying our own cause?

Youth work has always been politically led but now it is becoming overtly so; youth workers need to respond and tackle it.

CONCLUSION

People talk about Hip-Hop like it's some giant livin' in the hillside
Comin' down to visit the townspeople
We are Hip-Hop
Me, you, everybody,
We are Hip-Hop
So Hip-Hop is goin' where we goin'
(Def, M, 1999: 01:15 – 01:30)

In conclusion, I believe that youth work and hip-hop share similar traits from their birth, this is due to the intrinsic link between youth work and popular culture. Over the years, both youth work and hip-hop have shown themselves to be powerful adversaries but also allies to capitalism, which placed them unknowingly in capitalism's crosshairs. This resulted in both social movements being assassinated by way of corruption. Hip-hop with its 'bling bling' mentality and living to excess is the embodiment of a capitalist culture. The same is happening with youth work. One of my interviewees (Moria) said that, "Youth work at its best is when there is no money involved and it is done voluntarily". But there's always money involved – arguably not if one just operates on the street – but every facility means an effective donation – again to think otherwise is naïve – even the bus ride to where people are costs money.

This was confirmed when Moria went on to say, "I can only wax lyrical now because I have the car, house and can afford to live comfortably". This need to live comfortably and aspiring for more possessions in search of comfort can hinder people from speaking out and placing their head above the parapet. To quote a one of part-time youth workers circa 1980 – 'in this game you got to take shit and shoot shit'.

Youth work, being intrinsically connected by purpose and practice to national policy, state institutions, connected welfare and education, must be shaped, informed and confirmed by the same. At the same time youth work plays a part in shaping, informing and confirming these institutional structures. This has been so ever since youth work has been identified as such (at least). There has *never* been, and arguably could never have been (given the nature of the social form) a nationally defined and sanctioned youth service that was somehow not only organically separated from and independent of the nature of the state (from an Althusserian perspective) but also, practically unopposed or even encourage, to operate in direct contradiction of state ideology and function. To believe that this is not the case, the position effectively touted in much of the dialogue that surrounds our practice, has to be delusional; the product of false consciousness.

While young people's welfare has been consistently mooted as being at the centre of the purpose of youth work, their 'education' (they are seen as/assumed to be relatively ignorant) 'development' (from a state of taken-for-granted 'underdevelopment') and 'transition' (their effective 'reform' from non-conformist youth to compliant adult) have been part of the officialised social function of youth workers. However, as facets of the above research indicate, youth workers have been on the defensive since day one.

For all this, hip-hop has shown that it is possible to both have your opinion and still live comfortably, although it depends how comfortable you want to be and what you regard as comfortable. I believe that comfort is about more than possessions and money; maybe youth workers can find comfort in knowing that they are equipping young people with the skills to be questioning and critical thinking adults. However, they may already have the skills – they not unusually come to us with anguish – they often just need a place to express this and someone to listen and respond. This, in itself, is action and the start of something more than mere reaction (the likes of which was demonstrated in the UK in the riots of 2011).

I set out to discover what state youth work is in and whether, or not, it could be saved. What I discovered is that my expectations of youth work are actually what is considered to be radical youth work by reactionaries (what in another time and place might have been called 'the capitalist running dogs'). But radical just means going back to first principles – the soul and spirit of the work (not it's formularised 'history' but its essence) – bit like some of the new hip hoppers are trying to do?

Although my expectations are ideological, they have been built from my own experiences; therefore I have seen that this form of youth work is possible.

I have also discovered that both hip-hop and youth work have been infected by the capitalist rich soil in which they both grew up. Hip-hop critics are forever pointing the finger at rappers saying they sold out and that they are no longer 'keeping it real', as they become more and more successful. My initial thought prior to embarking on this research was that youth work had indeed sold out. What I have come to realise is that selling out is inevitable and it is not a reason to fall out of favour. Once hip-hop was adopted by the masses and was seen to exert power it was inevitable that it would be exploited by industries that have been built to enable that power to be harnessed. Youth work has also been a victim of this and has been led astray by the material elements of life, just like the girl Common was talking about in my introductory quote.

This said, it feels incumbent on youth workers to get away from asking those who have given up or effectively sold out what they think because that is always going backwards – 'we are what we are, we are where we are, the past is a foreign land they do things differently there' (to paraphrase LP Hartley's 1953 opening of *The Go-Between*) – a view of history from the standpoint of delusion, false memory and false consciousness is inherently retrogressive – the future is surely the field we need to plough?

Youth work has been, and will be, a tool in encouraging non-conforming young people to conform, which is now labelling people as NEET to EET. In 1857, the Ragged Schools had the aim of doing what they could to enforce an 'industrial education' on the poorest of young people. Although I have learnt that this is not the reason why youth workers come in to the field, it is what we are now effectively funded to do.

People I interviewed who spoke about youth work in a *Holistic* manner were accepting that we are part of the system but suggested we can learn the game in order to beat it. As well as bringing new *Energy* to youth work, no longer regurgitating the instructions of old and finally being *Resourceful* like in the past, youth workers can work below the radar to bring about change. This has always been a minority pursuit, hence the 'rebels' are living in nice big houses, with nice cars. While they head up departments or direct policy, they lament the loss of the revolution and blame it on the system they have always been part of – perhaps there is no justice, just us!

Understanding that H.E.R. (Holistic, Energy & Resourceful) can be something of beauty but can equally be easily corrupted. But trying to understand says that we are proud of what she stands for. Rapper Rapsody summarizes this by using Common's acronym where she states that, "Hip-hop in its essence is real; I'm still hearing every rhyme"[24] (Rapsody, 2011). I believe the very essence of youth work is 'Real'.

NOTES

[1] He had to change his name due to a band already having the name Common Sense.
[2] H.E.R. is an acronym which means Hear Every Rhyme.
[3] "Cause who I'm talkin bout y;all is hip-hop" (Common, 1994).
[4] Jimmy Hoffa disappeared in 1975, although his body was never found it was presumed he was murdered.
[5] 1990s is commonly referred to as the golden age of hip-hop.
[6] The word G.I. used to describe the *soldiers* of the U.S. Army.
[7] Rapper 50 Cent worked with Glacéau to create a vitamin water drink called Formula 50.
[8] Barack Obama joked about Jay Z on a trip to Cuba by saying, "I got 99 Problems and now Jay-Z is one".
[9] 'Nice' is often used to describe how good a rappers lyrics are.
[10] Public Enemy released 'Fight the power' single in June 1989.
[11] Ying Yang twins released 'Wait (The Whisper Song)' in March 2005.
[12] "Sometimes I wish it was dead, rather than look this stupid alive" (Ortiz, 2009).
[13] 50 Cent's album sold 691,000 in it first week in comparison to Kanye's who sold 957,000. However 50 Cent did not retire.
[14] "I hate to break it to you numbers always lie" (Budden, 2005: 04:20 – 04:25).
[15] "They fired everybody and labels stared merging" (Budden, 2005).
[16] "Was is it when Youtube came in the game, Now nobodys from their living rooms can make a name" (Budden, 2005).
[17] "1960s the company won a piece of work that was to shape its future direction – a maintenance contract for the UK Ballistic Missile Early Warning System" (Serco, 2014).
[18] The backpack is a feature of new rappers.
[19] "The group goes through a period of more outspoken disagreements as members feel 'safer' to reveal themselves" (Sapin, 2009: 129).
[20] "I mean, you made 'You Owe Me' dog, I thought that you could relate" (Cole, 2013). Nas's *You owe me* was a track made for the charts.
[21] Makaveli is an alias of rapper West Coast rap legend Tupac Shakur.
[22] Christopher Wallace best known as The Notorious B.I.G. to as the King of New York.
[23] Beef is wanting to start a fight or argument with somebody.
[24] Rapsody uses changes the H.E.R to mean Hip-hop in its essence is real while paying homage to Common's by saying I still hear every Rhyme.

REFERENCES

Abrams, Fran. (2010). *Learning to fail: how society lets young people down*. Abingdon, Oxon: Routledge.

Batsleer, Janet. (2010). *What is youth work?* Exeter: Learning Matters.

Beck, Dave, & Purcell, Rod. (2010). *Popular education practice for youth and community development work*. Exeter: Learning Matters Ltd.

Behrman, Harry. (1998). *The practice of facilitation managing group process and solving problems*. Westport, CT: Quorum.

Belton, Brian. (2000). *Developing critical youth work theory*. Rotterdam: Sense.

Belton, Brian. (2010). *Radical youth work: developing critical perspectives and professional judgement*. Lyme Regis, Dorset: Russell House Pub.

Blackledge, Paul. (2012). *Marxism and ethics freedom, desire, and revolution*. Albany: State University of New York Press.

Boyd, Todd. (2002). *The new H.N.I.C. (head niggas in charge) the death of civil rights and the reign of hip hop*. New York: New York University Press.

Buchroth, Ilona, & Parkin, Chris. (2010). *Using theory in youth and community work practice*. Exeter: Learning Matters Ltd.

Budden, Joe. (2005). *Who killed Hip Hop*. Unknown: Unknown.

CYPnow. (2013). Cabinet Office takes control of youth policy. *Children & Young People Now*, n.p., 3 July 2013. Web. 24 Jan. 2014. http://www.cypnow.co.uk/cyp/news/1077640/cabinet-office-takes-control-youth-policy?utm_content=&utm_campaign=080713_YouthWorkNews&utm_source=Children%20%26%20Young%20People%20Now&utm_medium=adestra_email&utm_term=http%3A%2F%2Fwww.cypnow.co.uk%2Fcyp%2Fnews.

Cleaver, Eldridge. (1968). *Soul on ice* (1st ed.). New York: McGraw-Hill.

Cole, J. (2011). Let Nas down. *Born sinner*, 00:010 – 00:20. New York: Dreamville,

Common. (1994). I used to love H.E.R. *Resurrection*, 00:20 – 00:30. New York: Relativity.

Cowen, Tyler. (1998). *In praise of commercial culture*. Cambridge, MA: Harvard University Press.

Davies, Bernard. (2009). Defined by history: Youth work in the UK. In *The history of youth work in Europe: Relevance for today's youth work policy* (pp. 63-86). Strasbourg: Council of Europe Publishing.

Def, Mos. (1999). Fear not of men. *Black on both sides*, 01:15 – 01:30. New York: Rawkus.

Department for Education. (n.d.). Youth contract provision for 16- and 17-year-olds not in education, employment or training. *Youth contract provision for 16- and 17-year-olds NEET*, n.p., Web, 23 January 2014. http://www.education.gov.uk/childrenandyoungpeople/youngpeople/participation/a00203664/youth-contract.

Dery, Mark. (2004). Public enemy confrontation. In *That's the joint!: The hip-hop studies reader* (pp. 470-486). New York: Routledge.

Doyle, Arthur Conan, & Freeman, Kyle. (2003). *The complete Sherlock Holmes*. New York: Barnes & Noble Classics.

Drake. (2013). Started from the bottom. *Nothing was the same*, 00:00 – 02:53. New Orleans: Young Money.

Electric Soul Show. (n.d.). Is Rnb music dead? – If it is can bought back to life again? – 2011. *Electric Soul Show – News 8*, n.p., Web, 22 January 2014, http://www.electricsoulshow.com/news/news8.

Fiasco, Lupe. (2012). *Food & liquor II: The great American rap album, Pt. 1*. New York: 1st & 15th.

Forman, Murray. (2012). *That's the joint!: The hip-hop studies reader* (2nd ed.). New York: Routledge.

Fraser, Julie. (2007). *Every child matters: Measuring moments of progress and inclusive assessment*. Armley, Leeds, England: Coachwise [for the Association for Physical Education].

Hill , Lauryn. (1998). Superstar. *The miseducation of Lauryn Hill*, 00:00 – 00:15. Philadelphia: Ruffhouse.

GOV.UK. (n.d.). Tell us what you think of GOV.UK. *National Citizen Service*, n.p., Web, 24 January 2014, https://www.gov.uk/government/get-involved/take-part/national-citizen-service.

Gilchrist, Ruth. (2013). *Reappraisals: Essays in the history of youth and community work*. S.l.: Russell House Publishing.

Greene, Roland. (2012). *The Princeton encyclopedia of poetry and poetics* (4th ed.). Princeton: Princeton University Press.

Grier, David, A. (2010, 27 January). Comedy central, chocolate news. *Comedy central, chocolate news transscript*, n.p., Web, 21 January 2014, http://livedash.ark.com/transcript/chocolate_news/6732/COMEDYP/Wednesday_January_27_2010/177066/.

Guevara, Ernesto. (2008). *Guerrilla warfare* (Authorised ed.). London: Harper Perennial.

Hess, Mickey. (2007). *Icons of hip hop (two volumes). An encyclopedia of the movement, music, and culture*. Connecticut: Greenwood Press

Howard, Sheena C. (2013). *Black comics: politics of race and representation*. London: Bloomsbury.

Ill manors. (2012). Dir. Ben Drew. Perf. Riz Ahmed, Ed Skrein, Keith Coggins. Revolver Entertainment, DVD.

Jay Z. (2003). Moment of clarity. *The black album*, 01:40 – 02:00. New York: Roc-A-Fella.

Jeffs, Tony, & Smith, Mark. (1996). *Informal education: Conversation, democracy and learning* (3rd ed.). Nottingham: Educational Heretics Press.

Jones, Mike. (1979). *Canoeing down Everest*. London: Hodder and Stoughton

Katz, Mark. (2012). *Groove music: The art and culture of the hip-hop DJ*. New York: Oxford University Press.

Kelley, Robin. (1998). Check the technique black urban culture and the predicament of social science. In *In near ruins: cultural theory at the end of the century* (pp. 39-67). Minneapolis: University of Minnesota Press.

Lamar, Kendrick. (2012). Bitch, don't kill my vibe. Good Kid, M.A.A.D. City, 02:45 – 02:50. California: Aftermath.

Ludacris, & Jay Z. (2007). I do it for hip hop. *Theater of the mind*, 02:40 – 02:50. Georgia: Disturbing tha Peace.

Mike Yi. (2013). Cole explains #LetNasDown. [Online Video]. 7 June. Available from http://youtu.be/wY5_0k2g-94 (accessed 10 February 2014).

MusicMP3.RU. (2006, 27 February). Hip hop is dead. *Hip hop is dead*, n.p., Web, 10 February 2014. http://musicmp3.ru/artist_nas__album_hip-hop-is-dead.html#.UvlbnGJ_tIE.

Nas. (2006). Hip hop is dead. *Hip Hop is dead*, 03:10 – 03:20. New York: Def Jam Recordings.

ONE, KRS. (n.d.). Temple of hip hop. *The official KRS ONE website*, n.p., Web, 20 January 2014, http://www.krs-one.com/temple-of-hip-hop/.

Ortiz, Joell. (2009). Cut you loose. *Slaughterhouse*, 02:09 – 02:20. Ontario: E1.

Plan B. (2012). Ill Manors. *Ill Manors*, 00:00 – 03:51. London: Atlantic.

Ragged School Union. (1857). Ragged School Union. *The thirteenth annual report of the Ragged School Union*. London: Ragged School Union.

Rapsody. (2011). Thank H.E.R. now. *The idea of beautiful*, 00:00 – 03:29. North Carolina: Jamla.

Saloy, Mona. (n.d.). African American oral traditions in Louisiana. *Folk life in Louisiana*, n.p., Web, 20 January 2014, http://www.louisianafolklife.org/LT/Articles_Essays/creole_art_african_am_oral.html.

Sapin, Kate. (2009). *Essential skills for youth work practice*. Los Angeles: Sage.

Savage, Jon. (2011, 26 October). Pop at the pictures: Wartime London dances to America's tune. *theguardian.com, Guardian News and Media*, Web, 14 January 2014. http://www.theguardian.com/music/musicblog/2011/oct/26/1940s-london-rainbow-corner-swing.

Savage, Jon. (2008). *Teenage: The prehistory of youth culture, 1875-1945*. New York: Penguin.

Serco. (n.d.). Serco. *Our history*, n.p., Web, 24 January 2014. http://www.serco.com/about/ataglance/history/index.asp.

Singer, Irving. (1987). *The nature of love*. Chicago: University of Chicago Press.

Smith, M. K. (2013). What is youth work? Exploring the history, theory and practice of youth work. *The encyclopedia of informal education*, Web, 14 January 2014, www.infed.org/mobi/what-is-youth-work-exploring-the-history-theory-and-practice-of-work-with-young-people/.

Smith, Mark. (1994). *Local education: Community, conversation, praxis*. Buckingham, England: Open University Press.

Third Sector. (n.d.). Serco consortium takes six National Citizen Service contracts. *Third Sector*, n.p., Web, 24 January 2014, http://www.thirdsector.co.uk/Social_Enterprise/article/1149871/Serco-consortium-takes-six-National-Citizen-Service-contracts/.

Verschelden, Griet. (2009). *The history of youth work in Europe: relevance for today's youth work policy*. Strasbourg: Council of Europe Pub.

Wale. (2008). The Kramer. *The Mixtape about nothing*, 01:58 – 02:08. Unknown: Unknown.

Wald, Elijah. (2012). *The dozens: A history of rap's mama*. New York: Oxford University Press.

White men can't jump. (1992). Dir. Ron Shelton. Perf. Wesley Snipes, Woody Harrelson, Rosie Perez. Twentieth Century Fox Home Entertainment, DVD.

Wood, Allen W. (1981). *Karl Marx*. London: Routledge & Kegan Paul.

Young, Vershawn Ashanti. (2007). *Your average nigga performing race, literacy, and masculinity*. Detroit: Wayne State University Press.

Zone, J. (2007, 20 February). 5 things that killed hip hop. *Hip Hop DX*, n.p., Web, 13 January 2014. http://www.hiphopdx.com/index/editorials/id.723/title.5-things-that-killed-hip-hop.

DANA FUSCO

THE SOCIAL ARCHITECTURE OF
YOUTH WORK PRACTICE

The Social Architecture of Youth Work Practice articulates the relational space for transformative work with young people, a space that good practitioners seem to know well, more by intuitive action than word. The model builds from the everyday lived experiences of youth workers, and others who work with young people, as well as from intellectual discourses in youth work and youth studies, and its cousin fields around the world. In this chapter, the author asks: *What is the space that youth work practice occupies? How is it created and why? Finally, what are the challenges to creating this social architecture today and what can be done so that transformative spaces with and by young people remain possible?*

INTRODUCTION

There was a time when physical spaces were designed for the explicit purpose of assembly. Spaces such as the Greek Agora or Roman Forum were the heart of public life. Here, meaning outside of self could be located; cultural, social and political forms of life could be created and expressed. Today, our physical structures are more likely to support assembly for capitalistic ventures than broader social good. People meet in malls, restaurants, movie theatres, and in ad-filled virtual environments. The abundance of consumer spaces where the vast majority of leisure time is spent not only makes it difficult to form a relationship to the broader social good but also masks its very necessity. Where does a young person go to engage in dialogue with and for social and communal purpose? With fewer physical structures *res publica*, there is an increasing need for understanding and constructing social, non-commoditized spaces with young people, as not only critical for their own development but as necessary for public life and engagement. In this chapter I ask: What is the space that youth work practice occupies? How is it created and why? Finally, what are the challenges to creating this social architecture today and what can be done so that transformative spaces remain possible?

First, Why 'Space?'

Couldn't one ask with the same effect, what are the programmes (or equally, settings, environments, conditions, or places) that successfully engage young people? Perhaps. But, the decision to discuss 'space' is not solely a linguistic choice. 'Space' has implications for practice that other descriptors do not. Space is

B. Belton (ed.), 'Cadjan – Kiduhu': Global Perspectives on Youth Work, 47–59.

nebulous. In its absence, one must work to create it; one equally, and with as much will and effort, can decide to dissolve it when as Marcus Vitruvius,[1] Roman writer and architect, advised with regard to a good building, it no longer serves the function of its people well, or has lost utilitas. Conversely, environments, settings, programmes, and the like, are relatively fixed structures, created for a purpose and rarely dissolved when they outrun their usefulness, or to take another of Vitruvius' principles, when they no longer delight and raise people's spirits (venustas). As durable entities, programmes are taken for granted as forever useful or worse, replicable. As soon as research determines a 'programme' is effective, the structures, features, and characteristics are duplicated, often with much disappointment (Schorr, 1997). Replication often fails because what is under-emphasized is 'space': the relational, on-the-ground, nuanced and responsive practice that is the soul and inside (or guts) of the 'programme'.

While there are times when understanding youth work as occurring within fixed and durable structures like programmes is helpful, e.g., when there is a need to establish the effectiveness of programmes and hence the worthiness of the investment, today we are at a collective moment in history, a crossroads, when new disciplinary perspectives might be necessary to preserve, reclaim and advance the field. 'Space' supports the notion that youth work requires a flexible and emergent sense of purpose and meaning that is discovered in relationship with young people, over and over again. Programmes, settings, and places do not ensure transformative spaces. One can employ 'science' to replicate the fixed traits of a thing much like one can replicate a Van Gogh painting. But, the art is to work with the blank canvas. The artist does not know in advance what she will create. She works in relation and in response to the medium and to her own imagination. Similarly, I would argue that the capacity to co-create space with youth is the most critical tool of youth work. Co-created space acknowledges the role of agency in human transformation. It does not assume that youth are subjects of conditions, environments, and settings, nor that they are objects to be acted upon, but are active and willing participants with the agency and desire to transform the conditions in which they live, learn and grow. It is from this central tenet that all else follows.

This chapter attempts to articulate three principles for co-creating transformative spaces with young people. Identifying principles allows us to find common ground across diverse practices of youth work but principles are not enough. Principles while grounded in the practice context do not articulate the purpose towards which such principles are aimed. It is the strong belief of this author that particularly at this time in history, when most if not all policies are aimed at efficiency and outcomes rather than human transformation, it is essential that youth work articulates not just how it engages young people but why! Here, I begin with what has emerged as three common principles of relational youth work practice (see Fusco, 2011, for earlier discussion). In the sections to follow, the principles are situated within a broader social purpose and design: within the Social Architecture of Youth work Practice.

YOUTH WORK AS RELATIONAL PRACTICE

I suspect few would argue against the point that youth work is, at its core, a relational practice. In fact, relationships are found to be the strongest ingredient within the developmental mix (Anderson-Butcher, Cash, Saltburg, Midle, & Pace, 2004; Benson, 2002; Fusco, 2007; Glover, 1995; McLaughlin, Irby, & Langman, 1994; Noam & Fiore, 2004; Stuart, 2008; Villarruel & Lerner, 1994). While the research on relationships is robust, there is much less in the way of a deep theoretical construct or model that would enable the teaching or research of working relationally as a necessary condition for youth work. Benson made a similar argument when he said, "Much more intellectual and research energy has been invested in naming developmental nutrients and demonstrating their role in youth outcomes than in studying the complex array of strategies and procedures for moving the developmental needle forward" (2002: 140). Moving 'the developmental needle' is what youth workers have been doing for decades but while the practice itself is sophisticated, the articulation of that nuanced, non-normative practice is only a more recent matter, and necessity.

In an earlier work, three common principles emerged as critical to youth work practices across settings, cultures, and geographies (Fusco, 2011). These principles are likely not the only critical factors within any given youth work practice, but they seem to be at the core of many existing descriptions. Davies (2010) argues that the uniqueness of youth work is not its value system but its process of engagement. Consistent with this argument, the three principles name how youth workers engage young people across a variety of settings providing a common starting point for understanding what makes youth work distinct as a practice and perhaps a profession.

The first relational principle is that youth work is a *contextual* practice. Youth workers can be considered social ecologists. They 'read' the social context of a situation first. Rather than seeing young people as individual problems, they see the broader social arrangements and are aware of the new arrangements that they are a part of creating with young people. The location of 'problems' is a sociological endeavour, not a psychological one. While youth workers may engage in problem solving and counselling that deal with individual young people, the central focus is not the young person in isolation. At a micro level, young people occupy groups; they are in 'youth', in association, in community, in space, in tribe, en milieu, in relationship. Groups occupy macro-associations such as, community, culture, and society. These macro and micro contexts provide important cues about young people, their issues, identities, and ideologies (Bejarano, 2005; Lareau, 2003; Milner, 2013). While some practice understandings are aimed at one sociological category at a time (e.g., gender, race, or culture) in the main they draw upon complex understandings that situate presenting issues within broader dynamic ecologies.

Context not only refers to collective space but to time and history, i.e., girls who attended clubs in the 1950s versus girls who attended clubs in the 1990s. Constructs of identity have different meanings in different communities at different points in history. Youth workers are keenly aware of the cultural, social and temporal conditions within which they work and the issues that young people are facing. This contextual and current understanding of young people is qualitatively different from a psychological or normative one because it leads to a response that is not only targeted at individuals but to changing conditions which at times might be inequitable, unequal, oppressive, and even violent. Sociological and political framing of issues affords opportunity for critique and transformation of the conditions surrounding youth, and in particular, for addressing youth inequities by inviting young people to become allies in social transformation.

The second principle is that youth work is *participatory*. Youth workers know that young people must be active participants in crafting their lives today and their futures. 'Participation' has a qualitatively different feel across youth work practices, but its presence as a common principle that guides practice, is undeniable. McLaughlin, Irby, and Langman (1994) found that, "a variety of neighbourhood-based programmes work as long as there is an interaction between the programme and its youth, that results in those youth's treating the programme as a personal resource and a bridge to a hopeful future" (p. 5). Youth workers co-create participatory conditions for 'voice and choice', leadership, action, and empowerment. Young people can be engaged in deciding on everything from their life goals to how the centre or programme will be governed, to what social issues should be addressed in the community and how (Roholt, Baizerman, & Hildreth, 2013). It is through the room to participate in such decisions that young people learn how to be active curators of their own lives and citizens of the world. Instrumental purposes for youth work run counter to the principle of participation, as discussed later in this chapter.

The third principle is that youth work is *responsive*.[2] Responsiveness begins with being present in the space, affected by what goes on there, by the unfolding of the scene, by what young people are saying, doing, feeling and experiencing (Krueger, 2007). And then, responding. Responsiveness is the other side of voice. It requires a reflective, informed, and mindful decision about what to do with *these* young people *here and now*. Responding is not reacting. It is the pause in reaction to consider how to respond given the context and in support of participation. Responses that are formed without understanding the context and without requiring participation are more likely to emerge from one's authority as an adult who turns to the rules, rather than the young people, for guidance. If one is committed to the principles of youth work, his or her response takes longer to form. It is unscripted, dialogic, and emergent. As good social workers know, every utterance can be a micro-intervention (Gaiswinkler & Roessler, 2009).

PROBLEMATICS, NOT PROBLEMS

An example might help elaborate on the embodiment of these three principles. Sam is a 15-year-old boy who lives in a public housing project in a community riddled with crime. One day an adult catches wind that Sam is carrying a knife. What happens? Well, that depends on who the adult is. Is the adult a police officer, a parent, a teacher, or a youth worker? Unlike most adults in Sam's life, the youth worker is more likely to engage Sam in a dialogue, searching for the contextual cues of Sam's 'behaviour'. Why is he carrying the knife? What does the knife mean to him? Is it protection, pragmatic, sentiment, bravado? In that dialogue, the youth worker is likely to remind Sam of the repercussions of his actions and help Sam make a choice that not only suits Sam but suits the relationships Sam has to others, including the youth worker, the family, the community. The youth worker does not see or define Sam's behaviour as 'bad' and therefore will not dole out punishment as a response. Rather, the youth worker looks to engage Sam in deciding his next actions, and responds to Sam where he is at (e.g. is Sam dealing with or is he a threat, is Sam angry, is Sam playing cool, etc.). The conversation and the actions that follow are not scripted but depend solely on Sam's reasons for carrying the knife, his intentions, and how open he is to avoiding a future problem. The knife is not treated as a problem but a 'problematic'. 'Problematics' do not have known solutions; they require dialogue to get at an understanding of context, instigate participation, and be responsive to the situation and the young person/people in any given situation. This is a distinctive, and likely very different, response to Sam-with-knife than would be socially expected from a parent, a police officer or a teacher.

The principles help us to test the strength of youth work, not as characteristics of effective programmes but as capacities of effective workers for creating relational space (see Figure 1). Contextual, participatory, and responsive is what youth workers do. It is how they co-create transformative spaces with young people. As the National Youth Work Network in New Zealand articulated, "Most other professions build relationships in order to deliver a service. Youth workers provide a service in order to build a relationship" (Barwick, 2006). In this view, youth work practice as delivered is not located in any particular setting. Setting is secondary to the 'space' that one works to co-create through the embodiment of the three principles.

Balancing relational principles in today's climate of accountability is a challenge, to say the least. With youth work becoming increasingly 'professionalized' and hence, mandated by external standards, accreditation, and short-term, measurable outcomes, little room remains for flexibility or professional judgment (Smith, 2003) a condition experienced also in nursing (Rafferty, 1996), psychology (Orange, 2011), child protection (Gillingham, 2011), social work (Cooper, 2011), and education (Tomlinson, 1995). It will be difficult to discuss and advocate for policies and provisions for supporting relational youth work practices without clearly articulating not just the principles, but the purpose. In the words of Malcolm X, "a man who stands for nothing will fall for anything".

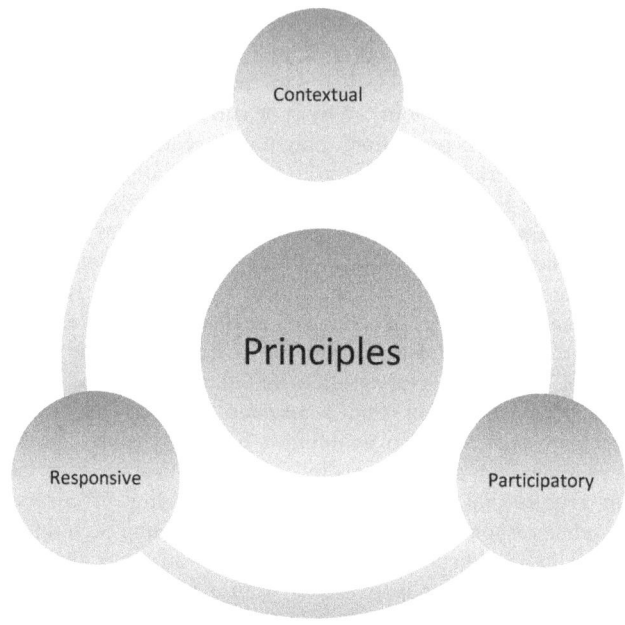

Figure 1. Principles of relational youth work practice.

THE PURPOSE OF YOUTH WORK PRACTICE

While youth work might have several common or core principles, its purpose is not only less clear, it is shifting. In the United States, 'youth work' is a term rarely employed these days. Practices with young people have shifted out of 'community centres' and into schools, away from youth work and towards youth development (National Research Council, 2002). The transition from youth work to youth development began in the United States but today is a global phenomenon (Smith, 2003) with those who recognize the difference being pushed to the margins and radicalized (De St. Croix, 2009). Does the transition matter in practice or is the shift from youth work to youth development merely semantic? Examining the purpose of youth work might illuminate the answer.

Following a 2005–2006 working paper and research seminar, the European Commission (n.d.) published a report on a multi-year study across ten European countries to define youth work. They found that "… most of the definitions contain two basic orientations reflecting a double concern: to provide favourable (leisure-time-orientated) experiences (of social, cultural, educational or political nature) in order to strengthen young people's personal development and foster their personal and social autonomy, and at the same time to offer opportunities for the integration and inclusion of young people in adult society by fostering societal integration in general or preventing the exclusion of disadvantaged groups" (17).

Attention to personal growth is a consistent theme in youth work's purpose. In Ireland, youth work is, "a planned programme of education designed for the purpose of aiding and enhancing the personal and social development of young persons", (DCYA, 2001). In New Zealand, a youth worker is a person who provides a service to build relationships with young people in order to foster wellbeing (Barwick, 2006). In England, youth work is explicit about its duty of care for individuals; committed to their greater self-realisation; concerned to help maximise their potential contribution to the greater good (Davies, 2005). The purpose of social inclusion is perhaps more contested space. Is youth work a supplement to education, a way to build community, a way to support individual development, a way to engage young people in public and community life? Is it the same across contexts such as afterschool, residential, foster care, juvenile centres, youth ministry, community centres, and Peace Corps? Does it matter?

Here I will argue that when youth work is viewed as a relational practice it does not neatly fall into one category; it cuts across services that might be considered the realm of education, mental health, physical health, labour, and/or justice. That is, youth work is not about this or that; it is a balanced and holistic approach (a gestalt) to working with young people that when balanced is where the 'magic' lies. The gestalt helps us to understand and capture the unique role of youth work in society – as a collective, co-created space that is transformative because it aims towards educational, therapeutic and socially-minded objectives while staying grounded in context, remaining participatory and responsive to real young people on the ground now. Such an architectural design of space is here captured as a three-legged stool. The Social Architecture of Youth work Practice positions the three central principles on the 'seat' of the stool supported by the legs (pillars) of the stool. The metaphor of the stool reflects the notion that to honour the principles you need a balanced model of youth work. When one leg is longer than the other two legs, the principles slide off the top of the stool.

Today the educational leg of the stool heavily dominates youth work in the United States. Many afterschool youth programmes, once located in community centres, where a range of social and cultural engagement was possible, now are housed within school buildings and have the explicit goal of improving achievement outcomes. Youth workers in these settings are having a difficult time engaging in authentic processes of youth work (Fusco, Ramos, & Lawrence, 2012). The new demands set up a system that replicates 'teacher gaze' over responsive practice or as Heathfield (2011) calls it 'school-lite'. Attention to broader contextual conditions surrounding young people's lives is 'relocated' to workers in other institutions. It is difficult if not impossible to stay responsive in an environment where the agenda, the outcomes, and the means to reach them have been predetermined.

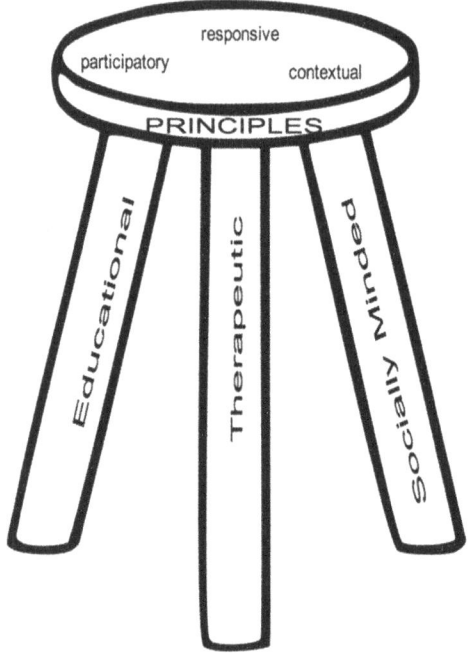

Figure 2. A balanced vision.

Educators working in the tradition of critical pedagogy have named a similar struggle to stay responsive to students in K-12 public education. Duncan-Andrade and Morrell (2008) state, it is, "essential for educators to move beyond the boundaries of prescribed educational practice to develop classroom pedagogy that serves their students' context-specific needs (cultural, linguistic, social, political, economic", (p. 30). The narrowing of youth works impact to the educational realm, particularly when that education is designed to reach academic targets and miss 'context-specific needs' ignores possibilities for human and social transformation and growth. In my visits to youth organizations around the USA I always meet at least one young person who tells me about how the programme saved his or her life. There is a healing aspect of youth work that reverberates from caring and supportive relationships. In fact, I have often found when working with marginalized youth that the space youth work gives them to be a kid, to explore, and to contribute in meaningful ways can be therapeutic. As they experience success, development and hope are re-ignited. While many equate a therapeutic aim with either doing therapy or psychoanalysis, this is not the intention here. To put it simply, a therapeutic role does not mean youth workers do therapy; it means that the relational, responsive process of youth work has saved lives. This healing function is often unintentional or unplanned (as such) but it should be named else we do not recognize the unique role that youth work plays in society.

In my own experiences as a youth worker and hearing the stories of youth workers, there appear to be two avenues towards the emotionally curative. The first occurs when young people with limited life experiences are provided with opportunities to explore and discover themselves in a psychologically and socially safe space. Limitations placed upon them by circumstance cause restricted sometimes harmful vision(s) of 'self'. Nurturing talents and strengths provides a platform to gain confidence in knowing one has something to contribute to the world and ignites new energies for navigating the world in new ways. The fractured self becomes a bit more whole as one sees oneself in a more positive (sometimes more accurate) light. A second path to healing begins when the inequities of one's life conditions are named, challenged and then worked on. If we take as the basic premise that societal inequities create multiple, painful experiences for young people, and we view youth work as a practice that provides a space for young people to voice those inequities and engage in social change, then how can youth work not be therapeutic for those involved?

The educational and the therapeutic legs help young people to grow as individuals. But 'having' without 'giving' negates that youth work is also and what it is often explicitly about; making the world a better place. Engaging young people in experiences where they lead the change they want to see in the world is powerful and there are many great examples of programmes that provide young people with that space. Here youth work is, "about making and developing a sense of meaning with young people, based on increasing commitment to searching out truthful information and understandings", (Batsleer, 2008: 7). The space that gets created when youth workers allow for learning, for healing, and for social justice is transformative for all young people, and particularly healing for marginalized youth (and their communities). However, caution is also warranted. There are other examples of social movements that engage young people in fighting for causes that are adult-led and adult-defined. These programmes are just as instrumental, including young people in a predetermined political agenda. While their participation may promote the development of a voice and leadership experience/skills, young people may never have the opportunity to talk about their personal goals or dreams thus limited in the role of youth agency.

REMOVING THE 'INSTITUTION'

Youth work has historically been institution free. It occurred on the margins of education, psychology and social work and for many, thankfully so. Over the past decade with increased attention to the practice, institutionalization has crept in. The space(s) for young people to learn and lead their learning is being replaced by educational curriculum and lesson plans that have adult-defined goals and targets. The space for acknowledging suffering and healing is being replaced by mental health record keeping. The space for socio-political dialogue and conscientization has become so marginalized against neoliberal (and oppressive) backdrops that even moderately political youth workers are deemed 'radical'. Any voice is considered anti-patriotic; the ultimately ironic disposition for the nourishment of a pluralistic democracy.

We should learn from decades of educational 'reform' that failed largely due to standardized policies that did not take into account the multiple layers of needs and issues in particular contexts (Milner, 2013). Conversely, culturally responsive pedagogy has worked for students living in low-income, under-resourced, and inequitable environments (Duncan-Andrade & Morrell, 2008; Ginwright, 2010). In such classrooms, students, "develop voice and perspective and are allowed to participate (more fully) in the multiple discourses available in a learning context by not only consuming information but also through deconstructing and reconstructing it", (Milner, 2013: 40). In this conception of the 'radical classroom' teachers learn about students' lived experiences, identify their strengths, connect to 'real' out of school experiences, building meaningful and sustainable relationships, and help students recognise and challenge injustices. They do youth work in the classroom.

Ironically, such conceptions are deemed radical today because the 'institution' of education disallows for real transformation, not by intention but by design. As Schorr (1997) has found over and over again, across multiple helping professions, systems get in the way of good people getting good work done. If we remove 'school' from 'education' we are left thinking about teaching and learning, not bureaucratic institutions, curriculum, test scores, or school buildings. When teaching transcends the institution of school, conversations become not only educational, but also therapeutic and socially minded (socially just) because students are seen in context, participate in meaningful and relevant dialogues, and teaching is responsive to student needs. Such teachers are 'the Stars' (Haberman, 2004); the 20% that students know care. Recently, I was reminded of the harsh realities of 'school' as anti-developmental space by a pre-service teacher reconsidering her career choice. In the midst of her final practicum, she said, "I can't be me". When I asked her who the 'me' was that she wanted to be she responded:

> I want to be open and fun with my students … in a respectful way. I want them to see education more than just another day out (of) their homes, but something that they control and can allow to create their own world-future! Due to the changes that are being implemented, the demand for programmes to be used in curricula and the politics of following (the) strategic plans of someone else, I do not believe I will be able to enforce such an idea … I want to be more than just the teacher who grades papers and neglects the responsibility of my students' education due to the politics but I want to be a mentor and that light that shines in that person's life – someone who both teaches and gives proper role model in well-rounded areas of life that goes beyond education.

Youth workers are facing similar ideological struggles that make contextual, participatory, and responsive practice challenging. Practitioners who once could meet young people responsively are now being asked to meet school-based agendas. As a practitioner recently told me,

In the cracks of the sidewalk, the grass is growing. We are the grass but it feels like somebody's following behind us trying to fix the cracks so that the grass can't get through. We're not an extension of school.

CONCLUSION

Youth work as a relational practice may be quietly disappearing, replaced by more narrowly defined opportunities to learn during non-school hours. The transition has been subtle, occurring slowly but steadily over the past decade. To those more recent to the field, the transition might go unnoticed because youth work in the United States is so diffuse and ill defined. Ironically, such a transition is occurring at the same time that there is a mounting body of evidence showing the impact of youth work on a host of developmental outcomes. With few institutionally supported contexts for youth-driven networking and activities, the 'soul' of youth work itself falls by the wayside supplanted by more formal, adult-led and academically focused structures. What is critical to understand is what might be lost when the balance of power shifts again towards an adult-driven agenda in the few community spaces where this was historically not the case.

The paradigm shift in youth work has not only occurred in the United States but around the world. The shift has led leaders in the UK to produce various documents re-claiming the youth work they know/knew (e.g., Bernard Davies 'Manifesto'; Janet Batsleer's book, *What is Youth Work?*; and 'In Defense of Youth Work' campaign's book, *This is Youth Work*). As a way to reflect on one's practice in relation to the principles spelled out in the Manifesto, Davies (2005) offers some anchoring questions: Is the practice respectful of and actively responsive to young people's wider community and cultural identities and, where young people choose? Is the practice encouraging them to be outward looking, critical and creative in their responses to their experience and the world around them? In the United States, we have not put forth one set of principles or one 'manifesto'. Perhaps the time has come more importantly to agree on such a set of principles internationally.

Youth work plays a role in a young person's life as part of a complex and dynamic system of supports that fluctuates with the needs and presenting issues of young people. It is always contextual, always participatory and always responsive to such needs. This means that it also has no singular target and cannot be neatly categorized within the typical narrowly defined span of youth services. Today, Sam presents a failing grade on a math test and asks for help; tomorrow he suggests he is overweight and wants to begin an exercise regime; next week, he presents as potentially suicidal. Teacher, coach, social worker, the youth worker is none these professionally but to an extent can be used and effectively regarded as all of these things practically. She will respond in the context of Sam, his peers, his community, and the larger issues that shape them in order to promote agency and equity.

In the centre of assembly, the youth worker is engaged in co-creating spaces where deep and meaningful work can get done. The future of youth work will rest on our collective capacity to create spaces for assembly, unconstrained by reductive and restrictive forces but not without intention and focus on the principles and the purpose of the work.

NOTES

1 De architectura was translated in 1914 as "Ten Books on Architecture" by Professor Morris Morgan at Harvard University.
[2] Originally this principle was named "fluid and emergent" (Fusco, 2011) meaning "an approach that is emergent and responsive to youth."

REFERENCES

Anderson-Butcher, D., Cash, S.J., Saltburg, S., Midle, T., & Pace, D. (2004). Institutions of youth development: The significance of supportive staff-youth relationships. *Journal of Human Behavior in the Social Environment, 9*, 83-99.

Baizerman, M. (2013). The quest for (higher) professional status: Second thoughts? *Child & Youth Services, 34*, 186-195.

Barwick, H. (2006). *Youth work today: A review of the issues and challenges.* Taiiohi, New Zealand: Ministry of Youth Development.

Batsleer, J. R. (2008). *Informal learning in youth work.* London: Sage.

Bejarano, C. L. (2005). *Que onda? Urban youth culture and border identity.* Tucson, AZ: University of Arizona Press.

Benson, P. L. (2002, Fall). Adolescent development in social and community context: A program of research. In R. M. Lerner, C. S. Taylor, & A. von Eye (Eds.), *Pathways to positive development among diverse youth* (pp. 123-148). New Directions for Youth Development, Vol. 95. San Francisco: Jossey-Bass.

Cooper, B. (2011). Criticality and reflexivity: Best practice in uncertain environments. In J. Seden, S. Matthews, M. McCormick, & A. Morgan (Eds.), *Professional development in social work: Complex issues in practice* (pp. 17-23). New York: Routledge.

Davies, B. (2005). Youth work: A manifesto for our times. *Youth & Policy, 88*, 1-26.

Davies, B. (2010). What do we mean by youth work? In J. Batsleer & B. Davies, *What is youth work?* (pp. 1-6). Exeter: Learning Matters.

DCYA. (2001). *Youth Work Act.* Ireland: Department of Children and Youth Affairs. Available for download at: http://www.irishstatutebook.ie/2001/en/act/pub/0042/index.html.

De St Croix, T. (2009). 'Forgotten corners': A reflection on radical youth work in Britain, 1940-1990. In R. Gilchrist, T., Jeffs, J., Spence, & J. Walker (Eds.), *Essays in the history of youth and community work: Discovering the past* (pp. 302-315). Dorset: Russell House Publishing.

Duncan-Andrade, J.M.R. & Morrell, E. (2008). *The art of critical pedagogy: Possibilities for moving from theory to practice in urban schools.* New York: Peter Lang.

European Commission and the Council of Europe in the Field of Youth. (n.d.). *The socio-economic scope of youth work in Europe.* Final report.

Fusco, D. (2007). Developmentally-responsive relationships during after school. *Journal of Youth Development, 2*(2), Fall,online.

Fusco, D. (2011). Framing trends, posing questions. In D. Fusco (Ed.), *Advancing youth work: Current trends, critical questions* (pp. 216-238). New York: Routledge.

Fusco, D., Ramos, S., & Lawrence, A. (2012, April). *The Accordion Effect: The squeeze between external pressures, increased expectations and reduced funding.* Annual meeting of the National Afterschool Association, Dallas, TX.

Gaiswinkler, W., & Roessler, M. (2009). Using the expertise of knowing and the expertise of not-knowing to support processes of empowerment in social work practice. *Journal of Social Work Practice, 23,* 215-227.

Gillingham, P. (2011). Decision-making tools and the development of expertise in child protection practitioners: are we 'just breeding workers who are good at ticking boxes'? *Child & Family Social Work, 16,* 412-421.

Ginwright, S. A. (2010). *Black youth rising: Activism & radical healing in urban America.* New York: Teachers College Press.

Glover, J. (1995). *Promoting youth development in a therapeutic milieu. Contract with America's youth: Toward a national youth development agenda* (pp. 22-23). Washington, DC: American Youth Policy Forum.

Haberman, M. (2004). Can star teachers create learning communities? *Educational Leadership, 61*(8), 52-56.

Heathfield, M. (2011). A Chicago story: Challenge and change. In D. Fusco (Ed.), *Advancing youth work: Current trends, critical questions* (pp. 85-99). New York: Routledge.

Krueger, M. (2007). *Sketching youth, self, and youth work.* Rotterdam: Sense Publishers.

Lareau, A. (2003). *Unequal childhoods: Class, race, and family life.* Berkeley: University of California Press.

McLaughlin, M. W., Irby, M. A., & Langman, J. (1994). *Urban sanctuaries: Neighborhood organizations in the lives and futures of inner-city youth.* San Francisco: Jossey-Bass.

Milner IV, R. (2013). Analyzing poverty, learning and teaching through a critical race theory lens. *Review of Research in Education, 37,* 1-53.

National Research Council and Institute of Medicine. (2002). *Community youth programmes to promote positive youth development.* Washington, DC: National Research Council and Institute of Medicine.

Noam, G. G., & Fiore, N. (2004, November). Relationships across multiple settings: An overview. In G. G. Noam, & N. Fiore (Eds.), *The transforming power of adult-youth relationships* (pp. 9-16). New Directions for Youth Development, Vol. 103. San Francisco: Jossey-Bass.

Orange, D. M. (2011). *The suffering stranger: Hermeneutics for everyday clinical practice.* New York: Routledge.

Rafferty, A. M. (1996). *The politics of nursing knowledge.* New York: Routledge.

Roholt, R. V., Baizerman, M., & Hildreth, R. W. (2013). *Civic youth work.* Chicago: Lyceum Books.

Schorr, L. B. (1997). *Common purpose: Strengthening families and neighborhoods to rebuild America.* New York: Anchor Books.

Smith, M. K. (2003). From youth work to youth development. The new government framework for English youth services. *Youth and Policy, 79.* Available in the informal education archives: http://www.infed.org/archives/.

Stuart, C. (2008). Shaping the rules: Child and youth care boundaries in the context of relationship. Bonsai! In G. Bellefeuille & F. Ricks (Eds.), *Standing on the precipice: inquiry into the creative potential of child and youth care practice* (pp. 135-168). Edmonton, Alberta: MacEwan Press.

Tomlinson, P. (1995). Can competence profiling work for effective teacher preparation? Part II: Pitfalls and principles. *Oxford Review of Education, 21,* 299-314.

Villarruel, F. A, & Lerner, R. M. (1994). Development and context and the contexts of learning. *New Directions for Child Development, 63,* 3-8.

HANS SKOTT-MYHRE

BUILDING A NEW COMMON

Youth Work and the Question of Transitional Institutions of Care

Youth work, it seems to me, is a field of endeavour founded on care. The question of how to care, who receives care, how to deliver care, and what is care, however, is neither simple nor uncontested. For many, if not most of us, caring and care are synonymous. However, I would argue that caring about someone and caring for him or her are not necessarily directly related. Both the affective relation of caring for someone and the practices associated with that sense of caring are both quite complicated.

In youth work, both the feeling of caring and the practices associated with and generated by such feelings are often conceived of as acts and affects centred within and between individuals. That is to say that I, as an individual feel a sense of caring within myself for another individual and, on the basis of those feelings, interact with the other in a caring manner.

CARE/COMMUNICATION

It might be argued that this is not dissimilar from the way many of us think of communication. I think of something that I wish to communicate to another. I send the other a message that they receive. They then translate the message within themselves, more or less accurately, and send a message back and so on. Caring, modelled as communication might be seen to operate in a very similar fashion; I experience caring, I communicate caring through words or deeds to another, the other receives my message of caring and translates it. Of course, this is where it gets tricky. The other person may or may not translate my caring in the way I intended. In fact, they may translate it in any number of ways I have not anticipated.

The contingent and unpredictable response of the other, to what we perceive to have been a clear message of caring, is a source of consternation and confusion for many youth workers. We simply cannot understand why our caring would be interpreted variously as an attack, a threat, a seduction or a deception. We look to discover the problem within the flawed perceptual field of the other. For many of us, this entails an archaeological project into the familial and social relations of the other. We investigate the extent to which previous relationships have shaped the other's misperception of our care. In some cases, we have elaborate theories of 'transference' and 'counter transference', borrowed from psychoanalysis, to help us to manage our disappointed expectations of what we would define as a caring

B. Belton (ed.), 'Cadjan – Kiduhu': Global Perspectives on Youth Work, 61–75.

relationship. If the rejection of our caring upsets us sufficiently, we may borrow diagnostic categories from psychiatry and psychology, such as borderline or sociopath, to assist us in neutralizing our sense of rejection.

All of these models and understandings of caring, however, are founded in what I would argue is an inadequate understanding of care. They each hold a common theoretical limitation. They are inadequate and limited as explanations, not because they are wrong, but because they are incomplete; both their definition of the subjects involved in caring and their understanding of how caring is shared, lead to theoretical formulations of the self and the other that actually reduce the possibility of actual care. Put succinctly, the binary formulation that posits two individuals with one communicating care to the other is insufficient as a model of care for youth work.

THE INFLUENCE OF LANGUAGE

To understand this, an alternate understanding of communication might be helpful. Deleuze and Guattari (1987) suggest that our understanding of communication as a simple transmission of information from one individual to another is both inaccurate and misleading. They propose that the way we commonly hope communication will work actually kills any possibility of what we would anticipate when expressing ourselves to the other. The problem lies in the nature of language as the model for communication. Language, Deleuze and Guattari (1987) tell us, does not simply transmit information. Instead it transmits commands or orders. This is because the nature of language is to define. It orders a certain world into being by structuring both the organization and the nature of that world.

When we think of caring, we bring a whole set of preconceived ideas about what caring is and how it operates. These ideas about what constitutes care do not originate with us, however. That is to say, we are born into a world of pre-existing linguistic structures and definitions. The way that we understand the nature of the world, and caring in particular, is not wholly shaped by us internally. It precedes us in the collective world of language shared by the group of people, in a particular geography, and the specific historical period, into which we are born. An individual, then, does not define the world. It is a collective process of ordering and commanding a world into being.

When we think of caring as a mode of transmitting information from one individual to another, we tend to assume that our communication will have a linguistic structure. In other words, even when we use touch or a certain look, tone of voice or other non-verbal modes of communication, we hope that these will be translated into something that could be called care. In fact, much of the conversation that takes place in youth work settings is in fact negotiating in language the non-verbal interactions that take place throughout the day.

Using the communications model, these negotiations have a highly charged political dimension. Each of us comes to the interaction with a set of definitions we have inherited and shaped through multiple interactions with others over the course of our life thus far. The way we have made sense of these interactions has been shaped by the definitions afforded us by the social field into which we are born and live our lives. Each of us believes that our definition of care is accurate and in some instances crucial to our safety and survival. When we communicate care, we intend to express something that is, we believe, commonly understood.

TRANSMOGRIFYING CAPITAILISM

This is a political interaction in several respects. First, our understanding of care is rooted in the norms and common sense of our society and/or culture. The very idea that we are individuals, who should care in certain kinds of ways, is something we are both overtly taught and absorb through observation and experience. Such learning, however, is not a neutral transmission of factual information about what constitutes care. It is shaped in ways that benefit and support the existing regimes of rule and domination within any given context and historical period. In our time, the system of rule to which we are subject is global capitalism. Thus the common sense that we bring to our expectations and communications about care and caring are riddled through with the logic of the capitalist system of value.

The logic and value of capitalism operates in important ways to influence the manner and means that we care both individually and institutionally. Let's begin with the fact that capitalism as a system has only one form of value and one overarching function. The form of value is money and the function is to make an infinite amount of it. The sole purpose of a capitalist economy is to make a profit. Its sole interest is in this endeavour. Money, of course, is an abstraction. It is an abstract system of sign designed to stand for other things. However, as Baudrillard (1981) and Deleuze and Guattari (1987) point out, signs have a way of taking over the thing they are designed to represent. They gradually begin to give the illusion that they are, first synonymous with the thing they represent and then often times actually appear as though they have more reality and value than what is being represented.

As noted above, language can work in this way. We can come to believe that the word for a thing named is the same as that thing. This is how common sense understandings within societies and cultures emerge. We mistake the name for the thing named and can be quite unsettled by any challenge to our understanding of what things are.

Foucault (1972) asserts that this process covers over what is actually a long historical struggle over what things mean. He argues, like Deleuze and Guattari, that the contentions relating to meaning are associated with revolutionary struggles against domination and control. To efforts made to defer the possibility of revolt and insure compliance, as Althusser (2006) points out, elaborate the endeavours made by and through schools, churches, governments and families to indoctrinate populations of people with the common sense understanding of the dominant system of rule. In our own time we can see this struggle in the contestations over the meaning of gender, race, sexuality, terrorism, nationality, and family.

Capitalism operates in a functionally similar fashion to language, but with a powerful twist. Language seeks to provide a final and essential definition of the world. That is to say, language (in effect) carries the claim that it has accurately named the thing it is identifying; we can say that this is a family, 'a girl' or 'a boy', etc.

For Deleuze and Guattari (1987) capitalism functions in such a way that it actually empties things of their meaning and replaces that meaning with one sign: money. Michael Hardt (1995) makes this point in his essay *'The Withering of Civil Society'*. He delineates the way in which our civil institutions, such as government, the courts, family, churches, schools have gradually been emptied of their civic function, which is to provide services to a given group of people. Instead, their function has been given over to the purpose of making money.

This conversion of civic institutions, designed by people to serve common interests, into fiscal agents, designed to serve the interests of capital, has been extremely effective as a transformation. One of the subtle and pernicious aspects of this gradual assimilation of our social institutions into cash machines for capital is the way in which the exterior veneer remains both familiar and recognizable. The government still looks like the government, courts continue resemble courts, schools maintain a likeness to an image of what schools might or should be and so on. The architecture of our institutions is left standing. It is the core values that drive their function that shifts.

This sleight of hand, like a magic trick, requires obfuscation and distraction to work. It is critical that our attention be directed anywhere other than towards what is actually happening. For this purpose, capital provides a dazzling and ever shifting array of alternative explanations for why our social institutions no longer provide the care they were designed to deliver. We are told that our system is failing us because of minorities of all kinds, immigration, big government, not enough government, single mothers, delinquent and out of control young people, greedy unions, Gay marriage and terrorists, the list goes on. We are given any explanation that will pull us away from the material actuality of the fact our global society is now run by addicts whose addiction is to money. Like all addicts, they have no regard for anything other than satisfying their addiction and have hijacked the very force of life itself to satisfy their endless craving.

As is the way of all magic tricks, however, the illusion produced by capitalism is unstable and falls apart the moment the machinery and sleight of hand is exposed and understood. Any challenge that seriously offers an alternative logic can break the trance and open the field of perception to both the profoundly 'un-magical' reality of the trick and to a much broader view of what is really happening. Such a challenge throws the entire system of the trick into crisis. A magician exposed holds little sway over those previously entranced when the mechanics of the trick become visible.

How might we break the trance of capitalism's trick? I would argue that we have already begun and that capitalism is in crisis across the full extent of its global empire. But, to understand the nature of the crisis and to offer an alternative, we must return the issue of how we conceive of care.

Our definition of care and the ways we organize ourselves to deliver it institutionally and personally are profoundly influenced by the system of distraction and monetization we have been describing. This is a complex process that has evolved over several hundred years, but there are some key elements that are pertinent to how we structure and conceive youth work.

CARE IN COMMON

Care is an activity and an affective relation we share in common. When we premise our care on our common desires and struggles, our practices are founded in the material actuality of real necessity. This is an anathema to the interests of capital as a system premised only on its own narrow set of abstract values; that is the money form. As a result, capital must undermine, devalue and then revalue our sense of commonality. We must be separated from each other and any sense of a commonality of purpose. Our allegiance needs to be shifted from what we share in common with all life on the planet, to a false relation to money as the primary motivation for what we do and what we value. Such a transformation shifts the function of care from an assertion of the value of life and the necessity to promote a diverse eco-system of proliferating and thriving living systems, to an obsession with producing a proliferation of signs that hold a parasitic relation to life, producing simulations of life while holding absolutely no regard for living things.

Under such a regime, our definitions of care become saturated with signs and significations of value utterly subjugated to the primacy of money. We can see this in the ways in which we discuss the value of social programming, education, living standards, medical care, environmental care, immigration, and so on. Our public discourse on such matters has been so infected with capitalist logic that it would be difficult to find a conversation, personal or public, which does not include a reference as to whether or not we can afford to functionally care. While our infrastructure crumbles, people live on the street, children starve and die of preventable disease, our schools fail to educate, violence and crime escalate, governments fail to govern, our air and water becoming increasingly poisonous, and eco-systems are thrown into crisis and collapse, capitalism thrives and profits increase. Throughout all of this, we are told that there simply isn't enough money to address the needs of the living. Through capitalism's sleight of hand, we have allowed ourselves to be fooled into thinking that care can be monetized and that corporations are people deserving to be prioritized and valorised above all other living things.

Of course, our lived reality under such circumstances has become increasingly painful and uncomfortable. We have begun to question what Marx (1978) referred to as the inherent contradictions of capitalism. As the symbolic fails to meet the needs of the actual, the magic trick is seen to be fraying at the edges and we begin to question the logic of the trick. The idea that care can be represented as a sign to be communicated between radically separated and alienated individuals, mediated by the money form, loses its lustre.

ENVISIONING THE STRUGGLE TO CARE

Across the planet young people have begun to realize that the promises made to them about their future are smoke and mirrors. They are re-opening questions about how and what should be valued that have lain dormant since the revolts of the 1960s. I would argue that the question of care is central to the re-invigoration of value during this crisis of capitalist empire.

In her provocative and inspiring book (2012) *The Next American Revolution: Sustainable Activism for the Twenty-First Century*, the 94-year-old activist Grace Lee Boggs asks the following question:

> Living at the margins of the post-industrial capitalist order we … are faced with a stark choice of how to devote ourselves to struggle. Should we strain to squeeze the last drops of life out of a failing, deteriorating, and unjust system? Or should we instead devote our creative and collective energies toward envisioning and building a radically different form of living? (134)

Central to the question posed here is the assumption of struggle. One of the illusions promoted by global capitalism is that of society as an endless and entertaining casino. There is no need for us to do anything other than to slip the coins of our life force into the endless slot machines of capitalist consumption and hope to win the jackpot and become one of the winners. While waiting to win, we passively endure the mind numbing, physically and psychically degrading lottery of insecure employment. At the same time more and more of us spend our lives catering to the needs of the capitalist ruling class.

Of course, we are promised that soon there will be a recovery and good and meaningful employment for all. While we wait in the line for a future, that according to Deleuze (1995) is infinitely deferred, we are endlessly entertained as passive spectators of a proliferating array of virtual realities that distract us from the actuality at hand. There is no struggle here, just the constant conflicted drive to mute our actual desires and stave off the colliding and conflicting experiences of boredom and anxiety.

Boggs, however, offers us struggle as a central characteristic of the creation of an alternative world to come. To care for ourselves under a system of exploitation and domination in crisis, she seems to suggest, is to move from away from the role of passive spectator watching the ever more desperate magic tricks of capitalism as it attempts to sustain its illusions of care. Instead, we must take a more active and creative role and be willing to struggle.

What kind of struggle though? Here, we come full circle to youth work and to the question of, what kind of world are we co-producing with the young people we encounter in our work? Are we working to shore up the increasingly shaky foundations of the existing system of rule? Are our programmes, practices and thinking still deeply embedded in the logic of what Boggs calls, "a failing, deteriorating, and unjust system". Can we call ourselves a system of care, if what we do is simply produce what Foucault (1977) saw as docile bodies to live in perpetual servitude at the edges of a dying empire?

Earlier, we delineated care as communication and found it lacking. We argued that when care operates as series of definitions, it doesn't nurture or promote life so much as ordering it as system of commands. Care in this sense is what Deleuze and Guattari (1987) call an, 'order word'; that is a word that tells us how the world is ordered and then how we are to behave in relation to that definition. However, Deleuze and Guattari also offer what they call 'passwords' beneath the order words. These passwords are the produced when language fails. That is to say, when language evokes, rather than orders our lived experience. This is the moment in any description of the world when we sense that there is more to be said, more to be thought, and more to be expressed. It is the crack in the seamless order of things, where the struggle over what things *might* mean is glimpsed.

This sense of the infinite possibilities of what could be, exceeds all capacity of language to contain it. Such an experience cannot be communicated in the old model of information transmission. It can only be experientially shared through experimenting with new forms of language, identity and mutual productions. In reference to this Deleuze and Guattari (1987) argue that we don't need clearer communication, suggesting that we have too much communication already. What we need they say, is experimentation that breaks down communication, with its endless proliferations of signs and significations. In this, we might engage what Boggs refers to as devoting, "our creative and collective energies toward envisioning and building a radically different form of living".

RESPONSIVE CARE

How do we, as youth workers break the mould and move ourselves into a position where our care is truly responsive to the actual lived conditions of the young people we encounter? For those of us saturated with the logic of the past century, can we let go the hope of liberal compromise and the dreams of global justice and democracy under the regimes of a kinder, gentler capitalism? As Laing (2011) might have it, can we awaken from the collective dreaming of a mythical and ever expanding bourgeoisie and face the realities of the 21st century? Are we willing to relinquish the idea that youth work should be designed to prepare young people to successfully enter society and become good and productive citizens? Do we have the courage to create youth work with an ethics of revolt and insurrection?

In her book, Grace Lee Boggs critiques the educational system in the U.S. for being obsolete and unresponsive to the actuality of life for young people today. She argues that the old notion of training young people in skills that will eventually lead to a, "good job and a lot of money", no longer makes any sense. She tells us that preparing young people to be workers and consumers is premised in an outdated paradigm better suited to the 20th century than to the 21st. It is not surprising to her that drop-out rates in many large cities are often as high as 50% in the neighbourhoods and communities on the front lines of economic crisis. She maintains that schooling has become irrelevant to an increasing number of young people, who recognize that the best the future will hold under current conditions is a life of debt induced indentured servitude in low paying, insecure and unsatisfying employment. For these young people, the lure of quick cash in underground economies or a simple withdrawal into the world of sustained indolence is far more attractive than offering themselves up to be in perpetual service to the ruling 1%.

Under such conditions, reform is not sufficient. Boggs argues that we must do more than, "supply workers for the ever changing slots of the corporate machine". We must go beyond any attempt to reform, what is in her analysis, a bankrupt, outdated and failed system of values. Instead, we need to explore the co-production of a new set of values, which transforms our social institutions in such a way as to, "provide children with ongoing opportunities to exercise their resourcefulness to solve the real problems of their communities ... Children will be motivated to learn because their hearts, hands and heads are engaged in improving their daily lives" (137-138).

Boggs proposes that schools move beyond producing compliant worker drones and consumer addicts. Alternatively, schools would, "incorporate learning into work, political organization, community service and recreation". (p. 140) Concretely, Boggs tells us that we might well,

> Imagine how safe and lively our streets would be if ... [children] were taking responsibility for maintaining neighbourhood streets, planting community gardens, recycling waste, rehabbing houses, creating healthier school lunches, visiting and doing errands for the elderly, organizing neighbourhood festivals and painting public murals. (158)

She describes how Martin Luther King had, "called for programmes to involve young people in direct actions, 'in our dying cities', that would be, 'self transforming and structure transforming'" (157).

RELATION TO EDUCATION

I would suggest that the critique Boggs levels at the educational system might well be worth consideration within our own field of social service as youth workers and academics. Let's begin with our relation to education and the question at the heart of Boggs' argument.

Do we as youth workers still believe that the education system serves the needs of the young people that we see? Do we still hold to the outmoded and obsolete idea that a high school diploma will lead to any kind of rewarding and fulfilling labour? Or perhaps we cling to the belief that a college or university education will provide the key to a lifetime filled with economic security and social mobility? Of course, statistically we know that neither of these beliefs are sustainable within the current economic regimes of global capitalism.

And yet, most of our programming regarding education is geared to supporting the idea that attendance at elementary, middle and high school is an inherently valuable activity. Day after day we send our children into a broken and obsolete system of education that cannot possibly offer them anything close to what it promises. We deplore the fact that children drop out of this system and we work hard to get grants and support to assist us in building ever more programmes to reduce truancy, drop-outs and recalcitrant behaviour. Even when we consider alternative educational programming, such as Charter schools or after school programming it is, more often than not, under the same bankrupt and obsolete set of beliefs and ideas about training children to become successful in the 20th century rather than the 21st.

Does this mean that I don't think that education is valuable? Quite the contrary, as a full time academic, I think education is extremely valuable. However, we must always ask, education to what end? Education is an inherently political process that can, as Paolo Freire (2000) points out, either obscures the ways that the ruling class sustains itself, or lay bare the mechanisms of oppression and point the way to liberation.

There is no such thing as value free education. All education systems are engaged in the production of a particular system of values. The question is, whose system of values is being reproduced and to whose advantage? The most cursory glance at the existing global system of education promoted by the dominant ruling capitalist class reveals that the only group truly benefitting from the current system are those who are now becoming to be known as 'the 1%'. Of course under the category education that supports the 1%, we must include the current efforts to 'reform' education by dismantling it and opening it to the predatory practices of the for profit private sector.

The majority of those of us who encounter young people on a daily basis know that this system does not serve the young people we encounter in our work. Even those young people who succeed or excel are increasingly relegated to lowered wages and insecure employment.

YOUTH WORKER AS SERVANTS OF THE SYSTEM

Of course, ironically, these effects also impact the youth workers, who work with the young people in our increasingly economically precarious programmes. So, why do we continue our unflagging support of a system that neither serves us, or the young people we encounter? How is it we have failed, as of yet, to provide an alternative premised in a different and more relevant set of values? I would argue that it is because most of us in the field of youth work continue to believe in the hopes and promises of late 20th century capitalism. In spite of the evidence that confronts us every day, as a field we sustain and perpetuate the values system of the ruling class. In fact, as a field we seem to want desperately to belong and be valorised by the system that dominates, exploits and controls us. In spite of the fact that most of us have been well trained to recognize, identify and even educate young people and families to the dynamics of an abusive relationship, we somehow fail to see how the dynamics of just such a relationship function at a systemic and political level when it comes to projects such as professionalization or standards of practice. We manage to believe that if we can just prove ourselves and show how well behaved we are, the system will grant us access and provide us with the resources we need.

If we believe this about our own relationship to the dominant system of control, it is no wonder that we pass this system of belief on in our programmes and practices. Instead of recognizing that the promises of compromise and accommodation made by 20th century capitalist social programming are finished, we continue to recycle the myth of social mobility and economic security, to the young people we engage and to ourselves.

Under these conditions, there is no viable possibility of the much-vaunted authentic relational encounter of care between youth worker and young person. As Laing (2011) points out, such an encounter can only occur between people who are awake and living fully within their actual experience.

I would argue that one cannot access the world of actual experience while living in a mythical past, like the promised world of 20th century capitalism, rather than the actualities of life under 21st century global capitalist rule.

WAKE UP AND RE-CENTRE

So, what would be necessary for the field and for ourselves as individual youth work practitioners and academics, if we wanted to wake up? How would our engagement with young people shift? First, I would argue that we would need to thoroughly examine and dismantle the 20th century capitalist beliefs and practices that currently structure much our practices and programming. How would we do this?

Grace Lee Boggs offers a vision of how we might re-centre our work if we took the world of 21st century capitalism seriously and realistically. She suggests that we would abandon any talk of the future in our programming. Instead of talking with young people about how to get ahead later in life, we would focus on engaging young people with us in concrete projects that create real change in our neighbourhoods and communities in the present. This, she tells us gives meaning to life now and offers actual and material reasons to believe in what we can do together.

On the basis of this, rather than an abstract promise of inclusion into the world of money, dreams of the future can be envisioned together. I would argue that this combination of community transformation though joint labour can then form the basis for the return of the functional care to the field of youth work. This renewed form of relationship, I would propose, holds the key to new systems of value that valorise life rather than money, love rather position or power, and creativity rather than conformity.

ORGANIZING OUR SOCIAL FIELD OF ENCOUNTER

However, the question remains, how do we as field move from our current 20th century practices and institutional structures and reconfigure them so they offer the possibility of the mutual co-production of care? In the midst of what Boggs calls a deteriorating and failing system, how might we form transitional institutions that can take from where we are to where the future begins?

To do this, we need to return to something noted in passing at the beginning of these explorations. That is, the necessity to reconstitute the field of what we hold in common. Under the logic developed under capitalism, there is an ethos of radical separation, alienation and individual assertion. One must look out for oneself and promote one's self interest against all comers. Our sense of a successful life is premised on the individual accretion of power, privilege and money. The fact that other people, species and eco-systems were significantly damaged or destroyed is an unfortunate and regrettable, but necessary cost of progress. If we are to shift our thinking, we must abandon this line of thought and rationale in its entirety. Instead, we might re-think youth work, as something other than a site for training young people in self assertion or the development of a coherent individual self. We might move away from developmental theories that valorise the importance of separating and individuating. Alternately, we might also consider moving away from models that subject young people to the rules and regulated behaviour of communities and families, founded in the exclusion of other ways of becoming.

This is, of course true of our own communities of exclusion that we call programmes or agencies. Instead we might begin to investigate what we do and how we form ourselves, based on a combination of what we hold in common and the unique and idiosyncratic capacities that each of us brings to the struggle to thrive and survive. What each of us holds as separate individuals is limited by the boundaries that we impose when we individuate from the other. In order to become an individual, we must determine what we are not. This negation of the other in ourselves radically restricts our available capacity for fully and creatively exploring all that we might do and become. In order to develop a coherent ego driven self, we must impose boundaries on who we are and who we might become. We must determine, on an ongoing basis, who we are not in order to determine who we are. The list of who we are not is infinite, while the list of who must be in order to be us becomes increasingly limited across the duration of a lifespan.

On the other hand, to determine who we are through the indeterminate entanglements with the all others, human and otherwise (Pacini-Ketchabaw & Nxumalo, 2010) is to engage in a rich and open field of possibility. This would mean re-thinking the ways in which we organize our social field of encounter with young people. It would mean thinking and practicing beyond the narrow confines of what we currently consider the institutional parameters of our programmes and institutions. Rather than thinking in terms of safety and protection, we might begin to think of opening engagements with the living systems of community and biosphere in which we are imbedded. We might engage the life that surrounds us in a spirit of inclusion, experimentation, creativity and affirmation.

To be clear, this is not a utopian project premised on anything as superficial as seeking a happy and harmonious involvement with those inside and outside our institutions. Instead, to return to the theme above, it means to engage in the creative struggle of developing dynamic and ever-shifting functional relations of care. Obviously, this would require a significant reconfiguring of existing institutional organization and thinking. First and foremost we would need to ask ourselves, what does a youth work institution do in the 21st century under conditions of deteriorating empire and impending global revolution? We might note that the encounters in our institutions as they stand already constitutes a significant site of social struggle between new and old modes of social production, subjectivity and appropriation, domination and creativity, rebellion and compliance, as well as refusal and obedience. Our programmes are sites of social production, where new modes of social interaction, knowledge, languages, codes, and information are produced in an ongoing contestation between staff and youth, staff and administrators, administrators and boards, youth, staff and community and so on.

In this sense, our institutions already hold the possibility of being laboratories for new forms of social and political production. However, in their current configuration, as sites of behaviour management and social control, they constitute an actual barrier to the creative possibilities inherent within them. The question becomes, is there a way that youth institutions/agencies might open themselves to becoming laboratories of the future rather than reactionary protectors of a rapidly deteriorating past? In short, can youth work join with young people across the planet in the revolution in progress?

In re-founding our institutions as sites of creative social production, youth work holds several unique intrinsic aspects. These might be delineated as:
– our focus on the importance of viable and functional relationship
– the dynamic nature of our daily encounters with young people
– and, of course,
– our focus on care

These are critical elements in development of any form of new a new social. They are what we hold in common as youth workers and they are the building blocks of an alternative institutional structure. However, all of these practices and engagements have fallen on hard times. Instead of being the actual centre of our work, they have become subject to the bureaucratic imperatives designed to mute and control their revolutionary possibilities.

ACCEPTANCE OF CONFLICT

In order to reverse and re-order the relations within our institutions/agencies so that they serve life and not money, we might well take counsel from Hardt and Negri (2009) in their thinking about how to create institutions that can transition us through the stormy seas of massive social change. To overcome the imposition of capitalist logic on our practices and thought, they advocate that we might well refuse to submit to any form of social contract that forfeits the right to rebellion and conflict in exchange for social stability. This would mean moving away from rules and regulations as defining structures for our programmes and agencies. Instead of avoiding conflict and struggle and aiming for a smooth, seamless and harmonious group, we might welcome the contestatory nature of competing desires and conflicting thoughts. In a broader sense this would mean an acceptance of conflict, not as an aberration to be managed, but as a normal part of living that is, "internal to and the constant foundation of society" (355).

In terms of our work this would mean a raucous awakening from the dreams of capitalism's worker drone existence. As youth workers, administrators and academics we would open ourselves to conflict, resistance and rebellion as healthy indicators of those things that need to change. We would see the institution or agency as composed of all of us together in struggle with accountability across all components of the institution.

In this struggle in common, it would be necessary to re-think conflict as a problem of individual behaviour. Conflict always takes place within a collectivity. In our current configurations we often seek to discover the individual or individuals responsible for conflict or crisis in hopes we can resolve the conflict and restabilize the group. Both the idea that the group needs to return to an externally defined status quo through management of behaviour and affect, and the idea that conflict is initiated by individuals for their own pathologically derived reasons needs to be re-thought.

Instead of holding any one person responsible for a disruption or a conflict, we would see any conflict as an indicator of our collective need to creatively respond. To do this, we would need to engage in a politics of difference premised not in hierarchy, but in equality, mediated by function. Instead of negotiating rules or contracts for certain behaviour with sanctions and punishments such as discharge, we would negotiate terms of creative struggle and conflict, open to the necessity of constant revision.

This institutional openness to conflict and struggle would require a different mode of decision-making. Hardt and Negri (2009) suggest what they call, "a myriad of micro political paths". By this we might imagine youth work practice as collective decision-making that occurs throughout the day, at multiple sites throughout the institution/agency. Decisions are premised contingently on the conditions present in any given interaction as it occurs, rather than on pre-set institutional values or rules. Common practices are arrived at and composed through conflict. Such practices are not delivered from an administrative top down structure, but are made up through the concretion of myriad and multiple creative exchanges, always open to transformation as conditions change.

While this may sound radical at first, it actually reflects what our field has valorised as the relation practice of the encounter and the magic of the milieu. In perverted and corrupted form these practices have been driven by the needs of dominant institutions, where relationships are bargained for privileges or acceptance and the milieu becomes a sophisticated form of group think and psychological bullying. Under the practices of functional care, interactions are released into autonomous and voluntary encounters in which we all struggle together to express our capacities without fear of conflict.

As we open ourselves to a more dynamic and actual set of relations, not artificially constrained by behavioural and ethical imperatives of a dominant system of top down control, the possibility of a form of caring far more responsive to all the bodies involved becomes a possibility. This kind of caring is shaped dynamically through myriad encounters through the institution/agency, rather than the institution defining a universal standard of care through regulation and fiat.

WORK OF ART

The tricky part of this new form of caring is to keep ourselves open to its inherently experimental form and not attempt to introduce new modes of domination and control. This means a radical re-thinking of who we are. Rather than seeing ourselves as individuals asserting our rights and imperatives for self-assertion, we would investigate the ways in which the unique and idiosyncratic capacities that each of us hold might contribute to the creative productions of our common good. This means, instead of training young people and ourselves in how to manage and control our behaviour towards pre-determined positive outcomes, we would need to learn how to become sensitive and more fully aware of how our desires and affects function within the broader context. In this sense our work together becomes less like work and more like art. We produce the world together through discovering, through conflict and struggle, what we hold in common. No one is denied their capacities or forced to use them in a way alien to their own desires. This would truly be a very different kind of institution than the ones in which we work now. Such an institution would be centred on functioning to the highest degree as a creative force for the assertion of the vitality and dynamism of living things.

Instead of being addicted to an abstract system of sign, such institutions would focus on breaking such addictions through immersion in the creative force of working in common struggle. In this, youth work would become a practice associated with waking from the trance of capitalism into the world of actual needs and desires. It would promulgate an understanding that we lack none of the things necessary to promote a joyful and full life for all living things on the planet. As transitional institutions, youth work programmes and agencies would aim to dissolve themselves into the broader world of democratic self-rule through the dissolution of categories such as adult, child and adolescent. This would release us from some of the saddest divisions in our existing social. No longer bound to the rules and regulations of externally defined development, those of us defined as adult might be able to re-engage the joy of play and imagination.

CONCLUSION

In the end, I am proposing that we utilize our existing institutions to move through the horrors and miseries of global capitalism to an uncertain, but possibly more joyful and loving community of life in common. We would hold as our goal the ability to experience struggle, conflict, joy and love. Our practices would be revolt, rebellion, creativity, and the building of new systems of values and a new world to come.

REFERENCES

Althusser, L. (2006). *Lenin and philosophy and other essays.* Aakar Books.

Boggs, G. L., & Kurashige, S. (2012). *The next American revolution: Sustainable activism for the twenty-first century.* University of California Press.

Baudrillard, J. (1981). *A critique of the political economy of the sign*. New York: Telos Press.

Deleuze, G. (1995). Postscript on control societies. *Negotiations, 1972-1990*, 177-82.

Deleuze, G., & Guattari, F. (1987). *Thousand plateaus: Capitalism and schizophrenia*. Minneapolis: University of Minnesota Press.

Foucault, M. (1972). *Archeology of Knowledge*. (Trans. A. M. Sheridan Smith). New York: Pantheon Books.

Foucault, M. (1977). *Discipline & punish*. Random House of Canada.

Freire, P. (2000). *Pedagogy of the oppressed*. Continuum International Publishing Group.

Hardt, M. (1995). The withering of civil society. *Social Text, 45*, 27-44.

Hardt, M., & Negri, A. (2009). *Commonwealth*. Harvard University Press.

Laing, R. D. (2011). *The politics of the family*. House of Anansi.

Marx, K. (1978). *Marx-Engels reader* (R. C. Tucker, Ed.). New York: W.W. Norton.

Pacini-Ketchabaw, V., & Nxumalo, F. (2010). A curriculum for social change: Experimenting with politics of action or imperceptibility. *Flows, rhythms & intensities of early childhood education curriculum*, 133-154.

BRIAN BELTON

COMPASSION AND THE 'COLONIAL MENTALITY'

Pretoria

In March 2013 I was in Pretoria, South Africa for an international conference on youth work. The day my plane landed, the National Executive Committee of the African National Congress Youth League was disbanded by the African National Congress. Of course, it had been the activism of young people, culminating in June 1976, in Soweto that had been pivotal in starting the last act of the defeat of apartheid. Less than 40 years later the first speeches I heard in conjunction with the conference were warnings that South Africa faced its own 'Arab Spring' unless young people were 'brought on board'. At this point, many in Europe understood the uprisings in Egypt and elsewhere, wherein the participation of the young seemed critical, as something of a spark of freedom, liberalism and modernization. As such, the mood seemed ominous from the start and as the days went by, from my perspective, the conference divided into two distinct camps; those who saw youth work as a means to work on young people in order to perpetuate forms of social adaptation and political conformity to a particular set of norms and others who understood the practice to ultimately be about almost the opposite – serving young people as they sought out the time, context and means to question and change the nature of society, developing their own political trajectory out of this.

Predictably, walking along the fault lines of this dichotomy were the apologists for 'nation building', mostly non-Africans, preaching a gospel of a species of 'covert evolution', apparently through which they believed serving the ends of establishment, a directed and politically regimented strategy could promote the ultimate expression of the particular individual and group interests of young people. This was counterintuitive strategy whereby advance might be achieved by retreat; that social progress might be achieved via forms of reaction and acquiescence with the current political orthodoxy. In short this doctrine suggested that obliged convention was a sensible path to libratory ends. However for many this felt, at best, more like waiting for the right bus at the wrong bus stop.

PREMONITION OR MEMORY?

For all this, I couldn't help but feel I had heard this all before, but wasn't quite sure where or how; a sense of being in a place somewhere between déjà vu and amnesia. Why would any state fund or tolerate work or professional intervention that brought its own rationale into question? Why would any capitalist country, with all the gross inequalities of the distribution of resources incumbent in that

B. Belton (ed.), 'Cadjan – Kiduhu': Global Perspectives on Youth Work, 77–105.

social formation (in 2006 the World Institute for Development Economics Research of the United Nations found that the top one percent of people in the world control 40 percent of the wealth) provide the means to alter or even temper its logical exploitative ends? Surely that state would look to endorse and support only forms of intervention that helped those same ends.

Capitalism requires a relatively compliant, relative flexible, relatively skilled, relatively cheap workforce, and anyone involved in youth work in say the UK over the last 20 years will be aware of just how the practice has been directed to this suite of tasks. But such considerations have to some extent always been present, one only has to look to see their presence (alongside a broad band of control and management oriented functions) in the history of youth work, it's just that in the last couple of decades these aims have been more obvious; they have been streaking rather than flashing.

As I left South Africa in the spring of 2013 I knew what I had experienced was not new at all or something unusual to that country or state. I was just involved in yet another incarnation of a social malaise, which I have come to understand under the tutelage of Franz Fanon, as a type of psychosocial disease, which has burdened world society for centuries.

COLONISED YOUTH

The worst thing about youth facilities is that they are 'youth' facilities. As a youth, the last place I, or anyone I knew wanted to go was a place designed for 'youth'. For most of the last quarter of the 20th century, a relatively small percentage of young people in the UK attended designated youth facilities for any significant part of their life before work. However, between the ages of 13 and 18, I didn't see myself as a 'youth' – that category, like 'adolescent', didn't mean a thing to me (and it still doesn't tell me much). Does it say much to anyone in any precise way? Where did it come from? Who invented this label? Well, it certainly wasn't 'youth' themselves.

How much room is there to make what there is for youth what youth want, if there are people employed to 'put on' what is seen to be good for or fit for youth, while they and others define what youth is and who young people are, what they need and want?

It's not surprising that as a society, with the colonization era being historically a comparatively recent period, wherein most of our institutions (education, health, law, etc.) were formed, the echo of the culture of colonization continues resonate. We are quite used to other people setting our social agenda.

Take education. We, as a society, tend to agree that education is 'a good thing'. But is it? Why? In our society, at best, to be educated is to be steeped in some field of knowledge, felt to be of use to society; at worst it is associated with being 'skilled up' for employment. When I have knowledge of something that is of little use to society I'm not really thought of as educated. I may know everything there is to know about West Ham United, and as such I might be thought of as an expert on the good old Hammers, but this would not make me educated in the eyes of society. However, if I had a great deal of information about mathematics in my head (and for me that's a big if) most people would say that I was educated.

In our society education is a commodity. This is logical as we live in a capitalist society where most things and/or people are either commodities (things; a bag, skills, or abilities to be sold) or consumers (people who buy commodities) and usually both. In general, the better educated I am (the more I have in terms of skills/useful knowledge that I can sell) the better I get on in society – in other words the more I adapt to this society the more advantages I have, although if I can buy stuff and sell it at a higher price than I paid for it (something which is astonishingly called 'fair trade') that will also provide me with financial advantages.

Education is, for the vast majority of people, a form of indoctrination, a particular slant on information and memorization. As such, to be well educated in a consumerist society is to be well instructed or trained and remembering a fair bit of what you were instructed about. Indeed, most folk would have trouble saying what the difference is between training and education is – that's indoctrination for you!

Training, indoctrination and instruction mean that you learn 'the way': the way to drive; the way to eat your dinner or the way to 'do' informal education (what some have tried to define as youth work). In turn, the ambition to get young people involved in informal education is based on the assumption that they need informal education (I'm not sure anyone has ever written to the council/local authority/government and demanded more informal education apart from a few unemployed informal educators perhaps). This is the working through of a deficit model of the type familiar within the colonial context. 'You, the native, need what I, the coloniser have. You have not asked me for it, indeed you avoid it, but one way or another, by reward or punishment, I will impart my notion of education, my religion, my values, my social norms (civilization) to you, and, in the colonial situation, the better you take these on, the better you will fare'.

This system or process gives rise to the attitudes that Franz Fanon observed in the colonial environment, what might be called 'the colonial mentality'. He pointed out in his books *Black Skin, White Masks* (1967) and *The Wretched of the Earth* (1965) a kind of social pathology, wherein the colonised have habituated reliance on the coloniser. The goods of society are distributed according to the values and norms not of my culture, but of the colonizing culture. I become a passive recipient of the favours given from what might be thought of as the active or controlling group.

The colonised in such a society, according to Fanon display a number of typical traits; they are apathetic, both politically and socially, showing little interest in the overall solidarity of society. In competition for the limited resources that the coloniser makes available, infighting between racial, tribal, family and other interest groups is constant. Ethnic or cultural boundaries become exaggerated in this rivalry (promoted and confirmed by the coloniser, aided by the media which they own, direct and operate) differences are pronounced while commonalities between groups are understated.

These traits are evident in current British and western, industrialised society generally, in particular among the young – indeed these reactions might be understood as the contemporary weapons of youth. It is hard to think of an era when the young have been so seemingly disaffected. However, from the earliest times the young have been a vibrant force in society. In the middle ages they were a major part of the workforce. Medieval times saw great pilgrimages of children, petitioning the Pope and visiting holy shrines. In the 13th century there was a children's crusade. In the 19th and early 20th century they were involved in industrial conflict and school rebellions. One of the first major industrial actions in world history was the Match Girl's Strike of 1888, this was a workforce made up predominantly of young women, and their action became the exemplar and inspiration for mass social and industrial unrest throughout the UK in the last part of the 19th century. Even as recently as the 1960s and 1970s students were involved in organised political action of the most dynamic and energetic sort (see 'When School Students Fought the System' http://www.workersliberty.org/node/7058). Of course the Teddy Boys and the Mods and Rockers played their part in scaring society into the (if only partial) implementation of the *Albermarle Report*, so creating the modern youth service in the UK.

Now the relatively young, apart from the politically almost meaningless drink induced frenzies of violence on Friday and Saturday nights in High Streets up and down the country, are the most passive of groups – the 2011 'riots' can, counter intuitively perhaps, be understood as a manifestation of this as the rebellion of the politically inarticulate. Alongside the seemingly long-term aim of 'NVQing' of the universe, the on going dismantling of unions and most forms of questioning/critical education, what little social will to resist is almost totally undermined.

What can we do? Despite what some youth workers seem to think, we are not in a position to change the world; we can't even change our job descriptions! But we can look to initiate a reassessment of our personal/individual position; we can become, as Malcolm X might have put it more like a 'field slave' (10 November 1963, in Detroit, USA, in his *Message to the Grass Roots* Malcolm X); someone who is supported by those we work with, rather than someone who comes in to do something to or with those people on the orders of 'the man' (the 'house slave').

However, Michel Foucault, notably in his work *Discipline and Punish* (1977), argued that the social interventions, carried out by the agencies of the State or organisations allied to the State (say via bureaucratic or legal and/or funding connections) whose aims and ambitions are often mediated by professionals, are premised on the need society has to control and/or create social conformity – to produce a compliant society and promote particular types of cultural norms that do not threaten or question the given social status-quo. The professional operating in the social sphere is part of and defined by this activity. The State, either directly or indirectly, will not tolerate or fund activity that is contrary to its values or which fails to confirm its basis; the inequalities inherent to any capitalist system.

From this perspective, what seems to be the professional youth worker's overriding ambition, to 'change' young people, could be understood as colonising activity wherein 'the client' becomes the object of 'cultural assault'.

Ivan Illich, particularly in *The Limits to Medicine* (1976) has pointed out that forms of professional intervention are ultimately damaging to those 'targeted' (effectively 'hunted'). The process starts by someone being seen to have a 'lack' that can be interpreted as pathological. I would suggest that this 'deficit model' is quite pervasive in terms of the professional focus. The excuse to introduce the change is set up by the portrayal of the targeted group as lacking elemental input, such as education or socialization, or they are assumed to have a psychological deficiency – youth workers not unusually have a set of these to apply (even though relatively few youth workers are qualified psychologists/psychiatrists) for instance the prognosis of 'poor self-esteem', 'lack of confidence' or 'ADHD' is made as if the professional was dealing with an endemic condition or disease and that the appropriate treatment is to 'change' the 'infected' person (expressions referring to 'betterment', ambitions to 'make them better' are openly used) to bring them into line with an acceptable norms of behaviour. The State aims for this are called 'effective change' in the professional realm and this is achieved by the client's movement towards 'commitment to change'.

Fanon (who was a qualified and experienced psychiatrist) recognised that the colonial mentality caused the colonised see themselves, their 'native identity', as having little if any value. Self- and group-worth are estimated on the level of approval that the coloniser gives. This approval is based on how close 'the native' has come to replicating the mannerisms, ways and cultural mores of the coloniser; black skins, white masks. However, it is always recognised that the approved actions are merely replicas and not 'the real thing'. Hence the very soul of the colonised is exterminated – they thus become the 'wretched of the earth'. How often, albeit entirely unintentionally, is the professional youth worker in fact an agent of this type of colonialism? Encouraged to see 'youth' as a problem to be solved.

What I would like to think is, if I enter an estate, local institution or work on the street, I will first look to be changed by and thorough that cultural context and the expressions of those I work with and amongst, rather than, in the first instance, seek to promote the ideas I might import, impart about how those people might, could or should be. Che Guevara in his *Guerrilla Warfare* (1961) tells us that it is not possible for the Guerrilla to support or define the groups or collectives. For the Guerrilla to be successful they must be ready to be defined (changed) by those who allow them to share their situation or context and look to be supported by them. This is the reverse, the antithesis of the deficit model, but it is not easy and maybe impossible for us to sustain. Cultural expressions involving what society might see as forms of vandalism, crime, drug abuse, copious consumption of alcohol, hooliganism, particular sexual practices, language forms that we might find abusive or even violent may need to be embraced rather than merely tolerated (toleration is a form of patronage and as such related to forms of deficit thinking – we tolerate everything up to the point will become intolerant of something).

This deficit thinking is prevalent in youth work, exposed by the labelling people as 'vulnerable', 'at risk' or 'NEET'. In *Deschooling Society* the reader is reminded by Ivan Illich of the wreckage wrought by professional incursions premised on notions of lack. We seem ready to append labels to people, such as 'at risk', 'vulnerable', assess that they 'lack self-esteem' and proceed to treat them in a way that suggests that the labels are in fact truth. Even if we are skilled/qualified enough social psychologists or psychiatrists to make such assessments, we might only see a person in a very limited context, maybe for a couple of hours a week and then usually as part of a bigger group, for a relatively short period of their lives. Few clinical specialists would risk 'treatment' on such a limited experience of another person.

Throughout my youth work career there seems to be at least as much skill in avoiding being invasive in terms of other people's experience, as there is in taking opportunities to label someone as 'vulnerable' as a means to make them an object of my 'professional attention', seeing myself as not only a potential but an actual 'helper'/'supporter'. From my earliest years in the profession I found myself asking how much of this sort of activity in practice creates vulnerability (or conjure it up). After reading another Illich book, *Disabling Professions* it seemed to me that my questioning was vindicated

ON COMPASSION

The control and manipulation of the social and political realm does not cover the whole panoply of colonization. As Fanon pointed out (1965, 1967) colonialism is reliant on the nurturing of a mentality (in terms of both the colonised and the coloniser) and as such is reliant on the capacity to reach into the psychological, emotional and even spiritual worlds of those hemmed into the colonial environment.

Over recent years there has been an on-going discussion across what are broadly referred to as the 'caring professions' about the place of compassion in practice. This is not altogether new. The contemporary discourse might be thought of a resurgence of the kind of attitude and thinking represented in David Brandon's book, *Zen in the Art of Helping* (1976, 1990), which has been described by Phil Barker as, "the most remarkable book of my generation" (1971, 2004). The real kernel of all our help', according Brandon (1990: 6) is, "that which renders it effective, is compassion". For him, caring and concern to alleviate suffering and the relationships that emanated from the same, needed to define helping more than managerial and technical concerns.

There has also for some time been a growing concern about levels of compassion within the caring professions, to the point where there have even been various prescriptions about the need to train potential practitioners to be compassionate. More contemporaneously Smith and Smith (2008: 15, 35-36) did much to introduce the same debate into youth work, calling on, amongst others, Brandon's perspective (although he comes from a social work perspective and background). But what might be the nature or shape of any skills involved in delivering compassionate practice? At what point does compassion become a form of patronisation and with this in mind, is there something colonial about the ambition to 'share suffering' (the meaning of the word 'compassion') particularly when one is not invited to do so? Is one not entitled to inhabit one's own emotional world or be free of having one's mental or emotional state defined and 'entered' by a professional other? Why should I think that I can or want to temper or alleviate (tamper with) the situation of another by way of my compassion?

In this following analysis, to an extent, I echo the position of Richard Sennett (2003), questioning what he sees as degrading forms of compassion that effectively undermine respect for those in need. However my position is inspired by the supplication made by Christopher Hitchens toward the end of his *Letters to a Young Contrarian* (2005: 140):

> Beware the irrational, however seductive. Shun the 'transcendent' and all who invite you to subordinate or annihilate yourself. Distrust compassion; prefer dignity for yourself and others ... Picture all experts as if they were mammals. Never be a spectator of unfairness or stupidity. Seek out argument and disputation for their own sake; the grave will supply plenty of time for silence. Suspect your own motives, and all excuses. Do not live for others any more than you would expect others to live for you.

However, like Sennett I would hope that mutual respect can create connections across the potential segregations of inequality, that are made more profound by effectively seeing some people as relatively pitiful, reliant on the bountiful compassion of those of us who imagine ourselves to be deep wells of this unconditional sentiment. This might be driven by the best of intentions, as were the colonial missionaries of the age of Empire, but as the proverb has it, the road to hell is paved with the same.

In the rest of this chapter I will look to make a case that our work, most often, in its best incarnation, is about dynamically taking responsibility for our professional status and role (taking it seriously) and not getting bogged down with seemingly meaningless rhetoric; indulging in an effort to disseminate boundless 'compassion' and 'love' to folk who may not need or have asked for the same. I find it hard not to understand this as a missionary exercise, premised on the kind of deficit assumptions outlined at the start of this chapter.

I will explore if we can, as professionals, claim to provide/extend compassion to, in Brandon's terms 'love' (1990: 48-50, 58-61; see also Smith & Smith, 2008: 15, 28, 29, 74) all those we work with? Is it 'unconditional' and available to all? Other questions that will be broached are

– Is it likely that this 'ambition' will be understood in the same way by everyone? and

– Will some not find it threatening or at least 'over-the-top'?

As the supposed 'kernel' of our practice does the position presented by Brandon (1990) and more latterly Smith and Smith (2008) offer a means for effective delivery of welfare, care (carefulness) or education or is it more akin to an ambition to psychologically and/or emotionally colonise?

A DUTY OF COMPASSION?

In the UK young people have a legal expectation of duty of care from professionals working with them, and in other national contexts similar rights, expectations and duties pertain. Care has been and is clarified in a range of contexts. For instance, Social care has been defined by IASCE (the Irish Association of Social Care Educators) as:

> … a profession committed to the planning and delivery of quality care and other support services for individuals and groups with identified needs.

It has been more officially characterised as being:

> … the professional provision of care, protection, support, welfare and advocacy for vulnerable or dependent clients, individually or in groups. This is achieved through the planning and evaluation of individualised and group programmes of care, which are based on needs, identified where possible in consultation with the clients and delivered through day-to-day shared life experiences. All interventions are based on established best practice and in-depth knowledge of lifespan development. (Higher Education and Training Awards Council Working Group on Social Care, 2001)

However, it might be difficult to frame or enforce an official/stated 'duty of compassion' in quite the same way.

The above definition mirrors many made in professional contexts around the world. As such, professional care might be thought of as logical benignancy, informed by knowledge of our role and a sense of justice that is evoked out of the consideration for and about individuals, as well as the groups and social settings they are part of. It sets a rational ethos for the management of services. This is very different to the effusive and pungently emotive response of Brandon;

> Compassion is being in tune with oneself, the other person(s) and the whole world. It is goodness at its most intuitive and unreflective. It is a harmony which opens itself and permits the flowing out of love towards others without asking any reward. (1990: 60)

For the most part the effectiveness of professionals working with young people will be judged by their ability to exert appropriate professional care. This apposite care is, in the best of situations, proportionate and measured rather than the letting loose of feelings and attitudes that some claim to involve 'loving' clients and/or promoting forms of 'intimacy' (see for instance Smith & Smith 2008: 39, 95; Brandon, 1990: 48) which may need, sooner or later, to be explained and justified, within the context of professional practice and safeguarding procedures, to those we aim be to be 'intimate' with or project this 'love' on – their parents/guardians, our managers, funders, inspectors, social services or the media.

So do we need to inform those we work with that we are going to be compassionate towards them? Should we make information and guidance about our compassionate action available in the same way as child protection procedures and standards of care are available for scrutiny? Is extending our compassion without the knowledge, consent or request of those who are the target of our compassion consistent with our ambitions to 'promote trust' and honesty, or act democratically and transparently? If we are compassionate covertly is there a risk that at least some of those we focus our compassion on might understand our actions as condescending or as some over kind of romantic overture? If we are frank about our compassionate intentions do we risk being seen to operate on a collection of assumptions, formed by way of a deficit model about individuals and their families (they don't get/give enough/any compassion)? Would this not betray echoes of missionary/colonial ambitions/suppositions?

MEANING

When talking about the potential relationship between compassion, love and intimacy to fellow professionals I have found that it is not unusual to be told something like 'that is not what I mean by compassion'. This is followed by attempts to formulate a picture of the person's approach, or what the harsher critic might call 'bias' (and the cynic 'prejudice') which in essence excuses attempts to develop levels of close or even a sense of personal familiarity with clients. Words like 'warmth' and 'empathy' are used interchangeably, alongside ideas about 'developing trust' and 'connection'. Now and then it is hard not to conclude, after listing the techniques and strategies deployed to achieve these emotive ends, apparently both purposefully and unconsciously, that a type of seduction is risked. There is almost invariably at least some hint of manipulation, fired by a seeming urgency to persuade or incline young people to 'open up' to or develop a 'sense of oneness' with a practitioner. This feels particularly questionable (at times unsavoury) when dealing with volatile and/or emotionally vulnerable young people.

For Brandon compassion involves, "… commitment, involvement, caring, love and generosity of heart". He claims, "Openness, intimacy and sensitivity are the herbs of compassion. Those qualities are concerned with seeing deeply and directly into the other person and feeling his needs and wants" (1990: 48); it is, "… the process of deep contact with primordial source of love"; compassion, "lies at the heart of all helping; without it relationships between people are like dry leaves in the wind" (ibid.: 49). He goes on to argue that compassion, "… embodies the fostering of love" (ibid.: 50) is "… a complete reflection of overall harmony. It contains, as Fromm pointed out in writing of love, the ingredients of care, responsibility, respect and knowledge" (ibid.: 59).

Putting aside the questions how one might determine 'overall harmony', how deep, deep contact might be (what is 'shallow' or 'average' contact?) and what 'generosity of heart' is and how it could be gauged (to some giving a beggar money ensures a place in heaven, for others it does not more than ensure the beggar continues to beg) for Brandon 'compassion' becomes a catchall word or practice that allows a sort of outpouring of affecting responses on the part of the practitioner, with the intention of creating a kind of emotional bonding with clients.

But this is a particular type of union wherein the (supposedly needy) client is the recipient of the practitioner's gushing benevolence.

Just as the colonised is defined by the coloniser (and vice-versa) so the function of giving compassion is realised by the supposed or enticed need for compassion; the compassionate person gains this status by the realization and concomitant giving and receiving of compassion – it is a complimentary relationship to that extent.

In truth the above type of translation of compassion is little more than randomly inventing personal meanings for words and the actions those words prescribe or elicit. This is a 'Humpty Dumpty' reaction; the meaning of words become more or less made up to persuade or inveigle others to adopt a point of view;

> *'When I use a word', Humpty Dumpty said, in a rather scornful tone', it*
> *means just what I choose it to mean, neither more nor less'.*
> *'The question is', said Alice, 'whether you can make words mean so many*
> *different things'.*
> *'The question is', said Humpty Dumpty, 'which is to be master – that's all'.*
> (Carroll, 1871)

Brandon, drawing more from his imagination than any definitive sources, inclines one to conclude compassion to be almost anything at all from a smorgasbord of emotive reactions, but it doesn't just follow that is what it is. He confuses and conflates 'compassion' – that is derived from two Latin words, *cum* and *pati* which translate as 'to suffer with'/'share suffering' – with a whole cavalcade of emotional trappings. He argues (1990: 49) that the presence of compassion is negligible in the realm of contemporary practice. However, we do call upon and use our emotions during the course of our work, but can our level of commitment to our clients be as 'total' or 'unconditional' as Brandon instructs?

While the general usage of words tend to define their meaning, perhaps we need to be aware of the dangers of simplifying and contorting language for purposes of defining situations to be as we want them to be (rather than managing situations as they are). This 'language of compassion' effectively appears to attempt to convert others to play a role in relation to particular ideas and attitudes, which can seem more about the psychological or emotional need of the giver of 'composite (the new improved) compassion' than the need their target audience might have for this emotive soup.

Words do have a life of their own to a certain extent, but perhaps the general meanings of words are less crucial than how and why a particular meaning of a word is chosen or deployed? You do not need to restrict yourself to Latin interpretations nor Brandon's subjective construals. You are able to build your own interpretation/understanding (based on your own experience and analysis) rather than relying on 'second-hand' perspectives. For all this, to confuse 'compassion' with Brandon's imagined and longed for Nirvana, wherein it seems we are expected to be all things to all people, all of the time, without reward of any kind, is not only fallacious it is unfair and risky in practice. Such indistinct fantasies, which conscript 'compassion', 'love' and 'devotion' to the professional cause, are dangerously free of all the fears and anxieties that social conditions have surrounded these affectations with.

Where is the client in all of this, the recipient of our benevolence? Some years ago I was told a story by an individual, let's call this person 'X', about how X's manager caught X in a very compromising situation, implicating the personal and private life of both X and the manager. The manager, a person prone to trading in words like 'love', 'forgiveness' and compassion, made X aware that they would take no action in response to the misdemeanour and that while they could not forget what had happened, forgiveness was given. This, understandably, evoked tremendous gratitude from X, which manifested itself in a fierce protective loyalty toward the manager. The years went by, the manager retired, but they had grown very close to X and X's family, often taking X's mother (after she had lost her husband) home for Sunday lunch and out for drives in the country, something X was again very grateful for. However X told me that as time had gone by he had learned to resent the former manager, feeling he could never criticise this person's ideas (many of which he found profoundly objectionable) or even be free of this person's benevolence, that hung around his neck like an albatross. He said he felt 'owned' by the situation and by this on-going, persistent compassion. For me, this story felt like a tale of one person colonizing another and the cost of missionary practice.

If we take the compassion gospel on board as the 'Zen' of practice, we can show how humane and compassionate we are, despite our organisation's inhumanity. We can, in our compassionate piety, highlight and complain about another's lack of compassion compared to our own stock of the same. We can invent a personal definition of compassion that complies with the formula, 'most things I do that are positive are compassionate, whilst practically everything my organisation does is not'.

This more or less uncritical approach seems mostly directed to justifying pretty questionable practice via insubstantial and rather vague sound-bytes (that are sometimes rendered almost meaningless in their generality). It also potentially sets up a 'compassion tournament' wherein practitioners compete to be seen or understood as the most compassionate, creating a hierarchy of compassion. One can only shiver as the cloying solicitude of such an environment is imagined.

THE CLAIM OF COMPASSION

One might claim to be, or want to be seen as 'compassionate' for all sorts of reasons. Of course, in particular situations the person who can establish that they are more compassionate than their peers may win the moral high ground. However, this can motivate feelings of guilt in those who, in the shadow of such munificence, appear less than compassionate or at least not as compassionate as the relative giant of compassion.

The other side of the coin of guilt is resentment. As the story above demonstrates to some extent, if you make me feel guilty (I must be guilty to be given and accept forgiveness) at some point there's a good chance that I'm going to resent you for it – albeit not consciously. This imposition of culpability in itself does not seem too compassionate.

The claim that one person is showing compassion for another, apart from making assumptions about another individual's relative suffering, the character of 'help', being 'nice', 'kind', 'considerate', 'empathetic', 'sympathetic', 'caring' etc. tend to be magically subsumed by this compassion; I have found that combinations of all of these sentiment connected verbs are used to describe what compassion is when delivered by youth workers.

It appears that it is not enough just to be 'considerate' or to show practical care; something more is demanded to prove one is compassionate. This promotes an all or nothing response; you are either 'compassionate' or you are not, and to be compassionate a full panoply of emotion based responses needs to be exhibited or effectively proved. If you fail to provide this voluble poignancy, you are not, by implication, effective, because you are in some way 'detached' and/or 'cold'. This in turn can convince that Thomas Szasz was not far wrong when he reputedly claimed that,

> We prefer a meaningless collective guilt to a meaningful individual responsibility.

If the central aim of our work is to be 'compassion' then it would seem compassionate to make this clear in job descriptions and policy etc. If we want to be this 'devoted' to other people's children do we have a duty to inform their parents/guardians of these aims, letting them know we want to 'give ourselves wholly' and have compassion for those they have (unlike us) full-time responsibility for in law? And should we tell them that these 'objectives' (at least partly) are based on our concern that their children may not be getting the compassion they need at home or elsewhere (although we have little if any concrete evidence for this conclusion)?

I doubt if most people would consider any of this as reasonable and, at least to some extent, understand it to be a fairly aggressive attempt at psychological colonization, even if they might not articulate it as such.

SHIFTING ARTICULATIONS

Is part of the difficulty of insisting that compassion be a central element of our practice perhaps that it is interpreted and/or articulated in a variety of ways by different people, at different times and places? There are models of professional care emanating from nursing, social care and social work that can be interpreted and agreed within practice arenas, as well as expectations in law (this in the past has been inherent and embodied in the UK by way of the Common Assessment Framework).

However, it is hard to identify anything like a generic consensus in the professional realm about what might constitute 'compassion'; it is probably difficult to establish in any meaningful way. For example, some people believe that euthanasia is compassionate; others see it as cold-blooded murder (however, under current medical care guidelines for most countries, whatever one's compassionate disposition, euthanasia is deemed unethical and theoretically disallowed).

How can we make this principle (compassion), a shifting and in places indistinct collection of notions, be integral to our work? How do we consistently, accurately (and so responsibly) judge when someone wants/desires/needs our compassion, across cultural, social or other divides? If we cannot agree what it is, how can we discern that we have delivered appropriate or inappropriate levels of compassion; too little or too much compassion? Do some people want/need more compassion than others? If so, how can we tell or do we just 'feel' (guess) and hope for the best? Can people be trained or educated to be compassionate or more compassionate than they are? Is a set of qualities required to be 'appropriately' compassionate, that we can simply take as fact that everyone has or that only some people are born with? If it is a central aspect of professional practice should people have a 'compassion test' before they are allowed to practice? What if it was identified that a practitioner was not compassionate enough, how might we explain this at a subsequent employment tribunal; that (for instance) they were unable to 'see into people' to 'share their suffering' to a sufficient depth?

For all this, as youth workers we often see people for little more than a couple of hours a week, perhaps for just a few months of their lives, sometimes in groups that might range in size from three to 40 – can we realistically say that we, as a general rule, have much of a chance to see 'deeply' into another person and 'feel' their needs and wants? Is that just a bit close to an ambition to read minds? How can one ensure that what one is 'feeling' is another person's wants and needs and not simply a subjective projection of one's own; the need to be needed or some other affectation? Indeed, a psychoanalytical view of certain seemingly compassionate acts might suggest they are in fact examples of the transference of the apparently compassionate individual's needs onto others.

Even if we can genuinely and directly feel the needs of others, can we do it for all, creating 'equal Access' to our compassion? This presents other difficulties, given that there is no clear accord as to what it (compassion) is? Or is compassion only for a special/lucky few that happen to be worked with by those able to extend to sort of 'deep', ethereal qualities that Brandon outlines? Would that not be a potential cause for jealousy, resentment and anger?

Are ideas about extending compassion in professional practice altogether clear or are they rather vague and open to what some might see as an 'unsafe' range of interpretation? Have the practices associated with what is an expansive human capacity been widely tested or evidenced to be in keeping with current accepted and profession wide agreed notions of 'best practice'; are there important cultural considerations/interpretations/understandings that need taking into consideration?

QUESTIONING COMPASSION

The above questions might be thought of as something of an example of energetic questioning of the notion that compassion may be a vital component in our work. One can of course use other definitions or generate one's own interpretation of compassion. But as a collection of activities proscribed for general practice (and so needing to be in harmony with existing professional standards, requirements and structures) much of the above might be of continuing concern.

Critical engagement is part of the development of professional judgement – the capacity not to just take on received knowledge or ideas, but explore and find possible flaws in the same, before we apply the opinions of others to the lives and experience of those we work for, with and amongst. Perhaps as carers of other people's children we are morally/professionally obligated to undertake such exercises just as a medical practitioner would examine the possible detrimental effects of a particular treatment on patients before administering that treatment. Indeed, to merely deliver received opinions in the professional context without appropriate, thorough questioning about the possible consequences of practice that might arise out of these ideas (how these have the capacity to potentially confirm or undermine existing professional standards and expectations) may be understood as irresponsible or perhaps within the framework of care, risk accusations of neglect[1] in terms of failing to meet the needs of clients.

While it is likely that most of us like to think of ourselves as being compassionate and probably experience compassion (both giving and taking) in our practice, is it incumbent on us to understand the nature of professional care as it is this, in the last analysis, that is the central expectation that society has of those of us who are entrusted with the welfare of young people; other people's children?

Our role is different to that of say the Dalai Lama; we are not professionally bound to particular interpretations of religious philosophy or 'Zen'. That said; we need to understand that we are most certainly subject to governmental, international and organisational policy and, in most national contexts, a huge raft of legislation as well as our job descriptions (relatively few of which might demand our compassion).

Realistically, isn't it very few of us who can boast being able to consistently live up to the standards the likes of Smith and Smith (2008) regard as necessary when they ask us to 'deepen our helping practice'? Is this a requirement, along a level or brand of compassionate enlightenment, for ethical and effective practice? How can it be, given the questions asked above? How might this make those of us who are unable to extend this prescribed quality of sensibility and emotion, which are effectively being marked out as the standard for our practice, feel? If this stipulated version of compassion became the required benchmark for practice, what would the consequences for those who admit to not being able to attain this spiritual/psychic summit? Could this incline others to understand and define their practice in such terms? What might be the upshot of this?

In the last analysis is it not the case that, for compassion to be compassion, it will be uncommon and notable on our emotional horizon because of its exceptionalness? As a pinnacle of sensitivity it cannot be everyday or mundane. To claim that compassion is commonplace and available to be dispensed at will, might be understood to undermine or even cheapen its meaning. But what is it to 'use' compassion in our work? If we can't just call on it, make it just happen; they one would assume it needs to be kind of 'acted out'. However, apart from this, how do we regard the receiver of our care? Are they the object of our benevolence or do they have an entitlement to appropriate standards of care. This is where Brandon's practice context might need to be considered. The America of his time of practice was very different to say the UK context of the last 70 years, with its welfare state that people in fact pay for via their taxes. With such a comparison come all sorts of questions about the relationship between rights to service and service at the behest of benevolence. Where welfare and education are a right in law the scope for colonisation via benevolence in these spheres is limited.

BORN AGAIN ZEN

If we unmask the fallacy/revelry/dream that Brandon (maybe unconsciously) clearly wants us to join him in, it would seem difficult to house compassion within any rational professional framework. This said he, by the title of his book, is openly not setting out to do this. Reading between the lines this is something of an evangelising treaties; the work of 'born again Zen' and to that extent he is a missionary trumpeting his faith.

However, Rastafarian teachings, with the proposition of 'oneness with Jah' might be understood to hold much more potential in terms of helping us think about our practice motivations than Brandon's somewhat prosaic, indistinct and at times crude attempts to accommodate Zen within a professional sphere.

Within the 'I and I' one could encapsulate many of the values organisations, and we as individuals in the profession strive to promote; diversity, equality, value for the other and what might be understood to arise out of this, not so much education, but the will to 'emancipate ourselves from mental slavery' and the insight that 'none but ourselves can free our mind'.[2] Although this might show no more than how easily our practice can be stuffed into a faith teapot of our choice.

> ... *the last time she saw them, they were trying to put the Dormouse into the teapot.* (Lewis Carroll, Alice's Adventures in Wonderland, Chapter 7: A Mad Tea-Party)

AN UNCOMMON SENTIMENT

Those in the 'compassion business' and the related 'helping' industry, seem to demand that we act in a certain way, but appear to be relatively unconcerned about how these actions might be translated or their possible consequences. Once more, this does not feel too compassionate does it? A more critical approach to such insistence seems necessary. This is the basis of developing professional judgement.

However, the somewhat indistinct doctrine of compassion should not lead us to a total rejection of compassion as a possibility. While compassion might be a rare form of transference or experience (depending on one's perspective) occurring within relatively heightened, passionate or intimate relations and probably not altogether appropriate or useful (and perhaps sometimes unsafe, unwarranted or potentially patronising and unwanted) in the professional context, it is a form of human experience, albeit uncommon, expressed in both actions and art.

As the sharing of suffering, compassion might be understood as a salve, premised perhaps on the notion that one person sharing suffering with another somehow lessens or alleviates personal pain. But how far can a youth worker take on the task of preventing or alleviating sorrow and pain? If we succeed in preventing people experiencing sorrow and pain are they, or society, necessarily the better for it? Are we more about working with people that they might use or translate their sorrow and pain, frustration and anger, ambition and joy, want and need to take themselves to places where they want to be? To some extent are people not just as entitled to the experience of sorrow and pain as they are to feel elation or pleasure? How might one know what happiness is unless one has felt sorry? This is not saying we should cause sorrow or give people pain, or even at times respond thoughtfully and caringly to the same, but both these sensory experiences are part of what it is to be alive and human; they are feelings and experiences that move us on sometimes.

It could be that compassion has the singular power to assuage suffering by way of sharing it, but how much suffering can we take a share of? Probably not the amount all of our clients might generate over years or decades? Is it likely that any one of us has a limited propensity for compassion?

COMPASSION FATIGUE

We might be thought of as living in an epoch of striking compassion. We appear to be able to see and feel each other's pain in a way that has not been experienced in other times as the social bonds of the family, the church, the nation and neighbourhood erode and snap. Our society seems prone to mass displays of empathy although they fail change the world to any notable extent; the poor are not better fed because of these committed displays, the sick are not cured due to them.

Figley (1995), Austin (2013), Florio (2010), West (2004) and Gabrin (2013) have all written about the phenomenon of 'compassion fatigue'. While much of this writing focuses on how we can become worn down by the giving of compassion (physically, emotionally, psychologically) some of it sees such 'outpouring' as a result of a need or a propensity to project our ego, telling the world and impress on others the level of our personal commitment to others. There is a 'feel-good' payoff in this; as such this is mass altruism but another expression of selfishness in an evermore individualised world. As West (2004) argues, sometimes this tendency can be cruel.

Looking at issues like this might demonstrate that professional and informed care, as part of a general welfare regime, is perhaps more central to our practice than emotive and vague pronouncements about what compassion might or might not comprise of (for instance 'intimacy', 'love' etc.)? Do professional situations, involving pain and suffering, have the potential (on examination) to allow us to define and demonstrate for ourselves how our emotions and/or our spiritual selves relate to practice? Does such experience have a role in our decision making about professional action (rather than the prescriptions made by writers remote from our practice)?

We might not be able to achieve perfect equality of care, but we are tasked with endeavouring, as far as we are able, to make sure that the delivery of services is carried out fairly and is consistent with the practice and spirit of equal opportunity. Personally I think it's time we referred to equal outcomes. This effort is part of the behaviour that marks us out as professionals, able to make judgements sensitive to diversity of considerations (encompassing ability, age, culture, gender, sexuality, faith etc.). Is not this capacity and need to make care judgements, based on the evidence we have gleaned from humane and human interaction with clients, which calls for our awareness of justice, best practice and relevant knowledge/theory? This is part of the qualities that might distinguish our activity from mere robotic responses.

INAPPROPRIATE ASSUMPTIONS

The motivation for compassion is often founded on assumptions about the help people might need are at times, essentially deficit models. As indicated throughout much of this chapter, this a bit like the suppositions applied by Europeans in the colonial period to South American, African and Asian populations. The colonisers and missionaries looked to target their 'help' on the then so called 'natives', applying the standards of European society, formulated with ambitions to 'educate', convert religiously, impose their particular brand of 'civilisation' and later 'democracy'. Objectives like these continue to cause tremendous damage in contemporarily situations such as Iraq and Afghanistan. This aside, the perception of the need for help might often be incorrect, maybe being a projection on the part of the would be 'helper' that has more to do with their needs than those they seek to patronise by way of a particular hypothesis (fantasies?) about a perhaps imagined deficit of an individual or group.

The use of what are basically instructions from various pious writers to extend 'love' and 'intimacy' to young people, although perhaps ok in terms of the majority of the population, could be misconstrued by some and as such might be interpreted as being out of place in serious efforts to safeguard children. At the same time because such words vary in meanings between people and over times of life, to say their use is playing with fire is probably not to underestimate the potential consequences of a scandal waiting to happen. This being the case such formulations might be seen to run very close to inappropriate in terms of responsible child protection – we can safely extend professional care as part of our appropriate concerns for young people; the means and parameters of this are usually made clear and understandable via shared organisational and policy guidelines. While compassion may at times be something we feel, like sympathy and empathy, surely the kernel of our effectiveness is the welfare of those we work with and amongst, which is mediated via a professional understanding and delivery of care?

'STRONG COMPASSION'

Recently I heard someone claim (in a youth work setting), that to be a volunteer one must start with a 'strong compassion'. How do we measure the relative strength of a particular person's compassion? At the same time, is it not the case that people volunteer for all sorts of reasons and combinations of reasons? They may become a volunteer because of politically founded concerns or a straightforward wish to contribute. They may also have a forcefully passionate drive, based on personal traumatic experience, although this type of motivation might not always be desirable, as it can be the root of strident or even fixated behaviour. Other motives might include loneliness, a wish to meet others, boredom, forms of projection or transference and curiosity; some might volunteer to satisfy voyeuristic tendencies or simply because they want to enrich their CV.

For example, Kanta wants to be a doctor so, in order to (in her words) 'build up her care-profile', while studying for her high-school exams, she volunteers at a local facility for the care of the elderly. Kanta is clear that she is not doing this out of compassion, although at times she might be said to show compassion to residents. She is however obliged to follow organisational guidelines (many of which relate to care legislation) about the care of residents. Kanta does not have 'strong compassion' for those she works with as a general feeling, but she does have an ambition to be a doctor. This aspiration, for her, is connected to;

a) *Her being good at science subjects at school.*

b) *Her determination to be a medical doctor (because it is a well paid profession).*

c) *Her aim to be a medical doctor (because she believes she will be able to gain employment anywhere in the world and does not want to feel 'expendable').*

Compassion, in practice and experience, is defined according to whatever our personal bias or individual understanding of the word might be. For instance, forms of corporal punishment have been defined as a means of caring; 'spare the rod, spoil the child'. Indeed capital punishment has often been depicted as a moral imperative for society; American Senator Orrin Hatch has argued *Capital punishment is our society's recognition of the sanctity of human life* (Steffen, 2006: 103).

If we are to straightforwardly accept personal and individual interpretations of the meaning of words, then it could be argued that both the above statements are compassionate in their meaning. Capital punishment could be understood as a stark example of 'being aware of a people's feelings' of fear, anguish, pain and loss of a murdered relative of friend; it is a recognition of their 'situation'. Likewise, refusing to mete out measured punishment to a child could be understood to be a blatant signal that the child can do whatever they want, regardless of the consequences for others.

But are such positions acceptable just because one person or a group of people (the majority or otherwise) might accept them as moral or compassionate? Can the state killing of someone ever be credibly 'compassionate'? Can organised brutality, even if some insist this might exemplify awareness of another person's feelings and situation (the person who has been seen to be wronged by an individual being punished for that wrong) be convincingly put forward as a means of extending compassion? Is it correct/appropriate/professional in the employment sphere to subordinate personal needs such as health and family to client needs (as an end-point of compassion might dictate)? Is that being compassionate in any sense of the word? Does it not feel just a little self-indulgent (redolent of Narcissism/a holier than thou attitude/martyr complex/concern with dominating the moral high ground)? Apart from anything else does it not contravene the logic and spirit of human rights/employment law?

JUDGEMENTS OF STREET WISE SAINTS

Youth workers may sometimes want to be 'street wise saints' but this stance might often betray that such individuals could be lacking in terms of personal emotional life and use work associations to compensate.

However, the moment you decide to extend compassion you are making a judgement, or probably more making assumptions about others:

> I have come to understand that compassion is an active form of judgment with the suffering of another being judged as bad. No wonder we dislike being pitied. We usually don't wish to relieve another of feeling something wonderful, do we? But we do tend to want to relieve another of a feeling that makes us feel bad too, i.e., pain. Sorrow and suffering are painful and therefore when we take pity on another's experience we are saying that what they are experiencing is not good, wouldn't you say? So with this in mind, would it make sense that compassion, as defined by the *Oxford Dictionary*, is a tool of judgment? Please keep in mind that this form of compassion being taught to us is all part of the game and we designed it to be disempowering so that we, as souls, could move into a disempowered state, figure out that we are disempowered and then take the steps to regain our power. (Starr, 2001)

Here Starr exposes a feeling that is often mistaken for compassion; pity. As Brandon himself had it (1990: 51) the energy in his helping, "came from feelings of pity felt towards others. Pity is one part arrogance and one part sympathy". The moment we see (suppose?) someone as being in need of our help, we understand them to be relatively helpless. This is when pity kicks in; we are seeing someone as comparatively pitiful.

I would argue we might be very wary of this feeling because of the massive assumptions of deficit it can encompass. Do you ever want to be regarded as helpless and/or pitiful? What have you got if that is what you evoke from others? We would indeed be in desperate straits if we saw ourselves in such need.

For all this I suggest that the vast majority of our clients are not helpless, in fact I have found that those colleagues and I have served in our work can not only help themselves, they can help us (to work with them). They are rarely pitiful; they are more usually potentially and actually wonderfully powerful.

The 'helping' approach encourages, taking our client group as almost totally being in need of help (generally helpless) is more than just a bit partial. Some people come to us for help, but others just want some guidance, a little advice or a bit of space and time to chill and/or express themselves. While we might understand all this as 'help', does it feel a tad patronising to see one group (the clients) as 'the helped' and another (the professional) as 'the helpers'? Once more, it seems we are in danger of mirroring the behaviour and attitude of the colonial missionary.

There is something of a debate in youth work around whether we 'work with or on' people. But in offering a service we are clearly working 'for' people. After all, if our clients were not around we would not exist as professionals. Whatever, is this notion of 'working' rather than 'helping' a more dynamic enterprise, especially when we are looking to facilitate situations and incidents wherein young people can discover their own potential, whether this be to 'help' themselves or express their ideas or help others? Does 'working' (that might be helpful to our clients or involve young people helping us) feel more like what we actually do most of the time in the practice situation? Might this be a premise of 'post-colonial' youth work?

What agenda might the practitioner regarding powerful and helpful people as helpless and pitiful have? Where does this perception put the practitioner (the insistent helper, the professional peddler of pity) in relation to those they see in such a dire situation?

For Brandon it seems to be a somewhat selfish pursuit of personal 'self-discovery'; the client's painful experiences (ibid.: 52) are apparently taken as part of the practitioner's journey towards enlightenment. What Brandon calls 'real compassion' (his piousness appears to enable him to see what is 'real' – others are seemingly blinded to this 'realness') this uninvited 'muscling-in' on the pain of others, 'enlightens' (ibid.: 59).

Starr has noted how we can set ourselves up as 'street wise saints', but who would knowingly do this; present themselves as the ultimate example of the 'compassionate' human being? Perhaps such self-proclaimed status is only possible by the practiced egotist? But if someone is going about bestowing their love, good will and goodness to each and everyone, maybe this tells us more about what such an individual might be lacking in terms of personal emotional life, as they effectively use work associations to compensate. Whatever your conclusion, the professional role needs a level of detachment to be and remain professional; otherwise we are confined to functioning as a sort of domestic friend or pseudo relative.

To disregard gradations of kindness, considerateness, thoughtfulness, generosity, care, empathy and concern (amongst other considerations) and name practically every positive human response an incarnation of compassion, conflates justice with compassion and hopelessly muddies the waters of practice.

As argued above 'compassion', is vaguely defined, but it often seems to be defined by being over defined, by applying other emotive labels or taking it as a compilation of sentiments, emotions, feelings and beliefs. The more that is added, the less clear the nature, function and meaning of compassion becomes. When something is everything it effectively becomes nothing; when the world is blue, there is no blue, because there is nothing that blue isn't. This is a poor world where the volume, tone, bass and treble can never be turned up or down.

Deficit/colonial models of practice inherent in the kind of stance Brandon insists on need to be challenge, building a response to the challenges and joys of our work based on distinguished, considered and appropriate care more than laying a foundation of pity. A few tin gods might be dented as the parable of *The Emperor's New Clothes* is deconstructed, and this of course will not win everybody over, particularly those stuck in the groove of the compassion mantras that ring around our practice, as some of us use work with young people to compensate for a lack of a personal emotional life beyond associations the organisation or agency. Definitely physician heal thy self.

But to be fair Brandon builds on his predecessors in the colonial realm. Justification of Christian compassion being slotted into professional activity via selective biblical references has a long and shameful history. While this might prove confirming to faith directed workers with a similar perspective to one's own, it is hard to see how it might be of significant relevance to the majority of youth workers who might not think like this or share such personal motivation.

However, like this well motivated but ultimately damaging response the use and meaning of the word 'compassion' and its delivery by Brandon has a consequence that any measure (large or small) of kindness, support, pity, care, concern, sympathy, empathy (amongst a range of other things) seems to mean anything he wants it to mean. This sort of moralizing declaration is underpinned by sweeping statements, opinions, assumptions and prescriptions relating to pity, hope and in the end it is all about what he desires; enlightenment. But it is not left there because this preaching is directed at convincing readers it is also what they *should* desire. However there is little in the way of guidance as to how much of this might be achieved.

For instance one youth worker after reading Brandon wrote "... compassion is an essential component in informal education and that the ability to cultivate compassion should be a desire of the youth worker ...". But this person, much like Brandon, provided no advice about how this might be realised; how might this desire be 'cultivated', monitored or measured (in order we might confirm 'it' had been achieved)? To repeat questions from earlier in this chapter in an attempt to embed the formless character of the instruction – what is the appropriate level of compassion; what is 'not enough' compassion and is there a point when we might be delivering 'too much' compassion? What does 'just enough' compassion look like, or does it change from case to case? If 'compassion is an essential component' of what we do how might we ensure equality of access to compassion (so avoiding potential jealousy or feelings of being left out or discriminated against in terms of compassion delivery)? When does the giving of compassion to particular people, seen to be in need of the same, by presumably some quite subjective criteria, become tantamount to a form of (on one side) favouritism and (from the counter perspective) prejudice? Unless we can at least come up with some practical responses to such questions how can compassion be a central element of professional practice?

COMPASSION IS NOT RELEGATED

Compassion, as a complexity of feelings and attitudes, is not relegated by its unwieldiness in respect of professional practice. In fact this emphasises its rareness and value as a human response – after all, if compassion is extended to all, all the time, everywhere, what is its value? Although Brandon emphasises centrality for helping (as do Smith & Smith, 2008) not all of the youth work role is related to helping (we are not social working monks/nuns). It maybe that there are times when we need to desist or even withdraw from helping to make room for our clients to be able to help themselves. This may not always make us popular or loved, but such decisions are part and parcel of the professional judgement of youth work practitioners; our role is premised on learning more than helping, keeping in mind the expectation of a duty of care.

SPONGES OF COMPASSION

With his 'musts' and 'shoulds' Brandon instructs us to adopt his way; his Zen. Yet again this does not feel terribly compassionate. However, the danger of this type of prescriptive writing is that the lazy practitioner, by just referring to it, can feel justified in the totality of emotional involvement (the harsh critic might say entanglement) such ideas espouse. This brand of over sentimental attachment to the people we work with takes 'compassion' to encompass (or be inseparable from) commitment, enthusiasm and empathy amongst other considerations. But are there not points in our lives when we are, for instance, 'concerned' or 'kind' rather than compassionate ('sharing suffering')? Or is the model for professional practice to be great human sponges of compassion, with no ability to turn down our emotional response below 11?

Whatever, is it not the case that what is often required of the giver of professional care is a level of appropriate detachment, to enable us to remain unclouded by emotive, or what some might understand as maudlin attachment, to our clients, that might not have been requested or expected? This is not to suppress feelings, but to be in control of the same, to manager ourselves, with the aim of providing appropriate and professional levels of care. This is perhaps part of what defines us as professionals, and some might argue that which distinguishes us from the perhaps well meaning, but maybe patronising missionary. However every profession recognises the risk of over identifying, or even transference with clients and we probably need to be aware of this

A DUTY OF CARE

In the above I am not condemning compassionate attitudes out of hand. It is my contention that humans have a need to show and can benefit from the extension of compassion. However, compassion is at the end of the continuum of the benign nature of humanity; it might be thought of as the ultimate benevolence, beyond the 'extra mile' – it is a powerful incarnation of kindness that by this power can be a force for salvation, but also as easily to overwhelm both the giver of compassion as well as those on the receiving end of this giving of one's all.

But more pragmatically, can the attachment to compassion as a central premise of practice, place us more at risk, in terms of our 'in-agency' behaviour, of becoming detached from practice parameters founded on sound professional judgment? Can we, sometimes, be unhelpfully drawn by motives (compassion, love, intimacy) more appropriately expressed in domestic, family and/or faith contexts?

The undertaking of practice means the adoption of a range of responsibilities, including the commitment to achieve organisational outcomes that are usually in line with state policy (and often the law). As such our duties encompass broad social considerations that impact on groups, localities, society, nation and are sometimes global in their motivations and effects. As such we need to demonstrate due diligence in promoting the welfare of the individuals we work with. Given this are we in a position (in terms of the expectations of professional conduct and appropriateness of the practice associations) to intimately devote ourselves unquestioningly to particular people in the way we might our own family or very close friends? Does this merely set up a potential (for both us and our clients) to (perhaps dangerously) confusion of roles and behaviour?

In the professional realm, while the expressing of compassion might not and indeed cannot be usefully expunged, its extremes might perhaps be more moulded and moderated than fired-up by the encouragement of compassion zealots. A fundamentalism of compassion is a form of extremism by which thoughtful and focused care, extended with simple kindness and consideration, can be confused and contorted into a sort of enthused amore; compassion can be seductive. As many readers may recognise, spiritual and physical giving has the capacity to draw us into a spiral of compulsion in terms of the response it can elicit and the vast, awesome feelings, which have both physical and psychological manifestations.

With this in mind, structured, thought through and appropriate care, might be understood as a more tempered mechanics by which we might deliver practice services, for we are indeed more servants than emotional relations or close friends of our clients. I here argue that care can and perhaps needs to be instrumental if it is to be fairly, effective (safe) and efficiently offered and taken up. The nature of the expectation of duty of care might be understood as a means to effect the latter. Below I have included an overview of the character of the duty of care in the UK. This is not to suggest this is taken on hook, line and sinker in other contexts, it is included to demonstrate something of the means we have to harness while effectively focusing care responses.

There are lengthy legal definitions available via a simple net-search but broadly duty of care in the context of the UK has four clear areas of application:
- Every organisation working with children and young people, whether they are paid or voluntary is subject to the right to extend a 'duty of care' to keep children and young people safe and protect them from harm.
- This duty of care rests upon the individual to ensure that all reasonable steps are taken to ensure the safety of a child or young person involved in any activity, or

interaction for which that individual is responsible. Any person in charge of, or working with children and young people in any capacity are considered, both legally and morally, to owe them a duty of care.

– The Children Act 2004 places a duty on organisations to safeguard and promote the wellbeing of children and young people. This includes the need to ensure that all adults who work with, or on behalf of children and young people in these organisations are competent, confident and safe to do so.

– Everyone working with children and young people should be familiar with local procedures and protocols for safeguarding the welfare of children and young people. Adults have a duty to report any child protection or welfare concerns to a designated member of staff in their organisation and/or report any concerns to the local Children Services/Police. Anyone who has a concern or is in doubt should refer to the document 'What to do if you're worried a child is being abused' and follow that guidance.

Duty of care is the obligation to exercise a level of care towards an individual, as is reasonable in all the circumstances, to avoid injury to that individual or his property.

Duty of care is based upon the relationship of the parties, the negligent act or omission and the reasonable foreseeability of loss to that individual.

A negligent act is an unintentional but careless act that results in loss. Only a negligent act will be regarded as having breached a duty of care. Liability for breach of a duty of care very much depends on the public policy at the time the case is heard.

Duty of care can govern relations with a wide variety of groups including, but not limited to, employees, users and even visitors to an agency.

The authority for duty of care is the leading Scottish case of *Donoghue v Stevenson 1932 SC (HL) 3.* The principles laid down by the Court in this case still form the basis for establishing a duty of care under Scots and English law.

The general principles for duty of care were highlighted in this case as:

DOES A DUTY OF CARE EXIST?

This depends on the relationship between the parties, as a duty of care is not owed to the world at large, but only to those who have a sufficiently proximate relationship. The courts have found that there is no liability if the relationship between the parties is too remote.

IS THERE A BREACH OF THAT DUTY?

Liability will only arise if the action breaches the duty of care and causes a loss or harm to the individual, which would have been reasonably foreseeable in all the facts and circumstances of the case.

DID THE BREACH CAUSE DAMAGE OR LOSS TO AN
INDIVIDUAL'S PERSON OR PROPERTY?

When Donoghue was decided it was thought that duty of care would only be applicable to physical injury and damage to property; however this has now been extended, in some circumstances, to where there is only pure economic loss.

WHAT ABOUT EMOTIONAL DAMAGE THAT SEEMS TO BE
RISING UP THE AGENDA?

Does a Duty of Care Exist?

The first issue, which must be addressed, is whether or not there is a relationship between the parties, which would establish a duty of care.

For example, in any further or higher educational institution there are a number of relationships in existence which may give rise to a duty of care. For example:
– Students.
– Employees.
– Governing Bodies of Professions.
– Visitors.

YMCAs (for instance) in the UK have a duty of care for their members, residents and service users. This is reflected in the need to constantly renovate and improve buildings and premises.

The ethos of this practice is not limited to the borders of the UK and is congruent with Human Rights legislation.

Brandon (1990), Smith and Smith (2008) pay little if any attention to how compassion and its component (as they see it) 'love' and 'intimacy' might be translated in relation to the expectation of a duty of care, which will consider not only (in youth work) young people, but the position of their parents, guardians as well as their wider family and social situation.

The notion and systematised duty of care is professional care translated as logical benignancy, backed up by knowledge relating to function and necessary skills, but tightly linked to a commitment to justice and fairness, which itself is induced by consideration for and about those we work with and amongst, as well as the families, groups and the social milieu they are part of.

To some or even many, setting out to be a font of compassion might sound sanctimonious or 'holier than thou', but as the supposed 'kernel' of our practice does it offer a means for effective delivery of welfare, care (carefulness) or learning? Is our work, as professionals, really more about providing clear guidelines about the services we can realistically offer and to extend the same in a responsible way, via best practice and in accordance with policy? If so, how do woolly, affecting notions, apparently defined in a random and emotional manner, help us do this? Does the insistence on such aims for our practice tell us more about the individuals looking to spread their 'devotion' than it does about the nature of our work? I argue that our generally demanding case load/client ratio and requirement to produce professional outcomes/initiate best practice (policy) makes

Brandon's point of view at least unrealistic and at worst fanciful and/or dangerously romantic.

CONCLUSION

Compassion as an all or nothing response is risky and probably at times dangerous. However, kindness, consideration, supportiveness, sympathy and empathy and the like, can be stand alone attitudes and feelings that do not necessarily demand that we share suffering. Indeed, if we follow prescriptions to give ourselves over to compassion as a first and last resort it is hard to see where there might be room to make some of the pragmatic and unpopular decisions/actions our work sometimes demands of us.

The compassion Brandon demands from us, as an end in itself, would logically make the taking of a salary incongruent. The implication is that we should share any income from professional practice with those who we judge to be 'suffering'? But how will we determine who is and who is not suffering? Do we defer to Brandon? How would we tell who is the most deserving of our 'compassion' (is it a 'first come, first serve')? Whilst we are busy with dealing out focused and 'deep' compassion to one person would others we have equal responsibility for be ignored? Should we take the homeless home with us? Would the adoption of this type of unlimited (untrammelled) sharing of suffering be seen to potentially expose vulnerable young people to possible abuse? How can we be sure that this 'compassion' is not more about meeting our own needs than any needs we might imagine others to have?

In the end, one person's compassion can be another's inconsideration or even wrong doing; while the son might see the switching off of his mother's life support as merciful compassion, the daughter may understand this as wicked, sinful murder – given this, how can it be at the centre of our practice?

This type of deficit oriented sermonising in the last analysis fails to clearly articulate what it is that constitutes compassion or 'help'; it fail to really define such terms. This said other than starting from the meaning of a word (say to 'share suffering') such a definition would seem almost impossible, given that the word has so many contested and often emotive definitions.

Perhaps because of these writers and those that have followed their example are unable to say how compassion or help might differ from forms of care, empathy, support, politeness or even the appropriate use of professional skill. If we follow the lead such preaching suggests, we need to take it that it is compassionate to show even the kind of concern and interest that might be mundanely expected of our role. Today I patted a dog, I took the time to do it; is that compassion? As such the emotional force that compassion might be is devalued as it is made commonplace.

But perhaps most importantly this species of analysis takes it for granted that people we deal with are looking for, or are in need of compassion; that in their lives there is a compassion deficit, not met by family and friends – how can we know this or just presume it? How do we tell a father or mother about our judgement that their child is running a 'compassion deficit' and/or we have decided to be intimate with them, presumably because they lack intimate relations, that this will include loving them, because we have judged that they in some way not getting the love they need? What response might we expect to this expression of the professional ego gone mad?

Can we totally give ourselves to each individual we work with by way of all embracing compassion? Indeed, is it not probable that over the course of our lifetimes there are relatively few people we will give so much devotion to? However, if, for a moment we imagine that we are capable of 'giving ourselves wholly' in the random and repetitious way that Brandon expects, can we avoid asking ourselves what our compassion is actually worth? In the same way, if you respect anyone and everyone without question, what is your respect worth to any particular individual? Your respect has been devalued because you just give it away (you appear to believe it is worthless) – no one has to earn or do anything to get your respect; this seems to demonstrate a lack of self-respect or at least have the potential to lead others to believe that your respect has no value. Could this valueless respect be taken as anything more than a pantomime? In the end is this 'total', unquestioning giving of respect likely to make you a generally respected person?

Professional expectations of our often brief encounters with the many young people we might work with during our careers do not allow for the kind of devotion that Brandon asks of us. To give of oneself totally might in itself constitute unacceptable professional behaviour and would neither be efficient or effective (as he imagines).

Perhaps we need to be wary of the level of compassion we show or use; that there are gradations of compassion. Can we just assume that each one of us will have similar compassionate responses to situations? Should we flippantly take it that people more or less respond (or should respond?) the same in terms of compassion to similar events or circumstances? But this of course would be incorrect. Some people feel little compassion for those who are homeless or suffer because of substance abuse (from coffee and cigarettes to hard drugs) maybe having more sympathy for foxes or donkeys. It is hard to envisage how one might 'front load' compassion or even train someone to be more compassionate. If we cannot do this, how do we make sure of equality access to, or that there are appropriate levels of compassion in our work?

The problem with compassion in terms of making it central to our practice is that it has no agreed professional or legal definition. However, we often do have an agreed, sanctioned and codified duty of care. Even though this might vary across or between contexts, something is expected of us and almost invariable it will be defined by law. How is it that this is not more central to our practice than compassion?

Brandon (1990) and his successors champion what is in essence an evangelical, missionary approach. It is hard for the detached reader to see this as much short of a sanctimonious moralizing, perhaps housing a covert, probably unconscious, colonial ethos, but it certainly promotes an indistinct attitude to professional practice, fuzzed and phased by contrived visions of what compassion might or should be. This encompasses collection of values, sentiments and emotions, which can produce an unpredictable range of responses and outcomes.

Are youth workers or social workers in a place to be able to say if a person suffocating their terminally sick spouse or society maintaining the heartbeat of the suffering and/or long brain dead individual has committed an act of compassion or evil? If you are unsure of the answer to this maybe you are not in a place to premise your work on the grounds of compassion.

Compassion can be cited as the reasoning behind both liberal and anti-abortion laws – it is for the most part an entirely subjective response, and its emergence into our practice will be shrouded in our own biases, prejudices, conscious and unconscious motivations. As such it is a volatile sentiment that is let loose by unquestioningly adopting the moralising of the likes of Brandon, shoe horning his somewhat naïve, and (from an organisational/policy perspective) apparently irresponsible point of view (ramblings?) into our practice situation. I would suggest the generation of personal professional judgement, tempered by the realism of the everyday might be the foundation of a more 'poised' practice stance. There are necessary boundaries that exist between professional attitudes and personal feelings. It cannot be questioned that we do indeed call upon and use our emotions during the course of our work, but if our commitment to our clients is to be as 'unconditional' is that healthy for anyone?

In practice we have responsibilities to achieve organisational outcomes that are sometimes connected to state policy (and often the law). This causes our careers to be attuned to broad social considerations. Compassion might be thought of as engendering essentially emotive and capricious responses, reflecting the nature of human conscience and experience. However, even in the most favourable light it is deeply subjective and as such spiced with personal moral imperatives about who deserves or needs to be subjected to or doused in its enormity.

Even when we know people well, after sharing our lives with them, perhaps for many years, compassion is sometimes hard to access as a constant resource. How can we promise it, front load it, and deliver it to all and sundry as a commitment, a guarantee of being the fulcrum of our service delivery? Even if we think that this is in our emotional, spiritual and psychological prevue, what does the ambition to do this mean? Yes, we are committed to care and the welfare of those we work with and amongst, those we serve, and some will evoke our compassion from time to time; we would be less than human to deny or be over defensive about this. But to judge the majority as in need of our deepest emotional resources and to look to impose the same of others without discernment or care, judgement or measure is, from a Fanonian psychological understanding of colonial incursion, a profound invasion; a disabling profession in terms of both client and practitioner.

> … soldiers armed with virtue – hearts afire with blind obsession, cannot see the difference 'twixt compassion and oppression. (Sabbat)

NOTES

[1] M. H. Golden, M. P. Samuels, and D. P. Southall (*Archives of disease in childhood*, 2003, vol. 88, pp. 105-107) define neglect as

> ... the failure to supply the needs of the child, including emotional needs. It does not include the deliberate and malicious withholding of needs, which is a form of abuse. Neglect has its roots in ignorance of a child's needs and competing priorities; it is passive and usually sustained. The carer is without motive and unaware of the damage being caused.

[2] From Marcus Garvey, speaking in Nova Scotia during October, 1937. These two lines from this speech were published in Garvey's magazine *Black Man*, 3 Number 10, July 1938.

REFERENCES

Ahmed, S. (2006). *Educational thinkers in India*. New Delhi: Anmol Publications.

Biko, S. (1987). *I write what I like*. Oxford: Heinemann.

Caracciolo, D. M., & Mungai, A. M. (Eds). (2009). *In the spirit of Ubuntu: Stories of teaching and research*. Rotterdam: Sense Publishers.

Davies, B., & Gibson, A. (1967). *The social education of the adolescent*. London: University of London Press.

el Saadawi, N. (2010). *The essential Nawal El Saadawi*. London: Zed Books.

Fanon, F. (1965). *The wretched of the earth*. London: MacGibbon & Kee.

Fanon, F. (1967). *Black skin white mask*. New York: Grove Press.

Gandhi, M. K. (1970). *My views on education*. Bombay: Bharatiya Vidya Bhavan.

Harber, C., & Serf, J. (2004). Exploring Ubuntu: Education and development – An introduction to theories and debates. Birmingham: Development Education Centre.

Marley, B. (1908). *Redemption song*. MYV Networks.

Nyerere, J. (1968). *Ujamaa*. Oxford: Oxford University Press.

ORGANISATION

HARINI AMARASURIYA

LEADERSHIP TRAINING FOR YOUTH

A Response to Youth Rebellion?

INTRODUCTION

The history of post-independence Sri Lanka has been turbulent and often violent. Yet, this turbulence and violence was far from obvious when Sri Lanka (then Ceylon) became an independent nation. Unlike in neighbouring India and Pakistan, Ceylon experienced a remarkably smooth and peaceful transition from a British colony to an independent state in February 1948. Building on initiatives that had already begun during the latter part of colonial rule, the newly independent state adopted a strong welfare model. Free healthcare and free education policies ensured that Sri Lanka performed well on conventional development indicators such as reducing maternal deaths and infant mortality, and increasing literacy in comparison with countries of similar economic strength. Gender disparities were also addressed in this regard, with as many girls as boys enrolling in education, creating gender parity in literacy rates and life expectancy.

More recently, however, Sri Lanka has been gaining attention for its violent internal conflicts. The conflict that gained the most global as well as academic attention was viewed as an ethnic conflict between the majority Sinhalese community and the minority Tamil community. Led primarily by the militant group, the Liberation Tigers of Tamil Eelam (LTTE), who claimed a separate homeland in the north and east of the country, the armed conflict lasted for 30 years. The less well-documented conflicts were led by a radical Marxist Party, the Janatha Vimukthi Peramuna (JVP), mainly in the Sinhala dominated southern areas of the country. The JVP led two insurrections, one in 1971 and the other during 1987 and 1989. The JVP insurrections have been largely described as caused by 'youth unrest'.

This chapter will consider these three armed insurrections against the state, youth involvement in these insurrections and state responses to these insurrections. It will also examine the way in which the involvement of youth in these insurrections shaped state-led youth development and youth work initiatives. Specifically, the chapter will explore the popularity of 'leadership training' programmes that are currently being implemented among youth in Sri Lanka as a response to youth problems, in particular the 'leadership training' programme for undergraduates recently launched by the Ministry of Higher Education. I will argue that the conceptualisation of 'youth problems' as caused by 'frustration' – leading

B. Belton (ed.), 'Cadjan – Kiduhu': Global Perspectives on Youth Work, 109–131.

to the manipulation of youth by political parties – has shaped how initiatives are designed for youth, particularly by the state. This has facilitated an approach to working with young people, which locates youth problems in the personalities and characters of young people, while dismissing and ignoring many of the structural problems of contemporary Sri Lankan society. It also reflects a particular relationship between the state and youth in Sri Lanka, where successive generations of young people have resorted to violence in order to capture state power.

THE POST-INDEPENDENCE SRI LANKAN STATE

When Sri Lanka gained independence in 1948 after almost 450 years of colonisation, the transition from colonial government to national government was comparatively smooth. The first national government in Sri Lanka was established by the United National Party (UNP), formed out of the Ceylon National Congress, which had existed earlier. The UNP consisted of a somewhat conservative, Westernised elite which had been agitating for self-rule for several decades. Unlike in neighbouring India, the independence movement in Sri Lanka was not a mass movement – it was led mostly by an elite community that had gained influence through their dominance in the professional sectors, as well as the planting and commercial sectors (Kearney, 1964; Jayawardene, 2000). Colonial dominance of the bureaucracy and government was deeply resented by this group who felt that they were eminently qualified and capable of governing the country themselves. Mass discontent and resistance to the colonial government was articulated mainly in the form of cultural and religious revivalist movements, which sought to establish cultural and religious identities in opposition to the Anglicised, elite culture and religion of the colonial power. There were also politically radical labour and franchise movements, mainly in urban areas, which emerging in the 19th century, mobilised people to resist the colonial government. These movements were not completely unlinked to demands for self-rule – the colonial government was very aware of the potential for these movements to develop into a struggle for independence and as such the leaders of these movements were subjected to close surveillance and control. However, the kind of mass scale independence movement that emerged in neighbouring India was not quite evident in Ceylon.

Ceylon granted universal adult franchise to all above the age of 21 in 1931 and was the first British colony to achieve universal suffrage. It hadn't been granted without a struggle. The traditional local elite were somewhat aghast at the thought of the newly emerging capitalist class and even women being granted the right to vote, leading one politician of the time, Ponnambalam Ramanathan to say that granting female suffrage would be like, "casting pearls before swine" (de Alwis & Jayawardena, 2001). The conservative elements in national politics fought for a narrower franchise, but strong support for extending voting rights for all came from the Ceylon Labour Union and the Ceylon Women's Franchise Union (de Alwis & Jayawardena, 2001). However, universal adult franchise did not bring about the expected social revolution: candidates (mostly men) with social influence from high caste and high-class families continued to dominate the political landscape in the country (Jayawardene, 2000).

During the almost 150 years as a British colony, Sri Lanka had undergone significant changes. Infrastructure development, especially of roads and railways, had connected various parts of the country, the plantation economy had given rise to wage labour and cash crops had replaced the mainly subsistence agriculture based economy that had existed earlier. An emerging local bourgeoisie and social reforms had expanded educational and employment opportunities.[1] These as well as electoral changes generated conditions that later created several divisions and tensions in post-independence Sri Lanka (Kearney, 1964). These growing tensions developed broadly along two lines: the rise of Sinhala Buddhist nationalism, resulting in ethnic tensions between the Sinhalese, the main minority community, the Tamils, and the growing aspirations of an increasingly educated youth, frustrated by the dominance of economic and political sectors by the traditional elite. There were certain moments and movements when these two lines crossed – however, for the most part, they developed independently of each other resulting in a particularly complex modern political landscape in Sri Lanka.

In this chapter, I will focus on three specific movements that emerged out of this complex, post-independence political landscape in Sri Lanka: the 1971 insurrection led by the mainly Sinhala Janatha Vimukthi Peramuna (JVP); the ethnic conflict between the mainly Sinhala state and Tamil militant groups; and the second insurrection by the JVP in the late 1980s.[2] I focus on these not only because of the impact these movements had on Sri Lankan society, but also because these were largely youth led movements. In the following sections, I will discuss each of these movements in greater detail – however, it must be noted that there is considerable overlap between these three movements and they should not be considered completely independently of each other, particularly the two JVP insurrections.

The First JVP Insurrection – 1971

The rapid expansion in educational opportunities, with the introduction of free education in 1945, has often been described as resulting in raising aspirations of young people, which were frustrated by slow economic and social reforms (Kearney, 1975). It is also largely believed that these educated, frustrated youth were behind the 1971 JVP insurrection.

There is no doubt that the introduction of free education, as well as the provision of education in the Sinhala and Tamil languages (the two local languages) led to significant social changes. Literacy levels rose from around 17.4% in 1881 to almost 59% in 1946. The expansion of Tamil and Sinhala medium education also meant that university enrolments, which had been previously dominated by those from English medium schools also changed, alongside growth in the number of people taking up university education. For instance, university enrolment increased from 3,000 in 1959 to 15,000 in 1966 (Kearney, 1975). But poor economic progress meant that unemployment, especially among the educated, was also rising. In 1970 for instance unemployment among those between the ages of 15–24 years with Advanced Level and higher qualifications was 60%, while for those between the ages of 24–35 years the figure was around 23%. Female unemployment in this age group was also extremely high (ibid). The promise of social and economic mobility offered by education had failed to deliver.

A striking characteristic among suspected insurgents in the 1971 insurrection is their age: 77% were between 17 and 26 years of age. The suspected insurgents were not just young – they were also educated, with around 80% having achieved a reasonable level of education. About 4% of those arrested were university students – although low in number, they had provided the leadership to the movement. The majority were also Sinhala and Buddhist – that is, from the majority ethnic and religious communities in Sri Lanka.

The 1971 insurrection has often been described as an attack not only on the government at the time, but on the elites who were in power. During the smooth transition from British colonial rule to independence, as described earlier, the reins of power passed over from the British civil service to an elite class that emerged during the colonial period. This class had access to political and economic power and were distinct from the rest of the populous over whom they ruled, by their life style. Mostly Western educated and cosmopolitan, they lived a life of wealth and privilege, associated with the aristocratic lifestyles of the older feudal class in Sri Lanka. A striking feature of this class was their command of the English language, which was a source of considerable power, despite the country's transition to education in the vernacular languages of Sinhala and Tamil (Obeysekere, 1975; Jayawardene, 2000; Gunasekera, 2005).

Education policy changes in the country since colonial times had considerably expanded educational opportunities. A good education was seen as the means to secure employment in the prestigious civil service. This was a high aspiration for those from the middle and lower strata of society. However, a stagnant economy resulted in shrinking employment opportunities. There was high competition for jobs and eventually, political patronage became the principal conduit to obtaining employment. Competitive examinations and other selection procedures were often meaningless, since the positions had already been secured through political connections. The frustration this generated among educated and unemployed or underemployed young people has been seen as the major factor in fuelling the 1971 insurrection. This was a period of severe economic torpor and deprivation, which caused considerable suffering among many sections of the population. Educated young people, particularly from the lower economic and social strata, were under tremendous pressure to find employment and provide a return on the investment made by their families in supporting their education.

The JVP insurgents were unsuccessful in capturing state power in 1971, although they caused much alarm among those in power. The UNP was no longer in control of the country and the Sri Lanka Freedom Party (SLFP), which had gained power was led by the world's first female Prime Minister, Sirimavo Bandaranaike. The resources available to the Sri Lankan military at that time were comparatively minimal and the JVP managed to push the military to its limits. The government response was severe. Apart from the thousands who were killed, many more were arrested and sent for rehabilitation. Estimates of the number of youth who were killed by the military during this time vary between 6,000 and 20,000; approximately 14,000 suspected of participating in the insurrection were arrested (Obeysekere, 1974; Kearney, 1975).

Stories from those who were sent for rehabilitation suggest that those in authority viewed these young insurgents as manipulated and misled by the JVP leadership. While the crackdown on the insurgents was harsh, there is also some evidence of sympathy towards these young people – who were considered to be educated and intelligent. Stories of jailors secretly passing on treats to prisoners; doctors ordering 'special' food for 'health' purposes; arrangements made for imprisoned university students to continue their studies and even sit for examinations are commonly heard in relation to the 1971 insurgency and its aftermath.[3]

It is interesting to consider the post-insurrection lives of those who came out of 'rehabilitation'. Several founding members of some of Sri Lanka's best known civil society organisations are former insurgents. Several more (particularly the university students) joined academia and there are many senior academics in the country today, including university administrators, who had been part of the 1971 insurrection. Others joined various political parties and some even served (and continue to serve) as Cabinet Ministers under various governments.

The core of the JVP itself was imprisoned and the movement more or less went underground. An important consequence of the 1971 insurrection was a concern about the potential for educated youth (particularly from rural and low-income backgrounds) in Sri Lanka to become radicalised and so lead or take part in militant actions. As a consequence of this a notion proliferated that youth needed to be carefully managed and controlled. The idea of 'youth unrest' – particularly among the educated, rural youth originated from this point.

The 2nd JVP Insurrection: 1987 to 1989

In 1977, the UNP swept back into power. Far-reaching changes were made in the political structure as well as the economy. A powerful Executive Presidential system was introduced and the first Executive President, J.R. Jayawardene was elected. That year also marked the introduction of open economic policies in Sri Lanka. As part of the strategy to further weaken the opposition, the battered SLPF, President Jayawardene offered clemency to jailed JVP leaders and released them in 1977. It was expected that the JVP would further weaken the embattled SLPF by eating into their votes among the rural Sinhalese, the traditional voter base for the SLFP. The JVP entered mainstream electoral politics thereafter, even contesting the 1982 Presidential elections; its candidate, the leader of the Party, Rohana Wijeweera, obtained 4% of the votes (Moore, 1993).

Ethnic tensions, which had been simmering since independence, were on the rise and in 1983 they came to a head. In July of that year an army patrol, in the Tamil dominated city of Jaffna, in the North of the country, was attacked and 13 soldiers were killed by the Liberation Tigers of Tamil Eelam (LTTE), one of the militant Tamil groups fighting for a separate state for the Tamil people. The government had declared that the slain soldiers would be buried in Colombo with full military honours. However, despite large numbers of people gathering at the cemetery, the funerals could not be held. Sections of the crowd started rioting, attacking the police who were trying to control them. The rioters set fire to Tamil homes and shops in the vicinity and tensions grew through the night. On the 25th of July, mobs went on the rampage, burning and looting Tamil homes and businesses, which resulted in the death of hundreds of Tamils. The riots soon spread to other parts of the country and thousands of Tamil families were displaced.

The UNP government blamed the JVP and two other left parties for the riots and proscribed them. This was widely seen as an unjust and totally arbitrary action since there was no evidence linking the JVP or the other left parties to the riots. In fact, several senior members of the government were later implicated in instigating the riots. What was evident, was that the government had no intention of allowing the JVP to participate in electoral politics and used the 1983 riots to once again proscribe the Party (Moore, 1993). The Party again went underground and started organising themselves for another insurrection against the state.

The JVP's platform when they re-emerged in 1987 was somewhat different from the 1971 insurrection. The UNP government in power had signed an agreement with the Indian government to deal with the North-East conflict. Among many other provisions, one of the most controversial was the Sri Lankan government agreeing to bring about changes to the constitution to devolve power to the provinces, enabling local governments to manage their own affairs. The demand for more independence had been a long-standing demand of Tamil political parties and this measure was seen as a way of meeting this demand. Indian involvement in Sri Lankan politics however also gave rise to suspicion among the Sinhalese, who believed that Indian politics used the Tamil problem to extend their influence over Sri Lanka. Indian expansionism was a theme that the JVP had been talking of for several years and they seized this opportunity to mobilise support against the Indian accord. The JVP were also politically opposed to any form of devolution on ethnic lines, which they argued was part of the imperialist project to divide the proletariat and destabilise countries. From then on the JVP opposed all ceasefire and peace initiatives between the LTTE and successive governments on the basis that they would result in challenging the unitary nature of Sri Lanka. This contributed to cementing the image of the JVP as a hard-line Sinhala group, although this is a claim that the JVP itself strongly resists (Moore, 1993; Venugopal, 2009). As Dewasiri argues, the more nationalist line pursued by the JVP in the 1980s marks a significant deviation from its strategy in 1971. Since the 1980s, the JVP has had to balance its Marxist roots with its support base among an increasingly nationalist Sinhalese constituency, leading to a dual strategy whereby what the JVP said in public was often not the stance taken by the internal Party members (Dewasiri, 2010).

What is of relevance to the present discussion is the marked difference in the nature of the insurrection in 1987 and the state response to it. The period between 1987 and 1989 was one of the most violent phases in Sri Lanka's post-independent history. There are estimates that, in the south alone, between 40,000 and 100,000 people were killed or disappeared during this time. The JVP too was responsible for assassinating those that they considered enemies and traitors, including members of rival left-wing groups and the armed forces. The response of the state was extremely harsh – several paramilitary groups were operating during this time under the protection of the state, alongside government forces, effectively crushed the insurrection (Venugopal, 2009; Hughes, 2013). Secret torture chambers were in operation in different parts of the country and the sight of mutilated bodies on the streets became distressingly common.

The level of violence during this period was significantly higher than in 1971. This was partly due to the fact that the JVP was far more effective than previously, managing to disrupt the functioning of the state quite considerably. JVP called *hartals* (strikes) directing people to refrain from going to work or opening shops, etc. These actions were very successful, paralysing public life regularly. Public transport for instance was severely disrupted. However, the JVP did not hesitate to 'punish' those who did not follow their instructions. In order to carry out these assassinations, the JVP created a front group Known as the Deshapremi Janatha Viyaparaya or the Patriotic People's Movement (DJV). Initiation into the JVP cadre followed a stringent process of recruitment and training, and in operation the cadre was subject to a strict disciplinary code. These were relaxed in the formation of the DJV and it was possible to absorb those into the DJV who were not politically educated or mobilised. This meant that the JVP cadre could and did distance itself from the activities carried out by this group and claim that it was not responsible for many of the assassinations and attacks carried out by the DJV. The violence intensified when the JVP ordered the military to resign while threatening members of the military and their families with death if they disobeyed. The ferocity of the state response reached a pinnacle with this threat.

There are very few records of the numbers or other details of those who were killed and disappeared during this time. Unlike in 1971, there are no census records of those who were captured by armed forces. Part of the difficulty was that there were several military groups operating at the time, and the disappearances and killings were often carried out by these shadowy groups, operating under the protection of the state.

The human cost to the JVP of the 1987/89 insurrection was huge – all except one member of their Central Committee were killed. The leader, Rohana Wijeweera was also captured and killed. Members of the second Central Committee, which was formed after the original members were eliminated, were also killed. Thousands of sympathisers and alleged supporters were tortured, disappeared or killed. The Party was almost decimated – its emergence once again in the 1990s is testament to its ability to survive and regroup despite heavy odds. The sole surviving member of the Central Committee (41 of the 42 members were killed), Somawansa Amarasinghe, worked from hiding in Paris and London and only returned to Sri Lanka just before the 1994 elections. While in exile, Amarasinghe fought off a rival to the leadership position, and managed to consolidate his position as Party leader. Since the 1990s, the JVP has joined electoral politics and in 2004 won over 30 seats in the national parliament.[4]

The 2nd insurrection of the JVP further consolidated the notion among Sri Lankan youth there was a propensity for violence. During the 1987–89 period, the JVP had managed to mobilise even schoolchildren, especially those in higher secondary school. The JVP's hold within the universities was also stronger during the 1980s – the Inter University Students Federation (IUSF) the largest student union, was commonly known to be linked to the JVP. During this period, there were also rival student groups, notably the Independent Student Union (ISU) and rivalry between these two groups led to violent clashes, including the killing of one of the most well known leaders of the ISU, Daya Pathirana, for which the JVP was held responsible. The IUSF too lost almost all its student leaders – many suffering unspeakable acts of torture and violence at the hands of the armed forces and state supported paramilitary groups. Many young people, particularly students, went into hiding during this time since the mere fact of being 'young' was sometimes sufficient for being detained.

Although a period of extreme violence, leading to months long closures of the education system, this time was also a period of intense student activism. Furious debates on the privatisation of education, the nature of science, the 'Indian question', rights of minorities, and Sinhala nationalism were taking place within the student community. Many student leaders went into hiding during this time to escape from rival groups, as well as from government forces. Although the government had banned student unions within universities, various alternative forms of associations were formed with university students organising themselves through a range of networks between and within the different universities.[5] For instance, Student Action Committees were set up in lieu of the banned student unions in many universities. These became the focus of political activism. The image of universities as radical sites of student unrest and violence was strengthened during this time.

The two JVP insurrections were largely confined to the youth in the south of Sri Lanka – and mainly Sinhala youth. In parallel, a conflict was raging in the north and east in Tamil dominated areas as well, and the armed groups operating there were also made up of mainly young men and women. The ISU which supported the self-determination rights of the minorities and were also not opposed to the Indo-Lanka Peace Agreement, made some efforts to link with these issues, but by and large, there was no significant interaction between these groups. Indeed, the JVP was strongly opposed to the idea of a separate homeland for which the Tamil military groups were fighting. The point worth noting in relation to this chapter is that the 1980s period marked a time when various youth groups from around the country were engaged in an armed struggle against the state and were fighting with the intention of capturing state power.

30 Year North-East Armed Conflict

The ethnic conflict in Sri Lanka is better documented and known internationally than the JVP insurrections described above. Ethnic polarisation had been simmering since independence, with post-independence governments catering to voter demands of the majority Sinhala community. One of the factors that fuelled the rise of Sinhala nationalism was the resentment felt by the Sinhala community that its culture and religion was suppressed by the colonial powers. There is also a perception among the Sinhala community that the minority groups were favoured by colonial regimes in order to propagate their 'divide and rule' policy. The dawn of independence was viewed as the moment for the Sinhala community to regain its 'rightful' place as the majority community. Consequently, many commentators have described the Sinhala community as a majority with a minority complex (Wickramasinghe, 2006).

The perceived failure of mainstream Tamil politicians to meet the demands of the Tamil community and various measures taken by Sinhala dominated post-independent governments, such as the Sinhala Only Language Act of 1956, which made Sinhala the official language of Sri Lanka, antagonised the Tamil community and gradually led to the development of a more militant Tamil nationalism. As Wickramasinghe (2006) has pointed out, the constitutions of post-independent Sri Lanka; "helped demarcate and define a majority from within the citizens, pitting them against non-Buddhists and non-Sinhala speaking minority communities" (2006: 182).

Mainstream Tamil politics was dominated by the Tamil elite. This group had many features in common with the Sinhala elite that dominated post-independent governments in Sri Lanka. The primary approach of mainstream Tamil political parties was to fight for entitlements from the state – dominated since Independence by mainly Sinhala governments (Wickramasinghe, 2006). From early times, there were more radical Tamil groups that organised themselves. For instance, prior to independence, there was a Youth Congress, a political movement that evolved into an anti-caste movement in Jaffna. Other small movements, such as the All Ceylon Minority Tamils Association, attempted to resist the dominance of elite Tamil politicians. However, these groups are rarely mentioned or discussed due to the focus on the rise of militant Tamil nationalism.

Tamil militancy first came into the spotlight when the former Mayor of Jaffna in the Northern Province, Alfred Durayappah, was assassinated by a group of young Tamil militants, led by Velupillai Prabhakaran. It was from this point that it became evident that Tamil youth had abandoned all hope of achieving their demands through electoral or parliamentary politics (Wickramasinghe, 2006). The goal was a separate homeland for the Tamils – Tamil Eelam. The Tamil Students Federation formed in 1970 and by 1975 had transformed into the Liberation Tigers of Tamil Eelam (LTTE). There were other militant groups that also emerged such as the People's Liberation Organisation of Tamil Eelam (PLOTE), the Tamil Eelam Liberation Organisation (TELO), Eelam People's Revolutionary Liberation Front (EPRLF) and the Eelam Revolutionary Organisation of Students (EROS). In the early 1980s, according to Wickramasinghe (2006) there were many as 30 such groups. Some of these groups, particularly PLOTE and EPRLF, articulated their demands in terms of Marxist political theory. Although there were brief and intermittent efforts to link with youth groups in the South, these didn't really materialise. The ISU, as mentioned earlier, supported the self-determination rights of Tamils and took the position that supporting the claims of Tamil youth was of paramount importance and should be a core issue for youth groups in the south. However, the influence of the ISU was not as great as that of the JVP dominated IUSF, which was opposed to the idea of a separate homeland. This was one of the major reasons for the bitter enmity between the ISU and the IUSF during this period.

The 1983 ethnic riots, sparked by the LTTE ambush of 13 Sinhala soldiers in Jaffna, marked the escalation of the conflict. By this time, many of the Tamil militant groups had been proscribed and had withdrawn to Tamil Nadu in South India for training and organising. But there was also bitter intra-group rivalry among the Tamil militants, particularly the main groups, LTTE, PLOTE, TELO, EROS and EPRLF. By the late 1980s, the LTTE had established its dominance over the others and leaders of rival groups were systematically killed.

Successive governments moved between declaring ceasefires, negotiations and armed response in dealing with the LTTE. It became the pattern for all newly elected governments to declare ceasefires and start negotiations, but eventually to resort to military action. Inevitably, after the failure of a negotiated settlement, the fighting would resume with renewed vigour.

The government of President Mahinda Rajapakse came into power in 2005 promising a negotiated settlement to the conflict. Despite the ceasefire, both the LTTE and the state military continued to arm themselves and engage in sporadic acts, frequently violating the ceasefire agreement. Previous LTTE responses to ceasefire agreements had also made governments suspect that the LTTE used the ceasefires to regroup, arm and strengthen themselves for further fighting. It was soon evident that the government was seriously considering a military settlement.

By 2006 the government was stepping up its military campaign despite the Norwegian negotiated ceasefire being technically still in operation. In January 2008 the government formally withdrew from the ceasefire agreement and declared its 'war on terror'. The war was declared at an end in May 2009, after the capture and death of Prabakharan, the leader of the LTTE. The last stages of war were particularly brutal, with both sides accused of using and targeting civilians who were trapped in the war zone. The final death count is disputed and the Sri Lankan government is facing increasing international pressure to initiate an independent investigation of the last stages of the war. The government has been resisting this pressure stating that local mechanisms are adequate to investigate any human rights violations; however, the United Nations Human Rights Commission (UNHRC) has been steadily pushing for an international investigation into human rights violations during the last stages of the war.

The LTTE was mainly constituted of young men and women and also children. The LTTE's suicide bombers were primarily young women and their use of child soldiers is well documented (Human Rights Watch, 2004; UTHR, 2008). While some child soldiers and youth were reportedly forcibly recruited, many joined voluntarily, leaving their homes and giving up on education for the sake of the cause of Tamil Eelam. Many were arrested, detained and killed over the years.

Over 10,000 LTTE cadre surrendered to government forces at the end of the war and the government launched a 'rehabilitation' programme under the Ministry of Defence. The former militants are purportedly provided access to education programmes, skills training, psychosocial support and loans before being 'reintegrated' into the community.[6] The rehabilitation process is closely monitored and managed by the Ministry of Defence and few details are available to the public. However, it is evident that the rehabilitation process is difficult. Ex-combatants face problems reintegrating into their communities after many years away and are subject to continued surveillance by the military. Livelihood opportunities are also scarce in the north and east, areas, which were directly affected by the war for several decades and lag behind the rest of the country in terms of infrastructure and economic development. Unresolved issues relating to land rights and the continued heavy military presence are other factors which continue to simmer in these areas over which formerly the LTTE had control.

SRI LANKAN YOUTH AND PROPENSITY FOR VIOLENCE

The violence perpetrated by the JVP and the LTTE, both of which were constituted primarily of young men and women, has contributed to the general idea that Sri Lankan youth have a propensity for violence. The JVP insurrections in particular are commonly referred both academically and in the public sphere as 'youth rebellions', which were instigated by 'youth unrest' (Hughes, 2013). These 'troubled' youth were seen to be those who had benefitted from free education and free health care policies and were thus educated, with high aspirations. High levels of youth unemployment are often cited as the reason for frustrated aspirations, pushing youth towards rebellion and militancy (Ministry of Youth Employment, 2007). Mayer for instance has argued, that the root causes of violence in the south, the north and east largely stem from similar problems faced by youth and that the grievances expressed by both Sinhala and Tamil youth indicate that the issues facing Sri Lankan youth go beyond the politics of ethnic identity (Mayer, 2002).

"Frustrated" and "unfulfilled" youth are considered to be prime targets for manipulation by groups such as the JVP and the LTTE, who are generally described as 'using' youth for their own political ends (Chandrprema, 1991; Gunaratna, 1990). This idea is also reflected in President Rajapakse's election manifesto of 2010, wherein he states that; "political parties with cruel and hateful tendencies soon took advantage of this situation and misled our youth and turned them into insurgents which led to hundreds and thousands of such youth being murdered" (Mahinda Chinthana – Vision for the Future, 2010: 18).

What is suggested here is that youth as a category have a natural tendency to rebel and a proclivity for violence and that such youth can be manipulated by unscrupulous individuals and groups who make use of the idealism and energy of youth for their own ends. Research among former JVP insurgents has shown that even they reflect on their participation in the insurgency using the same ideas – that their involvement was a reflection of their 'youthfulness' and the rebellious nature of being young. This explanation denies any agency youth may have felt in how they analysed their situation and responded to it, and also disregards any structural issues that may have shaped their experiences. Hughes for example, has argued that ex-insurgents may be borrowing from the official discourse of youthfulness and youth unrest to put some distance between themselves and their violent pasts (Hughes, 2013).[7]

When a Presidential Commission on Youth was established in 1990 in response to the devastation experienced in the 1980s, the Commission obtained statements from hundreds of young people and others who came forward to testify to the commission. According to the Commission report, Sri Lankan youth expressed several grievances in relation to the state. These were based on a sense of injustice in relation to the structure of Sri Lankan society, particularly its economic and political structures. Youth had described examples ranging from disparities in educational and employment opportunities to differences between urban and rural youth as evidence of the injustice experienced by youth excluded from economic, social and political centres of privilege and power. The Commission recommended several measures, including establishing independent commissions to ensure impartiality in law enforcement, electoral processes and other functions of the state. Essentially, the Commission strongly recommended measures to prevent the politicisation of state and other institutions and the establishment of processes that reward merit rather than social and political connections (Presidential Commission on Youth, 1990). Unfortunately, many of the recommendations, even though it has been almost 40 years since the commission made its report public, are yet to be implemented.

A National Youth Survey conducted in 1999/2000 found that only 20.7% of Sri Lankan youth felt that the society they lived in was just (Fernando, 2002). A similar survey conducted in 2009 provided somewhat more optimistic results, with about 60% of those interviewed saying they considered Sri Lankan society 'somewhat just' (Sri Lanka Youth Survey, 2009).[8] However, the 2009 survey was conducted soon after the end of the war, when society at large (certainly in the Sinhala dominated areas) was feeling more hopeful about the future.

The issue of youth unemployment (seen as a major cause of 'youth unrest') has also been rather simplistically described as a problem of 'skills mismatch' or the 'unrealistic' aspirations and expectations of youth. The preference of youth for jobs in the public sector has been described by successive policymakers and politicians as an indication that youth want 'easy' jobs which provide permanency, showing a lack of entrepreneurial flair among Sri Lankan youth (Amarasuriya, Gunduz, & Mayer, 2009; Amarasuriya, 2010). This is therefore an 'attitudinal' problem among youth. The responses to youth unemployment, which are based on such an analysis, emphasises skill building and training as a response for youth unemployment, with an emphasis on 'changing attitudes' of youth. However, closer investigation of youth unemployment shows serious structural problems, such as disparities in educational opportunities, unequal economic development within the country, stagnation of employment generation and social exclusion of youth who do not come from the 'correct' background, particularly in the private sector (Hettige, 2002; Amarasuriya, Gunduz, & Mayer, 2009; Amarasuriya, 2010). But explanations that locate the problem in the attitudes and lack of employable skills among youth, approach the problem of youth unemployment in terms of deficits within individual youth, which should be addressed through more effective training and awareness-raising.

YOUTH AND RELATIONSHIP TO THE STATE

Despite the often violent relationship between youth and the post-independent Sri Lankan state, the interesting factor about this relationship is that youth continue to have certain expectations from the state – their anger towards the state is directed by their disappointment that the state has *failed* to deliver on these expectations. To understand this, it is necessary to examine the way in which the Sri Lankan state established itself in relation to its citizens.

The Sri Lankan state's commitment to welfarism at the dawn of independence forged a particular and enduring relationship between the citizen and state. The most significant of those welfare measures was free healthcare and free education. Sri Lanka's good performance in education and health in terms literacy rates, school enrolment rates, infant mortality and life expectancy is closely linked to these policies. These are seen almost as part of what it means to be Sri Lankan. During a trade union action launched in 2012 by university academics, in public rallies to mobilise support for the academics campaign to protect state universities, particularly from the threat of privatisation, speakers often referred to free healthcare, free education and universal suffrage as corner stones of the Sri Lankan state. No government, they claimed had the right to take those rights away from the people. Thus, there is a very strong identification among people, with these policies and what it means to be a citizen of Sri Lanka.

Despite the gradual dismantling of the welfare state since the 1970s, particularly since 1977, there continues to be a deep conviction about and public support for a strong, benevolent state that takes care of its citizens (Wickramasinghe, 2006; Amarasuriya, 2010a). Successive governments have also been careful not to challenge the idea of the strong, benevolent state. Even governments that pursued strong neo-liberal economic agendas did not reduce the strength of the state as generally understood within neo-classical economic theory (Moore, 1993). The current government too, despite pursuing aggressive liberal economic policies, has strengthened the power of the state over all aspects of people's lives. Certainly political rhetoric reinforces the idea of the benevolent state, whatever the policy realities.

This has led to a somewhat peculiar situation, where while the state is rapidly divesting itself of its welfare role, it continues to present itself as the benevolent provider and citizens continue to demand this of the state. This is very apparent for example with regard to the question of youth unemployment. As mentioned earlier, the issue of youth unemployment has been a much debated issue in Sri Lanka, especially unemployment of educated youth. There are regular agitations from unemployed graduates demanding public sector jobs. And periodically governments launch 'graduate employment schemes' offering jobs in government institutions. What is also interesting is that young graduates (especially women) sometimes leave higher paid jobs in the private sector to seize the opportunity to enter the public sector. This is often perceived as an 'attitudinal problem' among youth (Ministry of Youth Employment, 2008).

However, what is apparent is that, employment in the public sector means something more than just a job – it provides people (especially those seeking social mobility) with respectability and status within their communities. Public sector jobs are also viewed as secure. These are often important considerations for young people and their families (Amarasuriya, 2010b). What this shows is the strong relationship that the public have with the state in Sri Lanka and their continuing expectations of the state as a caring provider of services as well as a source of security and social mobility.

It is in this context that repeated efforts of youth to take state power needs to be examined and understood. Others have also argued that that the anti-state (or the counter-state) element in much of the youth political activism in Sri Lanka is indicative of the evolution of the Sri Lankan state as the central agency mediating people's interests in a range of areas from economics to health to education and reflects the specific relationship of youth to this state (Uyangoda, 2003). Sri Lankan youth are not so much anti-state as fighting to establish a *better* state – one that is more responsive to their needs.

The criticism that is most often levelled against that state is that the largesse of the state is distributed unequally. This aspect of the Sri Lankan state – that its welfare and development benefits are unequally distributed – is an issue raised by successive generations of young people in Sri Lanka. Youth have argued that the benefits and resources of the state are distributed along lines of privilege. For the JVP the lines were drawn along class identities – while for the LTTE they were drawn along ethnic lines. A well-known slogan among radical youth in the 1970s was '*colombatakiri, apatakekiri*' which can be loosely translated as "Colombo (the Sri Lankan capital and its most prosperous city) gets the cream while we get the milk". In this conceptualisation Colombo is the symbol of privilege and power. This idea of Colombo as the centre of power and privilege is not new. Even during the colonial period, Sinhala nationalists in particular attacked Colombo as the symbol of elitism and Westernised, urban culture. Sinhala film and literature for instance regularly caricatured Colombo residents for their imitation of Western culture, pitting them against the 'authentic' Sinhala native rooted in a rural, agricultural society (de Mel, 2001).

Slogans like '*colombatakiri, apatakekiri*' reflected the distance felt by young people from the social, economic and political elite of Sri Lankan society. Within universities the English language was referred to as the '*kaduwa*' (the sword) which was used to cut down the aspirations of those for whom English was not the language spoken at home. Lines were drawn between those who spoke the *kaduwa* and those who did not. The English language in this context symbolised far more than competency in a particular language – it also signified power, privilege and opportunity. The practice of ragging[9] in universities, which pro-ragging groups defend as the means through which the differences between classes is erased, has its origin in this deep divide that exists between those who come from different socio-economic backgrounds.

The relationship between Sri Lankan youth and the state is therefore complicated – it reflects the disappointment felt when expectations of a caring, benevolent provider prove to be misplaced. It also reflects the distance felt by youth in relation to the ruling class. Both the JVP and the LTTE emerged as movements that were disillusioned by those who were elected to represent their interests. Both Sinhala and Tamil mainstream political leadership were regarded by the JVP and the LTTE as representing and protecting elite interests.

I now turn to discussing how this relationship between Sri Lankan youth and the state is reflected in youth work and youth development initiatives of the state.

YOUTH WORK IN SRI LANKA

In this section I will briefly outline some of the initiatives taken by the state to address youth issues. I will specifically focus on the recent 'Leadership Training' that was introduced to university entrants by the Ministry of Higher Education (MoHE).

As detailed above, the state response after crushing youth-led insurrections has been to 'rehabilitate' those who were suspected of involvement in these activities. This was particularly evident in 1971 after the first JVP insurrection as well as in 2009 after the war with the LTTE came to an end. Those who were arrested or surrendered to the armed forces, as well as those who were suspected of having links with the LTTE cadre, were placed in rehabilitation programmes coordinated by the Ministry of Defence. In the aftermath of the 1987 JVP insurrection however, there was less emphasis on rehabilitation: the conditions during that time were such that since there were multiple armed groups operating, the possibility of formally rehabilitating those who were arrested was more remote. Even then there were some rehabilitation centres where inmates were provided with vocational training and other skills development programmes. Most importantly those who were fortunate enough to end up in the rehabilitation camps escaped the torture and violence. Many more who escaped capture simply fled the country.

This idea of 'rehabilitating' or 'training' youth has permeated many youth work initiatives in Sri Lanka. The Ministry of Youth Affairs was established in 1979 and its first Minister was the current Leader of the Opposition, Ranil Wickramasinghe. The National Youth Services Act No. 69 of 1979 strengthened the existing National Youth Services Council (NYSC) to become the main state agency responsible for dealing with youth issues. One of the main initiatives of the NYSC was to start youth clubs at the community level. Currently there are over 10,000 youth clubs with around 400,000 members. The Sri Lanka Youth Service Federation is the apex body of the NYSC youth clubs. Apart from the clubs, the NYSC organises sports and cultural events, vocational training and annual youth awards. District Level youth officers are responsible for organising the youth clubs and NYSC events. The main purpose of the clubs and events are to provide opportunities for youth to learn leadership skills and display their talents. The NYSC also hosts the Sri Lankan Youth Parliament, which aims to, 'build a new breed of youth leaders with skills and confidence', (http://www.srilankayouthparliament.org/).

There is also a National Youth Corps, which was established in 2002, its website proclaims it to be the main state institution for providing training on 'personality development and vocational training for youth'. It goes on to say that it offers training in the areas of 'Squad Drill & Physical Education, Vocational Guidance & Management of Life Skills, Personal Leadership & Enhancement of Psycho-Social skills, English and Tamil Languages, Information Technology and especially Aesthetic Appreciation' (http://www.youthcorps.lk/english/aboutus/).

In a situation where thousands of Sri Lankan youth mobilised and organised themselves to challenge the Sri Lankan state militarily – and almost succeeded on three separate occasions – how is it that state led youth initiatives almost exclusively address deficits in the 'personality' and 'leadership qualities' among youth? Does this stem from the idea that Sri Lankan youth do not have the capacity to resist the manipulations of (in President Rajapakse's words), "political parties with cruel and hateful tendencies?" (Mahinda Chinthana, 2010). How do we reconcile this apparent lack of personality and leadership with the ideas expressed by youth of the injustice, exclusion and discrimination they experience in society? Are these then simply the perceptions of 'misguided' youth, who need to be 'rehabilitated' or trained so that their thinking can be 'guided' in more acceptable directions? I will explore these questions in more detail through the analysis of the highly controversial initiative that was introduced by the Ministry of Higher Education (MoHE) recently, which is 'leadership training' for university entrants.

Leadership Training for University Entrants

The Leadership Training for University Entrants (also called the 'Leadership Attitude and Positive Thinking Development Training' and hereafter referred to as the Leadership Training Programme) introduced by the MoHE programme, has drawn considerable attention recently. It is an annual leadership training programme for university entrants organised by the MoHE in collaboration with the Ministry of Defence and Urban Development. Although not compulsory, the MoHE has stated many times that it is necessary for all university entrants to participate in this programme; the Ministry provides a certificate of completion at the end of the programme. Several petitions filed by university entrants and their parents challenging the need for this training were dismissed by the Supreme Court. These programmes are held in military camps throughout the country over a period of three weeks.

This programme was launched in 2011 by the MoHE and immediately drew criticism from the academic community that was of the opinion that any training for university entrants should be conducted by the universities. The Federation of University Teachers Unions (FUTA), during its trade union action in 2012, demanded that the leadership training be halted. However, the MoHE refused to consider this demand, arguing that the leadership training is necessary and instead invited FUTA to propose what needed to be included in the training programme. Since the FUTA opposed the leadership training in principle, it did not provide input into the programme conducted by the MoHE. Furthermore, the fact that the training was being conducted in military camps and under the supervision of the military also led some academics to accuse the Ministry of attempting to militarise universities.

The rationale offered by the Minister for Higher Education and other officials was that the training was necessary to instil discipline among university students and that it is also a means of eliminating ragging in universities. In a veiled reference to the JVP's influence within universities, authorities further said that the leadership training would ensure that students are able to resist the manipulation of political parties. The Minister of Higher Education, Mr S.B. Dissanayake, has on several occasions also mentioned that university students need to be disciplined and trained on how to behave within the university, including learning such things as keeping their hostel rooms clean, working to a schedule and correct etiquette and manners. But when the leadership training was initially introduced it was presented as an attempt to stop the practice of ragging in universities.

The issue of ragging in Sri Lankan universities is a serious problem. There have been several instances where students who were subjected to severe physical ragging have suffered serious injuries leading in a few instances to the deaths of some students. Apart from physical ragging, new students are subjected to harsh treatment and humiliation by their seniors, ostensibly with the intention of breaking down all barriers between students, 'socialising' them into the sub-culture of universities. The rag is organised according to strict rules and regulations and is conducted under the supervision of senior students. At the end of the rag period the seniors organise a welcome Party for the new entrants, which is meant to symbolise the formal enrolment of new students into the university sub-culture. The rag is also a means through which students are enrolled into the student union. Student unions have said that the rag is the period during which new students are oriented towards student unions. The rag has been critiqued by many for its degrading and harsh treatment of new students and for the gendered practices, where female students in particular are indoctrinated into 'proper' behaviour within universities (Ruwanpura, 2010). A Prevention of Ragging Bill was introduced several years ago, making it possible for perpetrators of the rag to be punished legally. However, implementing the law has been extremely difficult, since often the worst forms of ragging takes place in hostels where staff are not always present, making it extremely difficult for perpetrators to be identified.

How the Leadership Training was going to prevent ragging was never very clear. The apparent rationale was that the personalities of university entrants would be sufficiently developed through the training, allowing them to resist ragging. In a statement released by a group known as the 'Friday Forum', which includes a former Chairperson of the University Grants Commission, as well as a former Vice-Chancellor among others, they the MoHE was questioned as to why it wasn't focussing on implementing the Prevention of Ragging Bill more effectively if the prevention of ragging was one of its goals. As the Friday Forum went on to say, the Leadership Training could cause even more aggressive ragging and incite violence between student groups, since senior students may feel that freshers who come through the Leadership Training must go through a more stringent socialisation process than those who do not (Friday Forum, 2011).

The syllabus of the Leadership Training caused further controversy. The cover page of the 2011 Leadership Training Programme curriculum has a photograph of the Secretary of the Ministry of Defence, Mr Gotabhaya Rajapakes, brother of President Mahinda Rajapakse, reflecting the close involvement of the military in the training. The syllabus is divided into two sections one which is titled 'Practical' and the other which is titled 'Theoretical'. The practical sessions consist of drills, physical exercises, First Aid, Appreciation of Art and Culture, Personality and Confidence building exercises (mainly physical activities, community service and food etiquette). The 'theory' component includes lectures on themes such as history and national heritage; leadership and positive thinking, psychological counselling, important laws in the country, personal hygiene and living in a hostel, culture and morals, conflict resolution, decision making skills, drugs and alcohol, sexual health and sexually transmitted diseases.

The history and national heritage component presents a particular Sinhala view of history, emphasising Buddhist cultural centres and monuments as markers of national culture. The section on leadership too focuses narrowly on well-known Sinhala leaders, including the current President, Mahinda Rajapakse. In the section titled 'Culture and Morality', the sub sections include, 'respecting the clergy and elders'; 'how to behave in public places', 'protecting one's culture', 'protecting public goods', 'fulfilling one's duties and responsibilities'. Interestingly, the section on law rather selectively discusses certain sections of the penal code, including unlawful assembly and destruction of public property. It is perhaps not coincidental that arrests during public demonstrations are usually made citing these sections of the penal code.

The syllabus conjures an 'ideal' university student. Such a student is disciplined, well-mannered, emotionally well-adjusted, moral, respectful of elders and authority and follows rules. This student is not expected to be a rebel or a dissenter. This is not a student who is expected to be politically active while at university or join radical student unions.

Academics protested that such a training is antithetical to university ideals of critical and independent thinking. As stated by the Friday Forum, 'Military type training is founded on a system of regimentation. University education is meant to encourage independent learning discussion and argument with tolerance and respect for disagreement and viewpoint difference' (Friday Forum, 2011). However, despite protests and criticism, the training has continued since 2011.[10]

The Leadership Training Programme has not prevented student activism. During the last few years, students have organised and protested on a range of issues from conditions in universities to privatisation of education. During the 2012 FUTA Trade Union Action, when the academics organised a Long March of five days under the banner 'Save State Education', the students organised a parallel march, which culminated in a huge protest in Colombo with the participation of both groups. The Leadership Training Programme is also being conducted in an environment where the state and university administrators have been coming down hard on student unions and student leaders. The current convenor of the IUSF, Sanjeewa Bandara, has been arrested several times and is even currently banned (under his bail conditions) from entering any university premises or participating in any demonstration.[11] Many student activists have been suspended from their universities and several universities have also suspended student unions under various pretexts.

In an environment where student led initiatives are being suppressed, the leadership training can be viewed as the state's alternative to student led organising – thus while the government makes claims about the need to develop suitable youth leaders and provide opportunities for youth, it is also adopting a stringently intolerant approach to student led initiatives, which it sees as inimical to its own interests. This dual approach to dealing with youth suggests that state led initiatives for young people reflect its own desire to control and manage a potentially dissenting group rather than as a means of empowering and enabling youth to articulate and advocate for their own interests. So, the state responds in different ways to different youth groups: 'good' or amenable youth are provided with carefully managed and controlled opportunities to display their talents while 'bad' or disruptive youth are dealt with harshly, and even violently. Suppressing the rights of 'bad' youth (such as their right to association and freedom of expression) are justified in the interests of public security.

LEADERSHIP TRAINING AS A RESPONSE TO YOUTH ISSUES

How do we understand the emphasis on leadership training, personality development and discipline in approaches to dealing with youth in Sri Lanka?

As discussed earlier, this perception that youth require discipline and 'guidance' appears to be founded on the perception that Sri Lankan youth are easily misled. Their involvement in violence, in radical politics and insurrectionary movements is seen as a form of 'youth rebellion' and 'youth unrest'. As mentioned previously, former insurgents themselves described their involvement in these terms. However, when considering the actions of these 'youthful rebels' in the past they were not mere looters or vandals. Those who were involved in the JVP insurrections, as well as those who fought for Tamil Eelam, were systematically working towards taking over state power. Their movement was articulated in terms of a rising against and a reaction to injustice. The movements were framed as movements for social justice. Both the JVP and the LTTE often won public support for the way in which they punished corrupt officials, errant husbands, and perpetrators of sexual violence. During the JVP insurrection in the 1980s, the public often assumed, especially during the early days of the insurrection, that victims of JVP violence had been 'guilty' of some misdemeanour, which led to their assassination. The discipline of JVP cadre is legendary, with stories of arrested cadre refusing to provide information, even when being tortured, gaining mythical status among Party supporters. People, especially in the Northern Province, continue to talk of the discipline that the LTTE maintained in their organisation and even within the community. The rise in criminal activity after the end of the war is sometimes attributed to the demise of the LTTE and its ability to maintain law and order in these communities. Of course, both the JVP and the LTTE gradually lost public support due to their authoritarian policies and the upsurge in violence, which led to horrific atrocities, but the 'boys' (as both LTTE and JVP cadre are often referred to by people) were not unusually attributed with an inherent desire for justice.

The disconnect between the intensity with which the insurrections were organised and fought and the idea of 'misguided' and 'manipulated' Sri Lankan youth without agency is significant. To what extent do these leadership programmes and other youth work initiatives appeal to youth who feel disgruntled and excluded? In some ways it can be argued that initiatives such as the leadership training are organised in an extremely paternalistic manner – with the intention of bringing people back to the 'right' path, reorienting youth who have gone astray. What is missing from this approach is a serious exploration of the basis for youth disenchantment. Recent research has shown that youth continue to feel disgruntled and discriminated against.[12] They continue to expect the state to provide them with certain entitlements, which they believe are being distributed unfairly. They continue to critique the political establishment for politicising state institutions and distorting the independence of these institutions (National Youth Survey, 2009). Yet the response of youth workers in Sri Lanka has not been to engage with these issues, but rather to attempt to address youth grievances as emanating from a personality flaw or lack of maturity among youth.

This approach to youth work is to locate the 'problems' of youth, in the personalities and characters of youth themselves. Of course, this approach is not limited to youth or even to Sri Lanka – since the 1980s there is a worldwide shift in how groups categorised as 'vulnerable' are approached. Problems people face are regarded as individual deficits – so parents require parenting skills training; children require obedience classes; families are provided with financial management training and youth are provided leadership training. All of these require the individual concerned to adjust his or her way of thinking and being in the world – of adjusting and accepting to the systems and institutions in society. Vanessa Pupavac (2001) has referred to this as the therapeutic model of intervention, a model that emphasises individual vulnerabilities and proposes capacity building or awareness rising as a response.

In the Sri Lankan context this approach requires serious scrutiny since it glosses over the structural inequalities and disparities that have shaped people's experiences in the post-colonial state. Even when the welfare state was at its height, factors such as caste, class, ethnicity and gender shaped how citizens were able to access their entitlements. The entrenched culture of political patronage further shaped the relationship of citizens to the state in terms of how people were able to mobilise political and social connections to their advantage. The leadership training approach that is offered to youth as a means of addressing the problems faced by young people in Sri Lanka does not take into account any of these issues. Rather, it frames youth problems as one of immaturity and youthfulness, which needs to be managed and controlled; it is based on a premise of a supposed deficit or 'lack' spuriously proposed as being inherent in young people.

CONCLUSION

Youth violence has been a feature of the post-independence Sri Lankan state. Since the 1970s, Sri Lanka has seen as many as three insurrections, led primarily by young men and women. Each of these insurrections were focussed on taking over the state and revealed the antagonism of youth towards those in power and their inability to respond to their needs. That these movements themselves were extremely violent and often authoritarian is without doubt – however they succeeded in mobilising thousands of young people to take up arms against the state. These insurrections have been met with a harsh response from the state leading to the death and disappearances of tens of thousands of young people.

At the same time, youth work in Sri Lanka has adopted an approach that views youth as lacking agency and requiring careful management in order to protect them from being misguided and manipulated. Such an approach ignores the structural causes of youth violence and the critique of the post-independence state that drove so many youth in Sri Lanka to take up arms. Another aspect that is important to consider, which I have not discussed in this chapter, is that the growth of the military in Sri Lanka is becoming one of the major sources of employment for young people. So while, one segment of the youth population is taking up arms in attempts to overthrow the state, another segment is being armed by the state to fight against their same age cohort. This is one of the most striking and at the same time, tragic aspects of post-independence Sri Lanka.

ACKNOWLEDGEMENTS

Dhana Hughes and DileepaWitharana read initial versions of this paper and provided useful comments and feedback for which I am extremely grateful. I also appreciate the many conversations I have had with my colleagues and friends in the Federation of University Teachers Unions (FUTA) and University Teachers for Democracy and Dialogue (UT4DD) regarding the Leadership Training for university entrants, which inspired me to write this chapter.

NOTES

[1] These changes were initiated in the Dutch period and continued under British Rule. For a detailed analysis of changes to traditional economic structures under the Dutch period see Nirmal Ranjith Dewasiri (2008).

[2] Although the 1971 and 1988/89 insurrections were both led by the JVP, I consider them as separate movements in this chapter due to specific differences in the nature of the two JVP led insurrections.

[3] Personal communication, Dileepa Witharana.
[4] More recently, the Party has been besieged by internal conflicts, with two groups breaking away. Its performance in recent elections has been poor and like the other main opposition in Sri Lanka, the UNP, the JVP too is struggling to hold its power base together in the face of the growing hold that the Rajapakse regime is wielding over the country.
[5] Personal communication, Nirmal Ranjith Dewasiri and Dileepa Witharana.
[6] http://www.irinnews.org/report/95525/sri-lanka-former-tiger-fighters-battle-for-a-normal-life
[7] See Hughes (2013) for an analysis of how such narratives are used to explain the JVP insurrection of 1987 even by those involved in it.
[8] The National Youth Survey was conducted by the Social Policy Analysis and Research Centre of the University of Colombo. This information is based on the author's access to the data generated by the survey.
[9] Ragging is a verbal, physical or psychological abuse on newcomers to educational institutions. It is similar to the American phenomenon known as hazing. Sri Lanka is said to be its worst affected country in the world – see http://www.sundayobserver.lk/2007/07/01/main_Letters.asp
[10] In fact, since the leadership training for university entrants, similar programmes have also been organised for school principals after which they were even conferred military titles.
[11] Since writing the chapter the IUSF has appointed a new convener.
[12] Unpublished data from Focus Group Discussions conducted by the author as part of the background research for the formulation of the draft National Youth Policy in 2012.

REFERENCES

Amarasuriya, H. (2010a). *Guardians of childhood: State, class and morality in a Sri Lankan bureaucracy*. Unpublished Thesis. University of Edinburgh.
Amarasuriya, H. (2010b). Discrimination and social exclusion of youth in Sri Lanka. In M. Vidopivec, R. Gunathilaka, & M. Mayer (Eds.), *The challenge of youth employment in Sri Lanka*. World Bank.
Amarasuriya, H., Gunduz, C., & Mayer, M. (2009). *Sri Lanka: Rethinking the nexus between youth, unemployment and conflict*. London: International Alert.
Chandraprema, C. A. (1991). *Sri Lanka, the years of terror: The J.V.P. insurrection, 1987–1989*. Colombo: Lake House.
De Alwis, M., & Kumari, J. (2006). *Casting pearls: The women's franchise movement in Sri Lanka*. Colombo: Social Scientists' Association.
Dewasiri, N. R. (2008). *The adaptable peasant: Agrarian society in western Sri Lanka under Dutch rule, 1740-1800*. TANAP Monographs on the History of Asian-Europeon Interaction (Leonard Blusse & Cynthia Vialle, Eds.), Vol. 9. Leiden: Brill.
Dewasiri, N. (2010). Mainstreaming radical politics in Sri Lanka: The case of post-1977 JVP. *PCD Journal: Journal of Power Conflict, and Democracy in South and South East Asia*, 2(1), 69-94.
Friday Forum Press Statement. (2011, 9 July).
Gunaratna, R. (1990). *Sri Lanka: A lost revolution? The inside story of the JVP*. Kandy: Institute of Fundamental Studies.
Gunasekera, M. (2005). *The postcolonial identity of Sri Lankan English*. University of Kelaniya.
Hettige, S. T. (2002). Sri Lankan youth: Profiles and perspectives. In S. T. Hettige & M. Mayer (Eds.), *Sri Lankan youth: Challenges and responses*. Colombo: Friedrich Ebert Stiftung Colombo Office.
Hughes, D. (2013). *Violence, torture and memory in Sri Lanka: Life after terror*. Routledge/Edinburgh South Asian Studies Series.
Human Rights Watch. (2004). Living in fear: Child soldiers and the Tamil Tigers in Sri Lanka. *Human Rights Watch*, available at http://www.hrw.org/node/11900/section/1
Jayawardena, K. (2000). *From nobodies to somebodies – The rise of the bourgeoisie in Sri Lanka*. Colombo: Social Scientists Association.
Kearney, R. (1964). Sinhala nationalism and social conflict in Ceylon. *Pacific Affairs, 37*(2), 125-136.

Kearney, R. (1975). Educational expansion and political volatility in Sri Lanka: The 1971 insurrection. *Asian Survey, 15*(9), 727-744.

Mahinda, C. (2010). *Vision for the future.* Election Manifesto of President Mahinda Rajapakse.

Mayer, M. (2002). Violent youth conflicts in Sri Lanka: Comparative results from Jaffna and Hambantota. In S. T. Hettige & M. Mayer (Eds.), *Sri Lankan youth: Challenges and responses.* Colombo: Friedrich Ebert Stiftung Colombo Office.

Ministry of Youth Affairs. (2006). *National action plan for youth employment in Sri Lanka.* Colombo: Youth Employment Network (YEN) Secretariat.

Moore, M. (1990). Economic liberalisation versus political pluralism in SriLanka? *Modern Asian Studies, 24*(2), 341-383.

Moore, M. (1993). Thoroughly modern revolutionaries: The JVP in Sri Lanka. *Modern Asia Studies, 33*(7), 593-642.

Obeysekere, G. (1974). Some comments on the social backgrounds of the April 1971 insurgency in Sri Lanka (Ceylon). *The Journal of Asian Studies, 33*(2), 367-384.

Report of the Presidential Commission on Youth. (1991).

Ruwanpura, E. (2011). *Sex or sensibility? The making of chaste women and promiscuous men in a Sri Lankan university setting.* Unpublished Thesis. University of Edinburgh.

University Teachers for Human Rights (Jaffna Branch). (1977). *Children in the North East War: 1985:1995 matters of violence: Reflections on social and political violence in Sri Lanka* (Jayadeva Uyangoda, Ed.). Colombo: Social Scientists Association.

Uyangoda, J. (2003). Social conflict, radical resistance and projects of state power. In M. Mayer, D. Rajasingham-Sennanayake, & Y. Thangarajah (Eds.), *Building local capacities for peace re-thinking conflict and development in Sri Lanka.* Macmillan India Ltd.

Venugopal, R. (2010). Sectarian socialism: The politics of Sri Lanka's Janatha Vimukthi Peramuna (JVP). *Modern Asian Studies, 44*(3), 567-602.

Wickramasinghe, N. (2006). *Sri Lanka in the modern age: A history of contested identities.* London: Hurst and Company.

JENNIFER BROOKER

CURRENT ISSUES IN YOUTH WORK TRAINING IN THE MAJOR ENGLISH-SPEAKING COUNTRIES

INTRODUCTION

Whilst youth work may appear to operate within similar parameters across the developed world, there are interesting differences, given the differing demographic youth profiles in each nation state. Youth workers work with young people, sometimes during very difficult times in their lives, helping them to become the best versions of who they are and can be. This chapter will compare the history of pre-service training for youth workers in Australia, Canada, New Zealand, the United Kingdom and the United States. It will outline their current similarities and differences, followed by a discussion on how their training impacts upon them and their potential to transfer their skills and knowledge globally.

Historically, youth work programmes have been delivered since the mid-1800s. These were either focused on education or physical fitness, usually provided by well-meaning, untrained individuals or Christian-based organisations such as the YMCA and the Boys' and Girls' Brigades, followed later on in the first decade of the 20th century by the Scouting movement.

However, formal pre-service training for youth workers only began during the Second World War in response to world events, initiated by two very different sectors of the community, namely, education in the United Kingdom and sport and recreation in Australia. New Zealand's youth work training was also influenced by the sport and recreation sector yet formally began much later, while in Canada and the United States youth work began within the social welfare system after World War II, based on a therapeutic care model, similar, yet different, to that of Europe at the time.

Today youth work has been considerably transformed to a targeted approach built around two predominant frameworks in operation globally: (i) positive youth development and (ii) therapeutic care. The only consistency to be found in training across the different countries is its primary focus – training workers to work with young people. But the differing frameworks and accreditation practices means that their youth training credentials are not transportable across national boundaries in many cases.

B. Belton (ed.), 'Cadjan – Kiduhu': Global Perspectives on Youth Work, 133–150.
© 2014 Sense Publishers. All rights reserved.

YOUTH WORKERS ARE.......?

What are youth workers? What do they do? What are the disciplinary and practice boundaries? A cursory review of the professional and research literature fails to provide a clear answer as to what youth workers actually do (Davies, 2005; Smith, 1988; Wisman, 2011). Some writers advocate integrating young people into their community (Martin, 2002); for others, it is about providing informal education (Banks, 1999). Vaughn Bowie, former lecturer in youth work at the University of Western Sydney, has described youth work and its dilemmas as having, "... a major role in working with young people in their personal and vocational and life development... (and) tends to have a reputation for working more with at risk kids... but that's not the whole picture" (Bowie, 2005a: 1).

The diverse and disparate nature of youth work is now complicated by the perennial ethical issues of confidentiality and balancing the autonomy and control of young people with the needs and requirements of funders, such as government agencies, philanthropic foundations, religious and other such agencies. Youth workers require a sound knowledge and both practical and administrative skills to successfully address the multitude of scenarios they face daily (Belton, 2009; Emslie, 2009; Gabb & Glaisher, 2006; Sercombe, 2007).

DEFINING 'YOUTH'

The confusion is exacerbated by the fact that there is no global consistency as to what 'youth' is. Across the world the age range spans across a moving scale of 0–40 years. In Victoria, Australia, *Positive Pathways*, a Victorian government youth policy introduced in 2010, increased the age range for young people from 12–25 years to 10–25 years of age. Nationally the Australian federal government works with the 12–25 age range, as does each of the other states and territories. Finland's youth become adults at 29 and in Canada youth workers care for children and young people aged between 4–18 years, though the range is fluid depending on who is creating the policy. Even the federal Canadian government is not clear, defining youth anywhere between 15–30 years of age depending on the department and/or organisation involved (United Way, 2011). In Malaysia and Sri Lanka a young person can be anyone under 40.

Nor are government youth work departments administratively located in similar arrangements. In Australia federal youth policy is managed by the Department of Education, Employment and Work Relations (DEEWR), whereas the Department of Human Services (DHS) is responsible for young people in the state of Victoria which houses the Office for Youth as well as Protective Child Services. In New Zealand youth are located within the Ministry of Youth Development while the United States does not have a federal youth portfolio.

This difference in arrangements is even more apparent in the United Kingdom where the current push towards devolution has meant that each of the four nations has been charged by the UK government with the responsibility of delivering their own education and youth policies. Hence, and not surprisingly, this has resulted in

I didn't feel prepared when I finished ... but being here now in the job I feel much more useful. I think in the course we need more practical experience... like writing grant proposals, writing child assessments, formatting, writing to government, etc. (Recent RMIT HE Youth Work graduate, 2012).

Initial interviews with industry in Australia and the United Kingdom highlight that graduates tend to be competent or capable but rarely both. To be competent, as deemed by the Australian Training Package Glossary (2010: 2), a student must show, 'the consistent application of knowledge and skill to the standard of performance required in the workplace ... to new situations and environments'. Capable students are expected to be able to, '... read, write, think critically and speak intelligently and effectively with the view of engaging reflexive citizens with contemporary issues that are within the broader public culture'. (RMIT University, 2010).

Numerous writers, including Benjamin and Harrison (2007) and Hartje et al. (2008) advocate for a mix of 'knowledge-based' and 'work-based' learning which Biggs (2003) called the creation of functioning knowledge. That is, content knowledge (knowing about things) is matched with procedural knowledge (practical and/or skills based knowledge). Jones and VanderVan (1990), speaking specifically about youth work education, echoed this, stating that

> To focus solely on practice-based knowledge, without incorporating into it an infusion of concepts related, even apparently unrelated, areas will ultimately diminish the richness of the field. (Jones & VanderVan, 1990: 118)

Corney (2004) names these concepts as the values, which underpin youth work because they influence and determine how people work within the sector. The National Youth Agency (NYA) of the United Kingdom identified these values as:
– Young people's voluntary participation
– Starting with the young person's view of the world
– Young people are treated with respect
– Developing young people's skills and attitudes rather than providing remedies for 'problem behaviours'
– Helping young people create stronger relationships and collective identities
– Respecting and valuing their differences
– Promoting young people's voices (NYA, 2010).

Corney advocates a youth work educational system, which highlights these values in its delivery. His several articles (2004, 2007, 2009) challenge the notion of Competency Based Training (CBT) which was determined to be value neutral. He and others (Corney, Broadbent, & Darmanin 2009; Grogen, 2004) saw CBT similar to imparting youth work skills to students without them receiving the necessary supporting contextualised knowledge. Kemmis (2009) and Chappell (2004) agree, both discussing the problems associated with reducing the role of the teacher to that of someone who follows a formula.

The identified knowledge necessary for youth workers, as suggested by Jones and VanderVan (1990), is best 'derived from direct practice' (118). Ord (2008) agrees and uses Dewey's experiential learning model to emphasise his case for the preparation of students for their chosen careers.

AUSTRALIA

Although currently a formal qualification is not required to work in the youth sector in Australia, industry is increasingly seeking and preferring qualified workers. Because the need and urgency to fill a position often takes priority, a large proportion of untrained workers, including volunteers continue to undertake many aspects of work in the sector, such as mentoring when working with those aged 10–25 years of age (Choy et al., 2008).

With no national youth policy, the responsibility for Australia's young people is given over to each individual state and territory, with each appearing to focus on an aspect of youth. Similar in their outlooks, New South Wales has Youth Health Policy 2011–2016: Healthy Bodies, Healthy Minds, Vibrant Futures while Victoria's Positive Pathways for Victoria's Vulnerable Young People. A Framework to Support Vulnerable Youth, supports the youth deemed most vulnerable in our society. One of the major differences highlighted in Victoria's policy is the nominated increased age range for young people in that state from 12–25 to 10–25 years of age while the rest of the country works with the former age range.

Delivered in December 2010, after widespread consultation with the community and youth sector, Victoria's policy sets out the state government's commitment to '… better support vulnerable young people and their families, moving towards improved integration of services, stronger localised approaches and earlier and more effective responses for these young people and their families' (Victorian Government, 2010: 1).

The government has determined that there will be five focus areas which will guide all current and future services for Victoria's young people at both the state and local levels:

Focus area 1: Engagement in education, training and employment
Focus area 2: Early identification of vulnerability
Focus area 3: Tailored responses to particular groups
Focus area 4: Local partnerships, planning and participation
Focus area 5: Effective services, capable people.
(Victorian Government, 2010: 1)

Coordinated by the Children's Services Coordination Board, which consists of eight members who represent various aspects of community interested in young people's lives, such as education, justice, welfare, government and Human Services, the idea is to connect '… vulnerable young people to their communities and enabling their active participation in family, school and community life is key to reducing vulnerability' (Victorian Government, 2010: 2).

With the hope that this policy will allow for the better coordination of services so that Victoria's vulnerable youth can be identified and supported earlier in times of crisis, it relies upon a positive youth development framework where the community supports the young person to achieve success in their life so they will become a successful adult in their community.

The emphasis on vulnerability clearly delineates this response from the notion of a generic service for all young people.

The first youth work training in Australia was a one-off course delivered by the YMCA in 1919, in response to a government initiative aimed at retraining returning servicemen. Offered only once (Board of YMCA Minutes, 1919; Ewen, 1981; Gurry, 1985; Johnston, 1985; Limbert, 1957), it was 25 years before youth work training in Australia became an ongoing concern. This was despite an enquiry by the National Women's Council (NWC) in 1935 into the possible training of physical education teachers to train Australia's youth to meet the health and/or fitness standards required by the armed forces in preparation for the anticipated impending war (Maunders, 1984).

In 1944, the University of Melbourne delivered a 10 month, full time course for youth workers of the day, in consultation with the National Fitness Council (NFC). Established in 1941 and representing the voluntary youth organisations, the NFC had been advising on possible leader training courses since its inception. Delivered for four years, the mantle of training was taken up by YMCA Sydney in 1947 when it introduced a two-year Diploma in Youth Leadership to train mainly YMCA and YWCA workers although candidates from other organisations and countries were accepted. It was the only youth work training course on offer between 1947 and 1963.

During the 1960s significant changes in Australian pre-service youth work training saw the introduction of a second provider, the Victorian State Government. The YMCA course continued, offering Christian-based training over two years (YMCA Minutes, 1964) while the Victorian State government training facility began awarding a qualification after 40 days of study in 1963, which became a 2-year course in 1966 (Social Work Department, 1971). Both courses became three years in length during the early seventies.

In 1977, the YMCA course was picked up by the State College of Victoria Coburg (SCV Coburg), which heralded all youth work training being delivered by tertiary educational institutions. Numerous educational amalgamations during the 1980s saw a growth in the number of youth work courses delivered, which now went beyond Melbourne to Sydney and Perth. SCV Coburg eventually evolved to become RMIT University in 1992.

In 1996 the Australian Federal Government developed a national vocational industry training package policy with the aim of developing a relevant set of competency standards comprising of the skills and knowledge required to perform a job with industry implementation guidelines for nominated industries (Youth Affairs Council of Victoria, 2004). Youth work was one of these. Updated regularly in consultation with the youth work industry to ensure the compulsory and elective competencies remain relevant (Corney & Broadbent, 2007) they are regulated for compliance by the Australian Skills Quality Association (ASQA). This provides a guarantee that all documentation, assessments and teaching staff meet the rigorous standards necessary for the successful delivery of each qualification.

In 2013, in Australia, there are currently three undergraduate degrees in youth work at recognised universities (RMIT University, Victoria University and Australian Catholic University) together with numerous vocational community college providers offering the Certificate IV and Diploma in Youth Work across the country, including a growing number of faith-based providers and Registered Training Organisations (RTOs).

CANADA

As in the United States, Canadian youth workers are known as Child and Youth Care Practitioners and experience varying levels of recognition. Similar to levels of training in Australia, Canadian workers can gain a certificate, diploma, advanced diploma and/or degree in the child and youth care sector. Many build upon a previous level of qualification, such as Selkirk College's, British Columbia, Human Services Diploma: Child and Youth Care. A two year course, it is advertised as providing, 'more advanced training and recognition to a certificate level' and allows graduates to articulate into the third year of the four-year degrees offered at the University of Victoria, University College of Fraser Valley, Vancouver Island University and Douglas College, B.C. This is only one example of pre-service training in youth work offered in Canada, where more than thirty courses are currently on offer (Selkirk University, 2012).

Canadian Child and Youth Care (CYC) encompasses 4–18 year olds. Although training does not appear to be necessary to work in the industry having a formal qualification is preferable, similar to the Australian situation today. An accreditation process, which is based on worker competencies for the child and youth sector in Canada, has recently been developed and is being implemented.

Youth work training began in 1957 when Lon Lawson taught the first course at Thistletown Hospital, Ontario. A decade later George Brown College offered the first official College programme and, 50 years on, numerous courses are offered through face-to-face, online and distance education delivery options at community colleges and universities across the country (http://cyccanada.com).

NEW ZEALAND

Hanna (1995) notes that youth work in New Zealand began with a predominant focus on outdoor camps and recreational programs for Pakeha (white) youth who were not deemed to be 'at risk'. First delivered by Christian-based organisations, such as the YMCA and the Boys' and Girls' Brigades during the 19th century, as they were elsewhere in the world, youth work remains an important aspect of reaching those aged between 12 and 25 by whatever means is most effective and is actively supported by the national Government.

Today youth work in New Zealand has a very high profile, which is reflected in the increased recognition youth workers have received from Government bodies, the media and funders alike after a concerted effort across the country to create a unified stance (NZYWNA, 2008). Like Australia, a formal qualification is not always required to undertake youth work and despite its positive recognition, New Zealand has a large unpaid volunteer work force and a small minority who hold a formal qualification.

Youth policy is the responsibility of the Ministry of Youth Development (MYD) for those aged between 12 and 24. Formerly the Ministry for Youth Affairs, the MYD promotes the *Youth Development Strategy Aotearoa* (YDSA), a positive youth development framework that upholds strengths over deficits for young people. Reflective of Maori youth development practices (NYWNA, 2011), it was introduced in 2002 and promoted as '… growing and developing the skills and attitudes young people need to take part in society, now and in the future' (MYD, 2013). Youth workers are an integral part of ensuring the YDSA is achieved.

Although the YDSA is the official government framework for youth work in New Zealand, the sector itself acknowledges that it works with four similar philosophies. These encompass and echo the positive youth development and community aspects of the YDSA.

'The Circle of Courage' is an integration of the best of Western education, positive youth development research and the traditional child-rearing values of the Lakota people of North America, where the whole village is responsible for its young people (Barnard, 2013, Martin, 2013, Reclaiming.com, 2013). Belonging, mastering skills, independence and generosity are the four developmental values depicted as quadrants on a medicine wheel. Dependent upon each other, and necessary for the creation of a healthy young person, if one quadrant is missing or damaged then behavioural problems can and are expected (Reclaiming.com, 2013).

It is a rare youth worker in New Zealand who has not completed the associated Response Ability Pathways (RAP) training, which teaches workers how to identify where the 'circle' is broken in a young person's life and how to respond to the needs of the young person rather than react to the problems.

The next framework identified by industry and training providers is based on the work of Urie Bronfenbrenner. His ecological approach to human development states that interpersonal relationships do not occur in a vacuum but rather as the culmination of the cultural, political, social and economic forces that impact our everyday lives. Thus, a set of stable relationships with trusted adults who believe in the young person, who is expected to contribute to the relationship, is very important and needs to be created and cultivated for successful personal development (Ceci, 2006; Martin, 2002; Martin & Martin, 2012).

New Zealand youth work focuses on the family, school environment, cultural community and the neighbourhood and geographical community, with peers acknowledged as part of each environment (Martin, 2002). The first section of the New Zealand Code of Ethics is titled '*Whanaungatanga. Quality Relationships*' and discusses how, 'essential (these are) to a young person's development and it is in this context that youth work exists' (NYWNA, 2011: 25).

New Zealand acknowledges it is a bi-cultural country through its laws and policies with all Government documents printed in both English and Māori. In acknowledgement of this, *Te Whare Tapa Wha*, the Māori health model developed by Dr Mason Durie in 1982, is a cornerstone for health and youth work in New Zealand. Similar to the Circle of Courage, it is a traditional, cultural model commonly known as 'The Four Walls' and drawn as a *wahrenui,* or traditional meeting house. A person's health, like the sides, walls and corners of a house, must be strong and established on solid foundations, if it is to remain standing and supportive. Psychological/mental, spiritual, physical and family/kinship health are the cornerstones and when these are out of alignment disharmony occurs (Kina Trust, 2013).

The first mention of training for youth workers appears during the 1970s with the delivery of the YMCA's *Diploma in Youth and Community Work*. As was the case in Australia, although youth work historically is based on its Commonwealth connections, youth work training was first provided within the model of the American YMCA recreationally based programmes delivered at Springfield College in Massachusetts (Hanna, 1995). Little evidence of its delivery and/or impact exists today.

A patchy delivery of training led to the creation of the National Certificates in Youth Work at levels three and four, and the National Diploma (level six) in 1995. Youth workers were finally able to take on nationally accredited training that was regulated by the New Zealand Qualification Authority (NZQA). Developed by national industry representatives, they are reviewed and updated regularly (NZQA, 2013). A nationally accredited, competency-based degree at level seven was introduced in 2011 after three years of intensive writing and development.

Taken over the duration of six, 12, 24 and 36 months respectively, they can be completed as stand-alone courses or in any progressive combination. All graduates must hold a current first aid certificate and undertake a successful police check before they can begin employment.

All youth work qualifications in New Zealand are competency based around industry desired knowledge and skills deemed necessary to be become a youth worker in New Zealand.

THE UNITED KINGDOM

Historically, youth programmes in the United Kingdom began in the early 1800s, as education programmes, both formal and informal, led by well-meaning volunteers whose main attributes were enthusiasm, energy and a willingness to support those deemed to be less fortunate than themselves. Stressing duty, obedience, loyalty and service, boys and to a lesser extent girls, were voluntarily organised into (literally) uniformed groups and taught the skills deemed necessary for becoming a fully rounded citizen of the day in numerous programmes, including The Girls' Friendly Society founded in 1875, The Boys' Brigade in 1883 and The Boy Scouts in 1908.

This remained the traditional format of youth services until the shift in political emphasis in the decade leading up to World War II saw a concern emerge regarding the state of Britain's youth, who were not expected to meet either the health or fitness standards required by the armed forces, the same complaint levelled at conscripts during the Boer and First World Wars.

Formal pre-service youth work training began after the publication of Circulars 1486 (1939) and 1516 (1940), the English government documents that are usually taken as the beginning of the youth service training sector in England and Wales. The proposed outline for these courses was set out in Circular 1598 (1942) with training beginning in 1945 when Westhill College, later the University of Birmingham, and University College, Swansea were granted the license to offer the first two courses.

Little changed in the youth sector, with regard to delivery or training until the Albemarle Report (1960). Although never fully implemented, this expanded the sector into a full-time training framework in England. Increased funds created a large building programme resulting in centres springing up 'everywhere'. Combined with the introduction of the Joint Negotiations Committee (JNC) which set the terms and conditions of youth workers' employment nationally, this led to youth work gaining the credibility and support necessary to grow as a full-time profession.

More centres meant more work for trained workers and in an effort to address the need, six new youth work courses were recognised by the JNC and approved by the Ministry of Education, for offer during the 1960s (National Youth Agency, 2011) and with eleven in total offered between 1970 and 1982 (Holmes, 1981; National Youth Agency, 2011).

Today the four nations of the United Kingdom, England, Northern Ireland, Scotland and Wales, work together politically on most things; however they have individual education and youth policies.

In England, the current policy and legislation which influences the daily lives of children and young people is *Positive for Youth* (P4Y) and the supplementary supporting documents. Bringing together nine ministerial departments including Education, Criminal Justice, and Health, the policy was billed as 'A new approach to cross-government policy for the 4.5 million young people aged 13–19' to become productive and successful adult members of their communities. Released in December 2011, by the Coalition government as their first statement on young people, it was said to continue the more 'targeted approach' of youth work begun by the New Labour Government (1997–2010).

Success through formal education and training is the central focus of the policy, with an acknowledgement that if young people are to be ensured higher levels of success in adulthood then they must successfully achieve in school and subsequent training. P4Y includes the areas of health (obesity, mental health and alcohol and other drug issues), volunteering and citizenship. Various national youth programmes have been created with the purpose of helping young people to achieve success including 53 'Myplace' centres; world class youth spaces built in the most deprived areas across the country, with the aim of encouraging young people to spend their spare time being productive (Bashir et al., 2013), and the National Citizens Service (NCS), a semi-residential programme of six weeks for

16–17 year olds, begun in the summer of 2001, which aims to create a more responsible, cohesive and engaged society.

In the last few years many youth work related undergraduate courses have been discontinued. This is partly in the face of austerity cuts impacting on local authority youth work programmes and the concomitant loss of employment opportunities. However, pre-graduate training has grown, providing a largely part-time workforce for voluntary agencies and commercial providers contracted by local government to undertake targeted work.

The National Youth Work Strategy for Scotland, *Moving Forward – a strategy for improving young people's chances through youth work* (2007) is designed to provide its young people with more services that will continue to enhance the recognised community strength found in youth work (Scottish Executive, 2007).

Because the primary focus for the policy's successful delivery is placed firmly on the youth work sector, the document continuously talks about the need for youth workers to be, '… equipped and empowered to achieve ongoing positive outcomes for young people now and in the future' (YouthLink_Scotland, 2013). Without the proper funding and support at both the national and local levels, the Scottish Executive understands that its policy will not be as successful as it could be, hence supporting those who already do the work is logical.

Northern Ireland's *Strategy for the Delivery of Youth Work in Northern Ireland 2005–2008*, worked towards ensuring those aged betweenfour and 25 years were able to reach their full potential as both 'individuals and responsible citizens'. The document guaranteed that all programmes worked towards helping to develop all aspects of a young person's development, whether that is personal, social, educational, political, cultural, spiritual, physical or vocational. Funded from the education budget, regular three year plans will be created by the appropriate boards and the Youth Council to ensure the priorities are met and guarantee that all children and young people are able to reach their potential.

This document was replaced with *Priorities for Youth. Improving Young People's Lives through Youth Work* at the end of 2013. After an extensive consultation process involving everyone who participates in the youth sector, including children, young people and those who work with them, the new document continues to fulfill the ideals and aims of the previous policy framework while acknowledging the importance of formal (education) and informal (youth work) education to achieve the vision of, '*every young person achieving his or her full potential at each stage of his or her development*' (DENI, 2013).

The Government acknowledges that this will not happen without properly trained workers so the recruitment and retention of good workers and volunteers, which has proven to be difficult for some employers, is a high priority. The Government has committed itself to ensuring there will be sufficient numbers of workers and volunteers to achieve its goals by creating alternative pathways for current workers to gain professional qualifications, the establishment of a coherent mapping of opportunities for youth work training in Northern Ireland, and the establishment of a joint Education and Training Standards Committee.

In January 2006 the North-South Education and Training Standards (NSETS) Committee for Youth Work was launched. It includes nine representatives each from Northern Ireland and the Republic of Ireland and brings together a wide range of youth work knowledge and experience, including voluntary and statutory sector employers, higher education staff, youth work trainers and trade union interests.

The NSETS Committee sets standards for the professional formation of youth workers throughout the island of Ireland and currently its work is focused on the professional endorsement of courses offered by Higher Education Institutions. However the Committee also has a role to play in raising the standards of training at all levels.

The North-South dimension offers the potential for the exchange of expertise, the development of new cross-border training programmes and sharing of resources. The NSETS sets the requirements for the achievement of professional endorsement, with the aim of ensuring that endorsed courses are adequately equipped to deliver the education and training essential for professional youth workers. The NSETS look to facilitate the creation of pathways for youth workers who may wish to progress by increments from basic training to professional qualification.

The national priorities for youth work in Wales are set out in the *National Youth Service Strategy for Wales* (2007). Built around the concept of 'The Five Pillars' of education, expression, participation, inclusion and empowerment, they enable, encourage, equip and support the young people of Wales, aged between 11 and 25, to be active participants in designing, creating and establishing services that will benefit them, wherever they see that is most relevant through wider skills development and enhanced emotional competence (CWYVS, 2013; Smith, 2007).

The government acknowledges that the success of youth work in Wales is dependent upon the delivery of a high quality youth work service that is based on the voluntary engagement initiated by the young person. Whether formal or non-formal, youth work in Wales is delivered through 22 local authorities, major voluntary youth organisations and independent local projects in a variety of locations, including youth centres, on the streets, in community and/or residential settings. The methods utilised can be as varied as the locales (CWYVS, 2013; Smith, 2007).

There are two levels of youth worker in the United Kingdom and eight possible qualifications. The first five, an award, three certificates and a diploma, are for Youth Support Workers, nonprofessional youth workers who are school students who wish to become youth leaders in settings such as church youth groups or volunteers. The latter are supported by their organisations to gain some recognised training. It is common for many professional youth workers in the United Kingdom to begin their careers in youth work as volunteers. To be granted professional worker status, students today must complete an Honours Degree (three years), which is supported by the National Youth Work Association (NYA). In 2011 there were almost 60 undergraduate courses in the United Kingdom recognised by the NYA (2011). This number has decreased dramatically over the last few years given the effects of austerity cuts to local authority budgets (the major single employer of full-time youth workers) and the effects of the global financial crisis on voluntary organisations.

Another important factor to remember when talking about youth services in the United Kingdom is that they are delivered by two distinct provider groups, the first being all levels of government, known as the statutory sector. The voluntary sector is used to describe all other service providers, which include private and not-for-profit organisations, such as churches, as well as their paid and unpaid workers. From an Australian (and other national) perspective this can be very confusing as 'volunteer' refers to those who work for a not-for-profit organisation or on projects that are undertaken without financial payment and that will benefit their community and the volunteers themselves (Volunteer Australia, 2013).

Industry requirements are seen in the National Occupational Standards (NOS), the identified competencies, skills, knowledge and understanding that underpin the values all youth workers require to successfully complete their daily jobs in the youth sector. Used by all levels of academia to shape course and training content, industry uses them to determine what duties and responsibilities match a position and fit them to new employment opportunities and professional development for current employees.

Created in 2002, by The Learning and Skills Improvement Service (LSIS), employers, practitioners and other stakeholders from across the UK, the standards were updated in 2008 and 2012 to ensure they continue to reflect current practice in the various contexts throughout the sector across each of the nations of the United Kingdom. With the disbanding of this body in 2013 the concern as to who will update the NOS (or if it will become defunct in the face of the effective demise of full-time professional youth work) has been raised.

THE UNITED STATES

In the United States, as in Canada, youth workers are known as child and youth care practitioners and experience varying levels of recognition. Although there are a number of very strong child and youth care-related programmes, training is inconsistent throughout the country with few university programmes available. Qualifications can be obtained at a certificate, two-year, four year and/or graduate level.

The Child and Youth Care Certification Board (CYCCB) administrate the Child and Youth Care Practitioner Professional Certification Programme, which is how American youth workers are accredited. Workers take an exam to demonstrate their competence in five domains deemed necessary for workers:

1. Professionalism
2. Cultural and human diversity
3. Applied human development
4. Relationship and communication
5. Developmental practice methods (Curry et al., 2011).

This list was narrowed down from 87 sets of competencies to the final five by a team of international youth practitioners brought together especially for this purpose between 2000 and 2007. Allowing for similarities in their approaches, residential treatment, juvenile justice, afterschool and day-care were brought together under the umbrella of child and youth care. The foundation document for this is the *North American Competencies for Child and Youth Care Practitioners* which identifies, 'the fundamental competencies' that underlie these workers' practice while, 'developing a reliable and valid process to assess competence by' (Curry et al., 2011).

Youth agencies in the United States of America agree that competent workers are an advantage to the sector but their reluctance to pay for higher skilled workers is hampering the push to ensure all workers gain this accreditation (Wisman, 2011). This can be overcome by courses offered being mapped against the competencies, as has been successfully achieved by Kent State University in Ohio (Curry et al., 2011). It is acknowledged that subjects such as psychology, human development, family and justice studies could be adapted to better address the needs of child and youth care worker training.

CONCLUSION

Investigating the pre-service training delivered in youth work across the English-speaking world has already proven that competencies can be delivered within university degrees, as seen in the Kent State University example provided above.

A number of themes have emerged from this chapter:
- The beginnings of youth work began in the middle of the 19th century with the formation of the YMCA and organisations such as the Boys' Brigades.
- In terms of youth work training, the YMCA was the key initiating agency towards the end of the 19th century.
- The original focus was on recreational and fitness activities, very much heightened during the various times of war to have fit recruits for the armed forces and at the end of wars in relation to repatriation programmes.
- The gradual evolution from Christian-based training programmes, to university-based programmes were under pinned by changes in government policy.
- The evolution inconstant of the training programmes occurred from a recreational focus to a more academic and service delivery focus.
- The national differences the detained curriculum content and age spread of the content for child, adolescent and young adult targets relate to the changing demographic and sociocultural context.
- The shift from generic youth work to more targeted youth work had a resounding impact on the youth work training curriculum.

While there is disappointment at the passing of generic youth work in the United Kingdom, it is essential that youth work students are able to take advantage of the new opportunities presented by targeted work and are knowledgeable and skilful in such diverse areas of practice such as and including education, crime prevention, health/sex education, drug and alcohol prevention work, mental illness and general wellbeing, accommodation including homelessness, work in hostels, working with those in and leaving care, school based youth work, including work with school exclusions, career advice and early intervention work.

To ensure graduates are work-ready upon graduation additional targeted areas of service delivery will need to be added to their education to ensure they are employable in their chosen career upon graduation as this is where there will be a growth of work with young people. The regular auditing and industry consultation, when placed next to the fact that all staff in both sectors has retained active roles in the youth sector ensures that, despite what is happening politically, youth services and the training of those working in the industry will continue to meet the needs of the young people in their care. This general strategy is also pertinent across international contexts.

REFERENCES

Barham, N. (2006). *Dis/connected. Why our kids are turning their backs on everything we thought we knew.* Sydney: Random House.

Belton, B. (2009). *Developing critical youth work theory.* Rotterdam: Sense Publishers.

Benjamin, C., & Harrison, R. (2007). *Across the great divide: Moving between theory and practice in foundation degree study.* United Kingdom: Open University.

Biggs, J. (2003). *Teaching for quality learning at university: What the student does* (2nd ed.). Maidenhead: Society for Research into Higher Education and Open University Press.

Board of Education. (1939). *In the service of youth.* London: HSMO.

Bowie, V. (2005). *Transcript of "Has youth work reaches (sic) its use by date?".* Life Matters, Radio National, Thursday 27 July 2005.

Broadbent, R., & Corney, T. (2008). A professional association for youth work in Victoria – The whole 'Kit Bag'. *Commonwealth Youth Development Journal, 6*(1), 425-434.

Bryman, A., & Burgess, R. G. (1999). Qualitative research methodology: A review. In *Qualitative Research, Vol. 1 Fundamental Issues in Qualitative Research* (pp. 160-179). London: Sage.

Cahill, D. (2010). *RMIT'S youth work program: An appraisal in historical perspective.* RMIT University, meographed.

Cahill, D. (2012). *Mind the gap! 2012 undergraduate intake: An analysis of the average score and range of ATAR scores for year 12 and non-year 12 entry students.* RMIT University, meographed.

Cahill, D., & Ewen, J. (1987). *Ethnic youth: Their assets and aspirations.* Canberra: Department of Prime Minister and Cabinet.

Ceci, S. (2006). 'Urie Bronfenbrenner' (1917–2005). *American Psychologist, 61*(2), Feb-Mar, 173-174.

Chappell, C. (2004). *Contemporary vocational learning – changing pedagogy.* AVETRA, [Nowra], Paper presented at the 7th Australian Vocational Education and Training Research Association Conference, http://www.avetra.org.au/Conference_Archives/2004/documents/PA013Chappell.pdf Accessed 30.7.2012.

Child and Youth Care Canada. http://cyccanada.com Accessed 21.04.2012.

Choy, S., Bowman, K., Billett, S.,Wignall, L., & Haukka, S. (2008). *Effective models of employment-based training.* NCVER, Australian Government.

Clark, C. (2007). *Hurt. Inside the world of today's teenagers.* USA: Baker Academic.

Corney, T. (2004a). Values verses competencies: Implications for the future of professional youth work education. *Journal of Youth Studies, 7*(4), 513-527.

Corney, T. (2004b). Youth work. The problem of values. *Youth Studies Australia, 23*(4), 11-19.

Corney, T. (2009). Participation and empowerment: Is youth work a form of community development? *Commonwealth Youth and Development, 7*(2), 1-11.

Corney, T., & R. Broadbent. (2007). Youth work training package review. More of the same or radical rationalisation? *Youth Studies Australia, 26*(3), 36-43.

Corney, T., Broadbent, B., & Darmanin, L. (2009). Why youth workers need to collectively organise. *Youth Studies Australia, 8*(3).

Curry, D., Richardson, R., & Pallock. L. (2011). Aligning educational program content with U.S. youth work standards and competencies. *Relational Child and Youth Care Practice, 24*(4), 24-32.

Curry, D., Eckles, F., Stuart, C., & Qaqisj, B. (2010). National child and youth care practitioner professional certification: Promoting competent care for children and youth. *Child Welfare, 89*(2), 57-77.

CWVYS. (2013). *Youth work in Wales. Principles and purposes.* Youth Work in Wales Review Group, January.

Davies, B. (2005). Youth work; A manifesto for our times. Reprinted from *Youth and Policy, 88*, September, 5-27.

Department of Education, Northern Ireland. http://www.deni.gov.uk/index/support-and-development-2/youth-service/19-priorities-for-youth.htm Accessed 17.04.2014

Emslie, M. (2009). Please sir, I want some more: Securing better pay and conditions for youth workers in Australia, *Youth Studies Australia, 28*(3), 32-40.

Ewen, J. (1981). *The education and training of youth workers in Australia.* A discussion paper. Office for Youth Affairs, Canberra.

Ewen, J. (1983). *Youth in Australia – A new deal and a new role.* Melbourne: Phillip Institute of Technology.

Gabb, R., & Glasiher, S. (2006). *Models of cross-sectoral curricula: TAFE and HE.* Victoria University.

Grogen, P. (2004). *That old chestnut: The professionalisation of youth work in Victoria.* Youth Affairs Council of Victoria.

Gurry, T. (Ed.). (1985). *Focusing on Australian history. An emerging identity* (revised ed.). Richmond: Heinemann Educational Australia.

Hanna, D. (1995). A background to youth work in Aotearoa/NZ. In *Real work. A report from the National Research Project on the state of youth work in Aotearoa.* Christchurch: National Youth Workers Network.

Hartje, J. Evans, P., Killian, E., & Brown, R. (2008). Youth worker characteristics and self-reported competency as predictors of intent to continue working with youth. *Child and Youth Care Forum, 37,* 27-41.

Her Majesty's Stationery Office. (1942). *Circular 1598. Emergency courses of training for those engaged in the youth service.* London: Board of Education.

Institute of Social Welfare. (1976). *Handbook. Social Welfare Department, Training Division.* Watsonia: Institute of Social Welfare.

Johnston, M. (1985). *A guide to HSC Australian history.* Melbourne: Longman Cheshire.

Jones, H., & VanderVan, K. (1990). Education and training for child and youth care practice: The view from both sides of the Atlantic. *Child and Youth Care Quarterly, 19*(2), Summer, 105-121.

Kemmis, S., & McTaggart, R. (2005). Participatory action research. Communicative action and the public sphere. In N. Denzin & Y. Lincoln (Eds.), *The Sage handbook of qualitative research* (3rd ed., pp. 559-603). London: Sage Publications.

Kemmis, R., Sutcliffe, S., & Ahern, S. (2009). *Making vet pedagogy explicit.* http://scholar.google.com.au/scholar?q=Kemmis%2C+R.%2C+Sutcliffe%2C+S.%2C+Ahern%2C+S.+2009+Making+Vet+Pedagogy+Explicit.&btnG=&hl=en&as_sdt=0%2C5&as_vis=1. Accessed 30.7.2012.

Kina Trust. http://www.kinatrust.org.nz/myfiles/PDF_E_-_Te_Whare_Tapa_Wha_Model.pdf. Accessed 17.04.2013.

Limbert, P. (1997). *Reliving a century. An autobiography.* USA: Baltimore Press.

Maunders, D. (1984). *Keeping them off the streets. A history of voluntary youth organizations in Australia 1850-1980.* Melbourne: PIT.

149

Martin, L. (2002). *The invisible table. Perspectives on youth and youthwork (sic) in New Zealand.* Palmerston North: Dunmore Press Limited.

Martin, L. (2008). Who needs training? *Te Ha O Te Aroaro, 2*(8), Winter.

Martin, L., & Martin, A. (2012). *Small stories. Reflections on the practice of youth development.* South Dakota: Circle of Courage.

McNair Report. (1944). *Teachers and youth leaders. Report of the Committee appointed by the President of the Board of Education to consider the supply, recruitment and training of teachers and youth leaders.* London: HMSO.

New Zealand Youth Workers Network Association. (2008). *Discussion document. What is youth work?,* Christchurch: NZYWNA.

National Youth Workers Network Aotearoa. (2011). *Code of ethics for youth work in Aotearoa New Zealand* (2nd ed.). Wellington: Ara Taioh.

Ontario Association of Child and Youth Workers. http://www.oacyc.org/index.php?page=8. Accessed 08.08.2011.

Ord, J. (2008). A curriculum for youth work. The experience of the English Youth Service. *Australia Youth Studies, 27*(4), 49-57.

Ord, J. (Ed.). (2012). *Critical issues in youth work management.* USA: Routledge.

Report of the Ministerial Review of the Training of Youth Workers in Victoria. (1995). Melbourne, s.n.

RMIT University. (2010). *Mapping the youth sector. Course guide 2010.* Melbourne: RMIT University.

Selkirk College. http://selkirk.ca/programs/hhs/humanservices/humanservicescyc/. Accessed 21.04.12.

Sercombe, H. (2007). Embedded youth work – Ethical questions for youth work professionals. *Youth Studies Australia, 26*(2), 11-19.

Smith, M. (1988). *Developing youth work, informal education, mutual aid and popular practice.* England: Milton Keynes.

Smith, M. K. (2007). Young people, youth work, youth service. The National Youth Service strategy for Wales. *The encyclopaedia of informal education.* www.infed.org/archives/gov_uk/young_people_ youth_work_youth_service.htm. Accessed 01.07.2013.

Social Work Department. (1971). *ISW: Youth leadership diploma course. Exam requirement.* Melbourne: Social Work Department.

United Way. *Environmental scan: Extended age definition for youth 15-24.* http://www.calgaryunitedway.org/main/sites/default/files/environmental_scan_extended_age_ definition.pdf. Accessed 18.10.2013.

Volunteering Australia. http://www.volunteeringaustralia.org/files/0WQ1A2EUTZ/Def_and_Princ_ English.pdf. Retrieved 02.08.2013.

Wisman, M. (2011). *Youth work practice. A status report on professionalization and expert opinion about the future of the field.* New England: ProYouthWork America.

Youth Affairs Council of Victoria Inc. (2009). *Taking young people seriously. Consulting young people about their ideas and opinions. A handbook for organisations working with young people.* Melbourne. N.D.: Office for Youth.

HELENA HELVE

YOUTH POLICIES IN THE NORDIC COUNTRIES

... the four main Nordics – Sweden, Denmark, Norway and Finland – are doing rather well. If you had to be reborn anywhere in the world as a person with average talents and income, you would want to be a Viking. The Nordics cluster is at the top of league tables of everything from economic competitiveness to social health to happiness. They have avoided both southern Europe's economic sclerosis and America's extreme inequality. (*The Economist*, 2013)

SIMILARITIES AND DIFFERENCES

All Nordic countries[1] know about the Nordic model of welfare systems and policy. It can also be detected in Nordic youth policies. For example all Nordic countries value coordination and investment in education and training as central strategy in the activation policy relating to young people. Nordic countries have often been in advance of other European countries in youth issues. From the 1980s and 1990s these countries implemented youth guarantees (in Sweden 1984, Norway 1993, Denmark 1996 and Finland 1996). More recently, in a time when youth unemployment is a serious problem everywhere, other countries have embarked on similar youth employment programmes, to help young people to gain access to education and employment. This activation policy means that for example the proportion of young people outside the education system and the workforce is relatively low. Across Nordic countries the proportion of young people completing higher and further education is high compared to many other European countries.

Policies relating to youth, education and the labour market are similar in the Nordic Countries, but they are not the same. The economies of these nations are also different. In the years between 1980 and 2011 the gross domestic product (GDP) per capita was higher in Denmark and Norway than in the other Nordic countries, partly because they were less severely affected by the economic crisis of the early 1990s, which had biggest impact to Finland. Norway's economy has benefited from oil. Since the crisis years of the 1970s, Denmark has experienced stable and relatively high growth. Explanations behind contemporary differences among the Nordic countries include the collapse of the Icelandic economy in 2008–2009, Norway's abundant financial reserves based on its high oil and gas revenues, Denmark's relatively low social assistance to unemployed youth below the age of 25, the relative high levels of job protection in Sweden and Finland, as opposed to Denmark in particular, where a very flexible labour market creates a relatively high number of job ('flexicurity'), a more academic vocational training system in Sweden and Finland compared to the apprenticeship-based vocational

B. Belton (ed.), 'Cadjan – Kiduhu': Global Perspectives on Youth Work, 151–164.

training system in Denmark and others (Björklund & Fredriksson, 2012; Olofsson & Wadensjö, 2012; International Labor Office, 2013).

More than twenty years after the fall of the Soviet Union (1991) the Nordic countries have developed close connections to Baltic countries Latvia, Lithuania and especially Estonia. Northern Europe has become culturally closer and socially, economically and politically less heterogeneous since Finland (1995), Sweden (1995) and Baltic countries (2004) joined European Union (EU). The Nordic countries have cooperated in many areas during their history, for instance religious, educational, social and political movements based on principles of enlightenment and egalitarianism. Contemporaneously the 'Nordic model' can be taken to refer to welfare states enhancing individual autonomy, ensuring the universal provision of basic human rights and stabilising the economy with similar goals by its emphasis on maximising labour force participation, promoting gender equality, egalitarian and extensive benefit levels, polices that result in the comparatively extensive redistribution wealth, and liberal use of expansionary fiscal policy. However each of the Nordic countries have their own economic, social and political models.[2]

The Nordic countries, since the Second World War, have adopted state regulated economic development programmes and organized targeted intervention into the lives of young people. Welfare state activities were aimed at young people and in all Nordic countries there was a determined expansion in secondary and vocational education, as well as a gradual growth in higher education. At the same time youth clubs and other forms of youth work were expanded. In Finland, for instance, youth houses were built to provide healthy leisure activities and for citizen education of young people (Nieminen, 1998). In Denmark, the Government appointed a Youth Commission in 1945, in order to examine the needs of young people and generate a youth policy. A Youth Commission conducted more general social research, and in 1956 an Institute of Social Research was founded. By that time such institutions had already been established in Norway, Sweden and Finland (Gudmundsson, 2006; see also Dahl & Björklund, 2008).

THE NORDIC YOUTH POLICY CO-OPERATION

The five Nordic countries have traditionally co-operated in terms of policy and development.[3] After the Second World War Nordic politicians strived for stronger international co-operation, this was at the same time as the United Nations was established and the Council of Europe was created. During this period closer Nordic co-operation started, the Nordic Council (NC) was formed in 1952. The Nordic Council of Ministers (NCM) was established in 1971. Denmark and Norway voted on membership of the European Community (EC) in 1972. One of the goals of the Nordic Council of Ministers was to maintain Nordic co-operation, in the event that some of the Nordic countries also became EC members. A long-term example of Nordic collaboration is the shared labour market, which had endured 60 years in 2014. One of the main focuses throughout that year was a determined effort to combat youth unemployment and unemployment among other vulnerable groups. Long-term unemployment and cooperation between educational institutions and labour markets are currently key issues in Nordic co-operation.[4]

Nordic countries have long cooperated in terms of policy effecting children and young people. Since the creation of Nordic Council young politicians have been encompassed into its work, organizing their own annual seminars. The first proper session of the Nordic Youth Council (*Nordisk ungdomskomité NUK*) was held in 1971. It was established as an independent Nordic Children's and Youth Committee *NORDBUK* in 2002 and became the youth policy body assisting the Nordic Council of Ministers. The Committee also co-ordinates Nordic youth research and is responsible for the funds earmarked for activities relevant to children and young people in the Nordic region and adjacent areas. The activities are administered by a Danish organization called CIRIUS. Among other schemes NORDBUK subsidizes projects, which also involve Estonia.[5]

NORDBUK's Committee consists of thirteen members, two from each Nordic country and one each from the three autonomous areas: the Faroe Islands, Greenland and the Åland Islands. A representative of the Sami Youth Council is entitled to participate in the Committee's meetings as an observer.

One of the aims of the Nordic Children's and Youth Committee is to strengthen the Nordic identity by supporting children's and youth participation in cultural, political and social activities in the North, and to enhance the possibility for children and young people to strengthen the Nordic profile in international relations.

The Nordic Youth Council (NYC) is a forum for the political youth organisations. The NYC deals with issues that are relevant to Nordic youth, such as easier access to education and jobs in the Nordic countries. However, the NYC also has a focus on affairs beyond its youth remit. The organization also lobbies for stronger Nordic co-operation relating to a range of concerns including environmental and climate issues as well as general questions relating to equality amongst others. Suggestions agreed upon by the NYC are sent to the Nordic Council. Members of the NYC board participate in Nordic Council meetings and the NYC chairperson is a speaker at the annual NC sessions. NYC's ideas are heard by the Nordic Council and have the potential to start debates amongst Nordic youth. This enables the NYC to affect agreements made by the Nordic Council and, by extension, Nordic politics. The NYC looks to further connections and co-operation between Nordic Youth.

The Presidency of the Nordic Council of Ministers rotates between the five Nordic countries on an annual basis. During the Finnish chairmanship in 2011 the activities of NORDBUK focused on promoting better living conditions, access to cultural creativity among children and young people, together with highlighting the potential of children and young people to influence decisions affecting their lives. The Presidency programme, called the Nordic Region: A Green Climate Leader, stressing the need to involve young people in the Nordic activities. For example, in the Presidency programme of Sweden 2013 among the four projects was strong action to combat youth unemployment.[6] The 'More young people in work in the

Nordic Region', project implemented a broad exchange of experiences between the Nordic countries on ways to facilitate young people entering working life.

NORDIC YOUTH RESEARCH AS A PART OF YOUTH POLICY

The Nordic Youth Research Information *NYRI* was founded in 1980s and it developed the Nordic bibliographic database of youth research and later also NYRI website. Nordic youth researchers took the initiative to organize the independent, multidisciplinary youth research network and host the first Nordic Youth Research *NYRIS* conference in Oslo January 1987. It was a start of the bi-annual Nordic youth research conferences. In 2011 the Finnish Youth Research Society, together with Nordic Scientific Committee of youth research in Turku, organized the NYRIS 11 conference on the topic *Global/Local Youth – New Civic Culture, Rights and Responsibilities*. The 12th Nordic Youth Research Symposium (NYRIS12) was held at Tallinn University, Estonia in 2013, under the title 'Changing Societies and Cultures: Youth in the Digital Age'. *NYRIS conferences are now global and the language of the conference is English.*

In the 1980s national youth research networks were developed. In Denmark two cooperating networks, in Copenhagen and Aarhus, started 1983 (Bay et al., 1985), in Sweden the *FUS* network (The Research Programme, Youth Culture in Sweden) in 1987 (Fornäs & Bolin, 1995; Jansson et al., 2003) and in the same year in Finland a Youth Research Society *Nuorisotutkimusseura ry* was founded (Hoikkala & Suurpää, 2005). It started to publish together with *Kansalaiskasvatuksen Keskus KAKE* (the organization before that in 1992 established Finnish Youth Cooperation *Allianssi* for youth workers and youth organizations) the Finnish Youth Research Journal *Nuorisotutkimus*[7] (founded in 1983). In Norway, in 1989, a state-financed research programme was formed called *Ungforsk*. During the 1990s a centre of youth research was developed in a unit of a larger institute of social research *NOVA* (founded in 2001). This is a research institute under the auspices of the Norwegian Ministry of Education and Research. *It publishes* a Youth *Research Journal, Tidsskrift for ungdomsforskning.*[8]

The Nordic youth research in Denmark and Sweden has focused mainly on youth culture. In Norway a social research approach has been taken from a generational perspective. Finnish youth research has more often taken cultural and social approaches. In Iceland youth studies have primarily been serving as an instrument of social control. Youth research has also been instigated in Faroe Islands and Greenland (Helve et al., 2005; Gudmundsson, 2006; Karlsson et al., 2010).

Nordic cooperation in youth policy and youth research increased when the Nordic Council of Ministers appointed an advisory group of youth researchers from all of the Nordic countries in 1992 and sponsored a Nordic coordinator of youth research.[9] The Nordic Journal of Youth Studies *YOUNG* was launched in 1991.[10]

NATIONAL NORDIC YOUTH POLICIES

Danish Youth Policy

The responsibility for the Danish youth policy is placed with the relevant national, regional and local authorities, as well as within the many voluntary (youth) organizations. Every policy sector has its own field of responsibility regarding measures and policy for young people. The aim is to support initiatives that help young people become active, democratic citizens who can participate constructively in the development of society; giving them real influence and responsibility in matters that concern them. The goal is to secure 95% of all young people a youth education by 2015. With this aim to the fore the Danish Parliament passed legislation giving young people with learning disabilities a chance to finish a youth education that qualifies them personally, socially and professionally to live an independent and active life, taking part in the labour market, in their spare time and in the family.

The Danish youth policy system is based on a decentralized model. The responsibility for providing information for young people's participation and voluntary activities involves the relevant national sectors on regional and local levels. Substantial funding is provided for nongovernmental organizations active in the youth field, including the Danish Youth Council (DUF), which is an umbrella organization for approximately 70 national youth organizations. The Ministry of Education plays a central role in increasing young people's participation in society, and the education system especially has a responsibility in educating pupils in the way democracies function, i.e. the political system and active participation in a democracy.

Finnish Youth Policy

In Finland the government adopts a development programme every four years with the aim of stepping up cross-sector youth policy action. The programme is prepared by the Ministry of Education and Culture in collaboration with other ministries, other relevant stakeholders and permanent experts from the field of child and youth research, child and youth organizations and youth work representatives from local governments (Helve, 2009; Peltola, 2010).

This co-operation is not only at governmental level but also at local level between youth workers and professionals from educational, labour and social sectors as well as policy-makers. Outcomes are recorded in the Youth Acts (the last ones from 2006 and 2011).[11] The Advisory Council for Youth Affairs (NUORA) mainly focuses on youth policy issues and it also submits to the Government annual evaluations and implementation of the Finnish Government's Child and Youth Policy Programme. The Programme for 2012–2015 places emphasis on enhancing participation and social inclusion, promoting non-discrimination. It follows up and supervises the management of everyday life of young people. In addition, the programme aims to strengthen co-operation as an implementation method. The Ministry of Education and Culture steers and develops youth policy by means of legislation, studies and reviews, budgetary and lottery funding (see also Helve, 2002, 2009). The aim of the Youth Guarantee – started in 2013 – is to offer for young under the age of 25 or recent graduates under the age of 30 a job, on-the-job training, a study place or rehabilitation within three months of becoming unemployed. Outreach youth work, which can be street work, detached youth work, mobile youth work, depending on target groups and environments, has been deployed.

The Finnish Youth Co-operation organization, *Allianssi*, has about 120 member organizations. Allianssi is involved in youth information with many web services. It maintains the *Youth Studies Library and Youth Info House*,[12] a web service for youth work specialists. Allianssi co-operates with the Finnish Youth Research Society and the Finnish Youth Research Network.[13] Allianssi publishes the national youth work magazine *Nuorisotyö*[14] and is also responsible for the youth election that is held in connection with the general election. Allianssi is active in the European Youth Forum (YFJ), the European Youth Card Association (EYCA), the European Youth Information and Counselling Agency (ERYICA), the Baltic Youth Forum (BYF) and the Nordic Youth Committee (NUK).

The Finnish Youth Research Society has about 260 members. The Society conducts its own research activities through the Finnish Youth Research Network, founded at the beginning of 1999. This Research Network is a community of researchers who work together with universities, research institutes and various professionals in the field of youth work and youth policy. The Youth Research Network's research has a clear connection to the field of youth policy, producing research information that can be used as support in decision-making. The yearbooks related to youth living conditions are issued in a series of publications of the Finnish Youth Research Society/Network and the Advisory Council of Youth Affairs. Publications on the Internet include memorandums that are mostly accounts of a certain theme, ordered by the Ministry of Education and Culture from the Youth Research Network. The co-operation between the Youth Research Network and the Advisory Council of Youth Affairs[15] has been realising projects and since 2001 producing the Young People's Living Conditions yearbook in collaboration with the National Institute for Health and Welfare.[16] The Youth Barometer published annually by the Council surveys young people's attitudes and values, future expectations and opinions of their social influence. For example, the Tuhti-seminar is organised every second year by youth work practitioners, administrators and youth researchers.

Finland has an Office of the Ombudsman for Children. The basic duty of the Ombudsman for Children is to promote the implementation of children's rights in Finland. Emphasis is placed on promoting children being heard and their participation.[17]

Icelandic Youth Policy

In Iceland the establishment of *Landssamband æskulýðsfélaga LÆF* was built on the idea that young people should be supported, and that the development of young people as active citizens can be best achieved through youth work. The Icelandic Centre for Social Research and Analysis *ICSRA* specializes in Youth Research.

Iceland participates in a large number of the European Union's collaboration activities in the field of education, training and youth, as well as culture and audiovisual services. These activities are to a large extent based on action programmes that are run for a number of years at a time. Through these programmes, funding is provided to support various kinds of activities that facilitate European co-operation in these areas.

In 2007 the Icelandic Parliament produced legislation on youth to support the participation of children and young people in youth activities. In accordance with this legislation The Youth Council *æskulýðsráð* is highlighting an evidence-based approach to policy and the cooperation with policy and research communities in youth policy implementation.

During the Icelandic presidency of the Nordic Council of Ministers in 2009 comparative research was conducted on the wellbeing and lifestyles among Nordic youth, from 16 to 19 years old. The research project was carried out in all the Nordic countries, as well as the Faroe Islands, Greenland and the Åland Islands. During Iceland's 2014 Presidency of the Nordic Council of Ministers the Council focused on green issues and sustainability. The promotion of Nordic culture was also emphasised, for example on co-operation on social media between countries.

Norwegian Youth Policy

In Norway *the Ministry of Children, Equality and Social Inclusion* has the main responsibility for coordinating the government's work related to children and youth. The goal of youth policy in Norway is to secure a good, safe environment in which children and young people can grow to adulthood. The Norwegian Directorate for Education and Training is responsible for the development of primary and secondary education. The Directorate is the executive agency of the *Ministry of Education and Research.* Norway has been the first country to establish a commissioner, or ombudsman, empowered by law to protect children and their rights. Since 1981, the Ombudsman for Children in Norway is charged with promoting the interests of children in both the public and private spheres, paying close attention to changes in the conditions of childhood development.

The Ministry of Culture, Ministry of Education and Research, Ministry of Labour, Ministry of Health and Care Services, Ministry of Justice and the Police, work together on issues related to welfare and living conditions for children and young people.

The Norwegian Children and Youth Council *LNU* is an umbrella organization uniting more than 90 nationwide non-governmental organizations for children and youth. The LNU represents youth in relation to authorities and other significant institutions. Regional Children and Youth Councils operate in 12 of Norway's 19 counties. These councils are umbrella organizations for regional youth organizations. They are consulted on youth related matters at the regional level.

The *NOVA* youth research section conducts research relating mainly to youth issues in Norway. It edits the only journal of youth research in Norwegian (*Tidsskrift for ungdomsforskning*, two issues annually), and organizes The Network of Youth Researchers *Nettverk for ungdomsforskning*, which has about 80 individual members around the country meeting up twice a year.

The Department of Children and Youth Policy is responsible for issues relating to the United Nations Convention on the Rights of the Child and the development of Norwegian child welfare and adoption policies. It is also responsible for developing and coordinating the Ministry's policies toward children and youth, including subsidy programmes to benefit children's and youth organisations, international youth exchanges and services for children and youth in urban environments. The department is also responsible for child welfare agency management at the national level and for administering laws and regulations related to children and youth.

Swedish Youth Policy

The National Council of Swedish Youth Organizations, the *LSU*, was founded in 1948 to increase contacts between young people in the Eastern and the Western Europe. Today the LSU operates as a platform on different matters, on international as well as national topics. Currently one of the most important actors in the youth sector in Sweden is the National Board for Youth Affairs, which is a government agency responsible for the implementation of national youth policy. *The Ministry of Education and Research* is responsible for the coordination of the government's youth policy, as well as issues affecting youth organizations and international cooperation in the youth field. The central government agency, the Swedish National Board for Youth Affairs *Ungdomsstyrelsen* is an important actor in the implementation of youth policy.

In Sweden the local authorities and county councils have a considerable degree of autonomy and many decisions that concern young people are taken at municipal level. The overarching objectives of youth policy are that all young people have genuine access to influence, and all young people have access to welfare. The follow up of youth policy focuses on how these two main objectives are achieved within education, employment, culture and leisure, participation, health and security (Ashing, 2010).

A knowledge-based youth policy is related with youth research and a systematic cross-sectorial follow up on the living conditions of young people are conducted regularly. The National Board for Youth Affairs produce a number of reports that are used by the Government in setting priorities in youth policy. These include the annual compilation of some 80 indicators of development with regard to the conditions of young people, an annual in-depth analysis of a priority topic and a study of attitudes and values among young people that is conducted every four years.

The Swedish Government has assigned to the Swedish Council for Working Life and Social Research *FAS* responsibility for the coordination of Swedish child and youth research.

CHALLENGES

The Nordic Youth co-operation organizations are involved not only with Nordic youth policy and youth research organizations and the Nordic Council of Ministers but also within the European Union, the Council of Europe, the United Nations, the Council of Baltic Sea States, and the Barents Euro-Arctic Council. The co-operation with Barents Council has appointed a Working Group on Youth Policy *WGYP* as a vehicle for youth policy and research co-operation. The Barents Youth Cooperation Office *BYCO* has established in Murmansk for multilateral co-operation in the youth field, which contributes to an improved situation for young people in the Barents Region, as well as a sustainable development of the region. BYCO is financed by the ministries responsible for youth in Finland, Norway, Sweden and Russia. The aim is to provide help, information, guidance and partners for youth groups, organizations and networks that are working with cross-border youth projects in the Barents region.

Although the Nordic youth policy has a long tradition of cooperation with other youth policy bodies it can be recognized that the main objectives, priorities and points of the Nordic youth policy are based on the national level policies of the five Nordic countries, which also guide their international work in the youth field. There are differences that exist with regard to industrial development, urban planning, immigration, asylum and refugee policy, youth segregation, integration processes and ethnic otherness and understanding of immigrant youth identity work. One challenge is how in future to create the conditions for a common Nordic youth policy that is able to reflect and consider the differences and similarities in the development of Nordic countries', and how to strengthen and connect youth across boarders and promote cross-national cooperation on education, employment, social entrepreneurship and political participation.

NOTES

[1] The five Nordic nation states are Denmark, Finland, Iceland, Norway and Sweden and three areas with home rule; the Faroe Islands, Greenland and the Åland Islands.

[2] See more Wikipedia. Korpi (1983) and Esping-Andersen (1990) have explained that the Nordic welfare states have their roots from the social democracy.

[3] The Nordic countries area was for hundreds of years politically based on the kingdoms of Denmark and Sweden.

[4] The Nordic governments' cooperation in the field of research and education is led by the Nordic ministers of education and research.

[5] The Nordic Council of Ministers' cooperation with Estonia, Latvia and Lithuania is directed by guidelines agreed by the Nordic Ministers for Cooperation in July 2013.

[6] The other three were: development of sustainable mining, reduced emissions and workplace-based learning.

[7] http://www.nuorisotutkimusseura.fi/nuorisotutkimus-lehti

[8] http://www.hioa.no/Om-HiOA/Senter-for-velferds-og-arbeidslivsforskning/NOVA/Publikasjoner/Tidsskrift-for-ungdomsforskning

[9] The Nordic Youth research coordinators have been Danish *Joi Bay* (1992-94), Norwegian *Ola Stafseng* (1994-98), Finnish *Helena Helve* (1998-2004) and Swedish *Elisabet Ljungberg* (2005-2009). Coordinators have engaged in the organization of the Nordic Youth Research Network (NYRI) and the biannual conferences (NYRIS), and they facilitated and raised funds for research projects that combined and compared studies in the five countries (e.g. Unga I utkant, Helve, 2003). A youth research coordinator is attached to Nordic Children's and Youth Committee NORDBOK to disseminate knowledge about children and young people.

[10] YOUNG has been published by Sage Publications from 2003; http://you.sagepub.com/.

[11] The Youth Act 72/2006 includes support for young people's growth and independence, promotion of active citizenship, social empowerment of young people and improvement of their growth and living conditions.

[12] http://www.nuorisotiedonkirjasto.fi/links/list; http://www.nuorisotiedonkirjasto.fi/english/

[13] They have published together a magazine *Nuorisotutkimus-lehti* ('Youth Research') and launched research projects relating to young people's living conditions and attitudes in their *Youth Barometers* from 1995.

[14] http://www.alli.fi/julkaisut/nuorisotyo-lehti/

[15] The Advisory Council for Youth Affairs represents expertise in young people's living conditions. Most of its members are nominated by national youth and youth-work organisations.

[16] http://www.minedu.fi/OPM/Nuoriso/?lang=fi

[17] http://www.nuorisotutkimusseura.fi/tapahtumat/tuhti

REFERENCES

Ashing, Inger. (2010). *Youth and youth policy – A Swedish perspective*. National and municipal youth policy at the Swedish National Board for Youth Affairs. Ungdomsstyrelsen.

Bay, Joi, Drotner, Kirsten, Jörgensen, Birthe, Nielsen, Elo, & Zeuner, Lilli (Eds.). (1985). *Årbog for ungdomskulturforskning* (Yearbook of youth culture studies). Copenhagen: Borgen.

Björklund, Anders, & Fredriksson, Peter. (2012). Economics of education: Policies and effects. *The Nordic Economic Policy Review*. TemaNord 2012:544 Nordic Council of Ministers, Copenhagen.

Dahl, Annica, & Björklund, Fredrik. (2008). Youth Policy of the Nordic Council of Ministers – Regional cooperation of great importance for the young people in the Nordic countries. Swedish Chair of the Nordic Children's and Youth Committee (NORDBUK), Stockholm, pp 50-54. Forum 21 [Policy]. http://www.coe.int/t/dg4/youth/Source/Resources/Forum21/Issue_No11/N11_YP_Nordic_council_en.pdf (March 2014).

Esping, Andersen, & Gösta. (1990). *The three worlds of welfare capitalism*. Princeton, NJ: Princeton University Press.

Fornäs, Johan, & Bolin, Göran. (1995). *Youth culture in late modernity*. Sage Publications Ltd.

Gudmundsson, Gestur. (2006). Wrestling with(in) the welfare state. An overview of Nordic Youth Research Papers 79, 2006. http://www.raco.cat/index.php/papers/article/viewFile/51824/57553 (March 2014).

Halvorsen, Bjørn, Hansen, Ole-Johnny, & Tägtström, Jenny. (2013). *Young people on the edge*. The Nordic Council of Ministers.

Helve, Helena. (Ed. and co-authored). (2003). *Ung i utkant. Aktuell forskning om glesbygdsungdomar i Norden* (Youth in fringe). TemaNord, Köpenhamn: Nordiska ministerrådet.

Helve, Helena. (2009). The Finnish perspective: youth work, policy and research. In Griet Veschelden et al. (Eds.), *The history of youth work in Europe: relevance for youth policy today* (pp. 117-129). Strasbourg: Council of Europe Publishing.

Helve, Helena. (2002). Finnish young people and youth policy in Finland. In Jean-Charles Lagrée (Ed.), *Rolling youth, rocking society* (pp. 93-102). Paris: UNESCO.

Helve, Helena, Leccardi, Carmen, & Kovacheva Siyka. (2005). Youth research in Europe. In H. Helve & G. Holm (Eds.), *Contemporary youth research. Local expressions and global connections* (pp. 15-32). Aldershot and Burlington: Ashgate.

Hoikkala, Tommi, & Suurpää, Leena. (2005). Finnish youth cultural research and its relevance to youth policy. *Young, 13*(3), 285-312.

International Labor Office. (2012). *Youth guarantees: A response to the youth employment crisis?* Employment: Policy Brief. http://www.ilo.org/wcmsp5/groups/public/-ed_emp/documents/publication/wcms_209468.pdf

Jansson, J. O., Helve, H., & Wichström, J. O. (2003). *Youth research in Sweden, 1995-2001. An evaluation report.* Report to FAS (Forskningsrådet för arbetsliv och socialvetenskap). 1 March, 2003, pp. 29-31.

Karlsson, Kristina, Olaison, Anna, & Skill, Karin. (2010). *Mapping and characterizing Nordic everyday life research.* Arbetsnotat Nr 343, Maj 2010. ISRN LiU-TEMA-T-WP-343-SE, Linköping: University Electronic Press.

Korpi, Walter. (1983). *The democratic class struggle.* London and Boston: Routledge & K. Paul.

Nieminen, Juha. (1998). *Nuorisossa tulevaisuus – suomalaisen nuorisotyön historia* (In youth is the future – The history of the Finnish youth work). Helsinki: Lasten keskus.

Olofsson, Jonas, & Wadensjö, Eskil. (2012). *Youth, education and labour market in the Nordic countries. Similar but not the same.* Friedrich Ebert Stiftung, November 2012, http://library.fes.de/pdf-files/id/09468.pdf

Peltola, Marja. (2010). *Youth work in Finland – Finding ways for intercultural opening.* National report for the project 'Moving Societies towards Integration?' Finnish Youth Research Network & Finnish Youth Research Society. Web publications 38.

The Economist. (2013). The Nordic countries. The next supermodel. Politicians from both right and left could learn from the Nordic countries. February 2.

INTERNET REFERENCES

Finnish Youth Policy

Finnish Advisory Council of Youth Affairs: http://www.minedu.fi/OPM/Nuoriso/nuorisoasiain_neuvottelukunta/?lang=en (January 2014).

Finnish Advisory Council for Youth Affairs NUORA: http://www.minedu.fi/OPM/Nuoriso/nuorisoasiain_neuvottelukunta/?lang=en (January 2014).

Finnish Government's Child and Youth Policy Programme 2007-2011: http://www.minedu.fi/export/sites/default/OPM/Julkaisut/2008/liitteet/opm21.pdf?lang=fi (March 2014).

Finnish Nuorisotyö-lehti. http://www.alli.fi/julkaisut/nuorisotyo-lehti/ (March 2014).

Finnish Office of the Ombudsman for Children. http://www.lapsiasia.fi/en/frontpage (March 2014).

Finnish Youth Research Journal. Nuorisotutkimus: http://www.nuorisotutkimusseura.fi/nuorisotutkimus-lehti (March 2014).

Finnish Youth Cooperation. Allianssi. http://www.alli.fi/english/ (March 2014).

Finnish Youth Studies Library and Youth Info House. http://alli.fi/nuorisotiedon+kirjasto/english/ (March 2014).

Finnish Youth Research Society. http://www.nuorisotutkimusseura.fi/ (March 2014).

Finnish Youth Research Network. http://www.nuorisotutkimusseura.fi/en (March 2014).

Finnish Youth Barometers: http://www.minedu.fi/OPM/Nuoriso/nuorisoasiain_neuvottelukunta/ julkaisut/index.html?lang=fi (March 2014).

Nuorisotiedon kirjasto. http://www.nuorisotiedonkirjasto.fi/english/ (January 2014).

International cooperation: http://www.minedu.fi/OPM/Nuoriso/kansainvalinen_yhteistyo/ kansainvaeliset_jaerjestoet_ja_organisaatiot/?lang=en (January 2014).

The Finnish Youth Act 72/2006: http://www.minedu.fi/export/sites/default/OPM/Nuoriso/ nuorisopolitiikka/liitteet/HE_nuorisolaki_eng.pdf (January 2014).

Youth Policy in Finland. A report by an international review group (1997). The Council of Europe (Ulrike Fremerey, Chairperson and Howard Williamson Rapporteur): http://www.coe.int/ t/dg4/youth/Source/IG_Coop/YP_Finland_en.pdf (January 2014).

Danish Youth Policy

Bertel Haarder Danish Youth Policy Forum 21 [Policy], pp. 59-69.
    http://www.youthpolicy.org/national/Denmark_2008_Youth_Policy_Article.pdf (March 2014).
    http://www.coe.int/t/dg4/youth/Source/Resources/Forum21/Issue_No11/N11_YP_Denmark_en.pdf
    Danish Youth Council DUF http://orgs.tigweb.org/danish-youth-council-duf (March 2014).

Icelandic Youth Policy

Landssamband æskulýðsfélaga Iceland Youth Council: http://www.aeska.is/en/federation-of-icelandic- youth-organizations/ (March 2014).

Youth – Voice of the Future 2010: Participation by all 2010. Youth Council æskulýðsráð http://www.menntamalaraduneyti.is/radherra/raedur/nr/5724 (January 2014).

Norwegian Youth Policy

Norwegian Ministry of Children, Equality and Social Inclusion. http://www.regjeringen.no/en/ dep/bld.html?id=298 (January 2014).

Norwegian Ministry of Education and Research: http://www.regjeringen.no/en/dep/kd.html?id=586 (January 2014).

The Ombudsman for Children in Norway. http://www.regjeringen.no/en/dep/bld/BLD-arbeider-for- at/Offices-and-agencies-associated-with-the-Ministry-of-Children-and-Equality/The-Ombudsman- for-Children-in-Norway.html?id=418030 (March 2014).

Norwegian Children and Youth Council LNU. http://www.lnu.no/pages/engelsk.aspx?nr=10332 (January 2014).

Tidsskrift for ungdomsforskning. http://www.ungdomsforskning.no/ (January 2014).

Nettverk for ungdomsforskning. http://www.nova.no/id/37.0 (January 2014).

The Ministry of Children and Equality in Norway: http://www.regjeringen.no/en/ dep/bld/Topics/Children-and-youth.html?id=1015 (January 2014).

NYRIS 11: http://www.nyris11.com/ (January 2014).

The Research Programme Youth Culture in Sweden:
    http://books.google.fi/books?id=kDgHYmVCehUC&pg=PP8&lpg=PP8&dq=The+Research+
    Programme+Youth+Culture+in+Sweden&source=bl&ots=HqYQD-8MRg&sig=F-
    qiwWhUAuDc6R9l7ApTkrlkVRA&hl=fi&ei=lIM8TYvOF8SOswbb_ezzBg&sa=X&oi=book_
    result&ct=result&resnum=1&ved=0CBsQ6AEwAA#v=onepage&q=The%20Research%
    20Programme%20Youth%20Culture%20in%20Sweden&f=false (January 2014).

Institute of social research NOVA. http://www.nova.no/id/1.0?language=1 (January 2014).

Swedish Youth Policy

Nyamko Sabuni. Priorities of the 2009 Swedish Presidency of the EU in the youth field http://www.coe.int/t/dg4/youth/Source/Resources/Forum21/Issue_No13/N13_Swedish_EU_en.pdf (January 2014).

The Swedish Government's youth policy (2009). Ministry of Integration and Gender Equality, September 2009. http://www.regeringen.se/content/1/c6/13/14/60/5fedc2f3.pdf (January 2014).

Youth Today. A description of young people's living conditions, The Swedish National Board for Youth Affairs. http://www.ungdomsstyrelsen.se/ad2/user_documents/Youth_Today_2009_ENG2.pdf (January 2011).

Introduction to Youth Policy – Swedish and Turkish Perspectives http://youth-partnership-eu.coe.int/youth-partnership/documents/EKCYP/Youth_Policy/docs/Better_understanding/Policy/Inlaga-ENG-1.pdf (January 2011).

The National Council of Swedish Youth Organizations, the LSU http://www.lsu.se/adimo4/Site/LSU/web/default.aspx?p=130&t=h401&AspxAutoDetectCookieSupport=1 (January 2011).

The Ministry of Education and Research. http://www.sweden.gov.se/sb/d/2063 (March 2014).

Ungdomsstyrelsen. The Swedish National Board for Youth Affairs http://www.ungdomsstyrelsen.se/english_main/0,2693,,00.html (January 2011).

National Report on Youth Policy in Norway (2003). Report by the international team of experts. The Council of Europe. http://www.coe.int/t/dg4/youth/Source/IG_Coop/YP_Norway_en.pdf. (January 2011).

Nordic Youth Policy

Barents Euro-Arctic Council. http://www.beac.st/in_English/Barents_Euro-Arctic_Council.iw3 (March 2014).

Barents Euro Arctic Working Group on Youth Policy: http://www.barentsyouth.org/the-barents-euro-arctic-working-group-on-youth-policy.72315.en.html (January 2014).

Barents Youth Cooperation Office BYCO. http://www.barentsyouth.org/the-barents-youth-cooperation-office-byco.375031-72314.html (March 2014).

Council of Baltic Sea States. http://www.cbss.org/ (January 2014). http://www.coe.int/t/dg4/youth/Source/Resources/Forum21/Issue_No11/N11_YP_Nordic_council_en.pdf. (March 2014).

NORDBUK – Nordic Children's and Youth Committee: http://en.iu.dk/grants-and-scholarships/nordbuk-nordic-childrens-and-youth-committee (March 2014).

Nordic Youth Council. http://www.norden.org/en/nordic-council/nordic-youth-council-nyc (March 2014.)

Nordic Council of Ministers: http://www.norden.org/en/nordic-council-of-ministers (January 2011). http://www.norden.org/en/nordic-council-of-ministers/the-presidency/sweden-apos-s-programme-for-the-presidency-2013 (March 2014).

http://www.norden.org/en/nordic-council-of-ministers/ministers-for-cooperation-mr-sam/estonia-latvia-and-lithuania/guidelines-for-the-nordic-council-of-ministers-cooperation-with-estonia-latvia-and-lithuania-2014 (March 2014).

http://www.nordiclabourjournal.org/nyheter/news-2013/article.2013-12-08.2538298704 (March 2014).

http://www.norden.org/en/nordic-council-of-ministers/council-of-ministers/nordic-council-of-ministers-for-education-and-research-mr-u (March 2014).

Nordic Region: A Green Climate Leader. http://www.norden.org/fi/julkaisut/julkaisut/2010-768 (March 2014).

Nordic Youth Networks and Programmes: http://www.ookpik.org/youth-networks-and-programs/ (March 2014).

Nordic Youth Research Information. http://www.childwatch.uio.no/research/youth-issues/nordic-youth-research-institute.html (March 2014).

YOUNG – The Nordic Journal of Youth Studies: http://www.sagepub.com/journals/Journal201637 (March 2014).

MIRIAM TEUMA

THE DEVELOPMENT AND IMPLEMENTATION OF YOUTH POLICY IN MALTA

Up until the 1990s, there was no youth policy in Malta. There were education policies, health policies and other related policies that impacted on and influenced the lives of young people, but there was no dedicated and coordinated policy for youth.

What prefigured the development of such a policy in the 1990s was the role of the Catholic Church and the British presence in providing youth work and related services for young people. But this tended to be at once paternalistic, directional and what was deemed character forming in light of Christian morals and mores. Youth work and related youth services in Malta had their antecedents in the work of the Catholic Church and its voluntary organisations such as the Society of Christian Doctrine, Catholic Action and the Salesians.

After gaining independence from Britain in 1964, the emerging state was too preoccupied and distracted by other issues to adopt a more assertive role as regards youth policy. What resulted was a patchwork; a miscellany, of youth work practices and youth service provision. As such, services and programmes for young people were delivered piecemeal by a voluntary sector that lacked the organisational capacity, financial resources and professional human capital to implement a coherent and effective youth policy.

In 1993, the newly established Ministry of Youth and Arts published the first document on youth policy. This coincided with a number of other significant developments. Following on a National Youth Conference – the first of its kind in Malta – the National Youth Council was established in 1991. Independent of government, it initiated discussions and work on a range of issues including international relations, social action, education, employment and their relation to and relevance for young people. In 1992, the University of Malta established an Institute of Youth Studies (now the Department of Youth and Community Studies), to provide training for those who wished to pursue a professional career as youth and community workers. The first group of graduate students founded the Maltese Association of Youth Workers (MAY) in 1998, which subsequently published a Code of Ethics for Youth Workers in 2001. In addition to campaigning for state funding for youth work, the association also advocated full professional recognition and status for youth workers as well as enhanced employment opportunities.

Malta's first National Youth Policy (1993)[1] sought to provide young people and policy makers with clear objectives in the political, social and economic development of the nation and also provided for periodic revision of the policy in

B. Belton (ed.), 'Cadjan – Kiduhu': Global Perspectives on Youth Work, 165–172.

light of changing circumstances – a national conference on youth policy and youth affairs was envisaged every three years. The Ministry for Youth and Arts had responsibility for implementing the policy. In addition to its own actions and initiatives it was to support those of the National Youth Council and voluntary youth organisations as well as promoting a cross-ministry approach in addressing youth related issues. The roles of the National Youth Council and that of the University of Malta were formally recognised. The policy also set out a number of areas for action in relation to youth: information, employment, culture, equal opportunity, health, participation, values, special needs, family and parenthood, intergenerational communication, enterprise and mobility.

The new policy, while reasonably comprehensive, was largely aspirational, weak on specifics and lacking in details. These deficiencies might have been overcome if the policy had been accompanied or followed by a comprehensive strategic implementation plan. While positively recognising and asserting the role and place of young people in Maltese society, the tone of the document was patriarchal, circumspect and cautious, as evidenced by some of the principles underpinning the policy – 'seek to understand the just aspirations of youth', 'assist young people to overcome the inherent difficulties of adolescence', 'seek to create an awareness of their responsibilities towards the family and towards society'.

However, due to change in government and other contingencies, the policy was never effectively implemented. The National Youth Policy published in 1999,[2] was in large part a reiteration of that of 1993. The tone and approach of the document was more open and youth oriented in some respects: account is taken of 'youth culture' and the need to promote 'social justice' and for 'sensitivity to the needs and aspirations of youth'. There was recognition of the need to create an environment in which 'youth find fulfilment' and for understanding the potential of young people 'to make responsible choices in their lives'. The rights of young people, including the right to work, were recognised and the role of non-formal education acknowledged. However, there was an increased focus on 'problem youth'. An entire section of the policy document, which also included education and employment, was devoted to 'social problems affecting youth'.

In 2001, resulting from its representation on the European Steering Committee for Youth, a review of youth policy in Malta by an international team of experts was initiated. The policy review team visited Malta in 2003 with three primary objectives:
– to advise on the national youth policy
– to identify components of youth policy for a general European approach to youth policy and
– to contribute to a learning process about the development and implementation of youth policy.

The National Report on youth policy was presented in late 2003 and formed the basis for a revised National Youth Policy that was published in 2004.

The National Youth Policy (2004)[3] continued with the themes and concerns of the previous policies. It aimed to ensure social justice, opportunity and equity; to promote the authenticity of the identity, diversity and responsible independence of young people; and to promote the active citizenship and participation of young people. The approach to those deemed at risk – 'young people who require particular attention' – was softened but remained a matter of focus and concern. The influence of 'the European' approach to youth issues was reflected in reference to such issues as empowerment, access to information, lifelong learning and the role of European Union programmes in youth mobility.

The most significant feature of the 2004 policy document, however, was its reference to the 'need' for a national youth agency. The agency would co-ordinate and monitor a cross-sectoral policy on youth that included advocacy, research and data collection, support for youth organisations, enhanced local youth activities, participation in international activities, and provide for the monitoring and revision of the National Youth Policy.

Despite these advances in youth policy development however, the period 1990–2010 was to witness little progress 'on the ground' in terms of provision and coordination of services and opportunities for young people. The services and opportunities available remained the responsibility of traditional mainstream providers: ministries and government agencies in areas such as health, education, and the environment, as well as the voluntary youth sector. There was also no coordinated process or instruments put in place to implement youth policy. While the new emphasis on policy development mirrored similar trends at European Union level, the approach in Malta continued to be characterised by a more paternalistic and traditional view of young people and their place in society, with an added focus on those deemed at risk. Throughout the period, youth policy in Malta remained consistent in its vision. While the policy evolved towards a more youth centred approach and the growing influence of European youth policy becomes more evident, it remained a policy that sought to balance what might be described as the 'rights and responsibilities' of young people.

Malta's accession to the European Union in 2004 provided it with new sources of funding, through *Youth in Action*, as well as a new and expanded policy horizon, through the Youth Working Party and the Council of Youth Ministers. But Malta continued to lack a coordinated and focused response to meeting the needs and aspirations of young people. Policy implementation was effectively left to individual ministries and state agencies, much of whose focus was sectoral, system based and thematic rather that youth orientated, and a voluntary youth sector that lacked both the professional and organisational capacities as well as the financial and human resources to implement policy.

It was partially in response to these concerns that a new National Youth Policy for the period 2010–2013 was initiated.[4] The policy had a number of significant features. First, it was based on an extensive consultation with all the relevant stakeholders. Second, it established an instrument for policy implementation, Agenzija Zghazagh, the National Youth Agency. Third, it emerged against the background of a new policy initiative at European Union level, the renewed framework for European cooperation in the youth field (2010–2018). It was the first policy approach to embed youth policy in the context of UN Conventions and European policy documents and to adopt a particular vision:

This policy sets out a vision of young people who are enthusiastic to be successful and empowered to achieve their potential, while living in solidarity as active citizens. It is aimed at improving the quality of life of young people by promoting their initiatives, participation in decision-making and social life, as well as by supporting easier transition from youth to adult status and the world of work and lifelong learning.

Its mission statement was

to endeavour to address the holistic development of young people and advocates young people's needs on behalf of our community.

In formulating the policy, young people and youth organisations including the National Youth Council, other youth organisations and relevant stakeholders were consulted, and previous policy approaches were considered and evaluated as well as European Union youth policy. The policy aimed at empowering young people to achieve their potential while living in solidarity as active citizens, as well as seeking to address their holistic development. It advocated underpinning principles of accessibility, sustainability, solidarity, diversity and equality; while also seeking to promote efficiency, effectiveness, accountability and research.

The policy was based on an interwoven tapestry of eleven vertical themes to facilitate mainstreaming of youth issues and five horizontal cross cutting threads that informed all the themes. The vertical themes included education, employment, health and wellbeing, youth justice, transitions and vulnerability, culture and the arts, community cohesion and volunteering, sport, leisure, the information society and environment. The horizontal cross cutting threads were participation, youth information, social inclusion, the family and mobility. For each theme a policy statement was presented as well as a strategy that sought to promote and encouraged various actions and desired outcomes. The policy also emphasised and provided for policy mainstreaming, monitoring and evaluation.

While the policy remained largely aspirational, even idealistic, it did contain within it the potential for a more practical approach to implementation. The means for such a practical approach was Agenzija Zghazagh, the National Youth Agency, which was established in late 2010 and commenced operating in February 2011.

The aim in establishing Agenzija Zghazagh (the agency) was to develop youth services and mainstream youth related policy issues. Its overall objective was to provide a coherent, cohesive and unified approach to youth related policy issues. For young people, it was to enhance participation, empowerment and dialogue as well as expand supports and services. For policy makers is was to bring about a change in attitudes and work culture to include a youth perspective, greater coherence in policy making and better data and information on youth. The mission statement of the new agency was to 'manage and implement the National Youth Policy to promote and safeguard the interests of young people'.

Whatever the aspirations and declarations, the intent in establishing Agenzija Zghazagh was clear: it was to be the national instrument for implementing the National Youth Policy and for effectively ensuring that the policy impacted directly, consistently and positively on the lives of young people and, if not determining their future, playing an active role in supporting young people in shaping that future both as individuals and citizens.

But what do we mean when we speak of Agenzija Zghazagh as a national instrument of youth policy implementation?

Youth policy aims, objectives, principles, instruments, tools, processes and methods have been the subject of much debate and reflection. The renewed framework for European cooperation in the youth field (2010–2018) in seeking to meet its aims of creating more and equal opportunities for all young people in education and in the labour market and in promoting the active citizenship, social inclusion and solidarity of all young people, adopted a dual approach: specific initiatives in the youth field (i.e. policies and actions specifically targeted at young people in areas such as non-formal learning, participation, voluntary activities, youth work, mobility and information) and mainstreaming initiatives (i.e. initiatives to enable a cross-sectoral approach where due account is taken of youth issues when formulating, implementing and evaluating policies and actions in other policy fields which have a significant impact on the lives of young people). As was the case with Malta's National Youth Policy, the renewed framework provided guiding principles as well as a number of fields of action. The renewed framework also presented implementation instruments both for the youth field and other related policy fields: knowledge building and evidence-based youth policy, mutual learning, progress reporting, monitoring, consultations and structured dialogue, and mobilisation of EU programmes and funds.

The experiences of Agenzija Zghazagh since its establishment in 2010, affords us the opportunity of considering and analysing the nature of youth policy instruments and their roles in youth policy implementation and development.

As the instrument of national youth policy implementation, Agenzija Zghazagh set itself two inter-related tasks: one relating to specific initiatives in the youth field and the other relating to youth policy mainstreaming. With regard to specific youth initiatives, the agency initiated direct and indirect services, programmes, projects and opportunities for young people and youth organisations as well as the provision of facilities and other material supports. These included the first youth cafes and youth hubs in Malta where young people could associate in a friendly and safe environment as well as avail of support services; youth activity centres where youth organisations and groups could conduct training and other non-formal learning activities; an extensive youth empowerment programme at both national and local level; and targeted projects for young people in the arts, literature, music, drama, volunteering and community activism.

In providing such direct and indirect supports it has often worked in cooperation with other ministries, state agencies, voluntary youth and other organisations and associations as well as with the private sector.

As well as the provision of services and programmes, Agenzija Zghazagh has also sought to communicate and listen to young people and youth organisations and to strengthen the evidence-base for future policy development and implementation. One of its first initiatives was to establish Youth Information Malta, an interactive web portal that both disseminates and accesses information and data, as well as Kellimini.com, an online personal support service and a Youth Information One-Stop Shop. It also oversees and coordinates the Structured Dialogue in Malta. Research has been prioritised with the publication of the first ever study of Maltese young people's perceptions of themselves, their families, communities and society as well as a study of leisure activities among young people. Other initiatives have also been actively pursued at European level through Agenzija Zghazagh's engagement with, among others, the European Youth Information and Counselling Agency (ERYICA), the European Knowledge Centre for Youth Policy (EKCYP), the European Youth Card Association (EYCA) and the Euro Med Youth Platform (EYP). The agency also oversaw the drafting of a Youth Work Professional Bill that provides for the statutory recognition of youth work as a profession in Malta.

It was perhaps inevitable that in its first years of operation Agenzija Zghazagh would focus, in addition to strengthening its corporate base and identity, on 'core' youth policy activities: provision of direct or indirect services, programmes and initiatives and the promotion of youth participation and non-formal learning through youth work. As a consequence perhaps, the agency has been less focused on its other stated task: policy mainstreaming. While it has participated on a number of policy related committees and working parties as well as on a cross-sectoral policy implementation group on youth issues, policy mainstreaming has lagged behind other policy initiatives in terms of implementation priorities.

The reasons for this, other than the aforementioned, are perhaps understandable: policy mainstreaming is more challenging, more problematic, and less amenable to direct control, action and impact. But there is perhaps another reason. All organisations have a tendency to revert to type. Each has its own bailiwick, its particular expertise, its comfort zone, its raison d'être, generally recognised and often unchallenged by others. In its own field, Agenzija Zghazgh can exercise its remit and prerogative through direct and indirect action, but when dealing with ministries, peer organisations in related fields of activity, such as education and training, health and wellbeing, arts and culture, it cannot act as a primus inter pares. It must adopt a different approach: one of cooperation, advice, support and advocacy.

Agenzija Zghazagh gives evidence of fulfilling many aspects of effective policy instruments. It is at once a provider, both direct and indirect of a wide range of general and tailored programmes, projects, initiatives, opportunities and campaigns for young people, often in cooperation with other stakeholders both public and private. It provides not only information and personal support services, but also communicates effectively with young people and actively engages with them in seeking their views on policies and issues that impact on their lives. In addition, with its focus on research, reporting and data collection it provides for an evidence-based approach to future policy and decision-making. Lastly, it offers the potential of being an instrument for mainstreaming youth issues and promoting a cross-sectoral approach.

If the agency is to be an effective national instrument of policy implementation and development it needs to be a flexible and innovative one: a provider, a communicator, a listener, a coordinator, a leader, a compiler, an evaluator, a researcher, a supporter, an adviser, an advocate and a repository of knowledge, expertise and experience. How these different facets interact with each other, how some take precedents over others in shifting contexts and situations, how they are all to be kept in equilibrium can only be a matter of conjecture. The result however should not be a cacophony of policy aims, instruments and processes but rather, as in Yeats's phrase a 'great melody' in helping and supporting young people to fulfil their needs and aspirations.

CONCLUSION

Up until the 1990s, Malta lacked a dedicated and coordinated youth policy. Such a policy took form in the period 1990–2010, along with the emergence of a professionally trained cohort of youth workers. However, an effective instrument for implementing youth policy was lacking until the establishment of Agenzija Zghazagh in 2010. Agenzija Zghazagh gives evidence and hope that it can provide Malta with an effective instrument not only in implementing existing youth policy but also in the development and implementation of future policy.

However, the agency's focus to date has been on what might be described as 'core' youth policy activities such as those set out in the renewed framework for European cooperation in the youth field: youth information, participation, research, youth work, non-formal learning. The greater challenge is to develop more varied, dedicated and selective support instruments that will both share the burden and expand the capacity of effective youth policy implementation in terms of youth work, service provision and practice. The public sector, relevant ministries, government agencies, educational and training institutions, the voluntary sector, youth NGOs and other voluntary organisations, and the private sector – including banks, businesses, and enterprises – all have a role to play.

Given Malta's size, history, resources and capacities, Agenzija Zghazagh may prove an effective instrument for youth policy implementation. Other larger countries, with different historical experiences and cultures, greater resources and more capacity must determine their own instruments for policy implementation. What does not appear to be in doubt is that such instruments are necessary. "Covenants without sword are but words", commented Thomas Hobbes, the supreme political realist. Youth policies without effective instruments to implement such policies are but words. What such instruments can or should be is a matter for those who make and decide on policy.

NOTES

[1] www.agenzijazghazgah/downloads/policy_93_english_final.pdf
[2] www.agenzijazghazagh/downloads/yp_99_1_merged.pdf

TEUMA

[3] www.agenzijazghazagh/downloads/National_Youth Policy_2004.pdf
[4] www.agenzijazghazagh/downloads/0662_001.pdf

EMINA BUŽINKIĆ

BRIEF ON YOUTH IN CONTEMPORARY CROATIAN SOCIETY

One might argue that Croatian youth does not differ from youth in other countries; neighbouring nations, other European states or any other youth population anywhere in the world. However, sociologically and politically speaking, Croatian youth have a history of being caught up in political, social and economic crises and transitions. The disintegration of Yugoslavia followed by violent armed conflicts burdened the young with an inheritance of loss, crime, corruption, robbery and death. This experience has left a legacy of deep social trauma and insecurity that together challenge and affect the quality of the everyday life of young. The history of contemporary Croatian society since its independence has given root to huge social differences, economic instability and lack of opportunities and prospects for young people.

A quarter of the Croatian population is aged between 15 and 30. Many are socially marginalised, politically underrepresented and economically disempowered. Over the course of the past twenty years politicians have created a notion of socio-economic development that emphasises the role and strengths of young people and their potential as a social resource, but daily, youth are mainly perceived as a social problem or a social group that causes problems, being principally described via words and images relating to delinquency, alcoholism, smoking, misbehaving, irresponsibility and like attitudes and behaviour.[1] This discourse ignores or fails to understand youth as a current or actually present resource, requiring social trust and political investment.

There are over a million young people in Croatia who are burdened with the 'social greying' process, which to some extent also pertains in other European contexts, together with an effective prolonging 'youthhood' (which might be thought of as the time between childhood and adulthood). However, also like other societies, Croatia is deeply threatened with a rapid decrease in the number of young people since many of them, primarily due to economic insecurities, do not plan to have more than one child. This is not sufficient for the demographic renewal of society. However the generation between 30 and 40 experience much the same life conditions as those between 20 and 30 (later independence connected to insecure employment, low wages, lack of housing, prolonged education, etc). According to 'Youth in Time of Crisis' 73.5% live with both or one parent (Ilišin et al., 2012) and are unable to become independent, which would include starting their own families.

There is a need to be aware of different needs, aspirations and expressions; subcultures and age-groups exist within the Croatian population. However, at the

B. Belton (ed.), 'Cadjan – Kiduhu': Global Perspectives on Youth Work, 173–176.

same time common social characteristics and interests exist, but one of the abiding concerns of contemporary society is adequate social integration of youth, which requires appropriate social conditions (Furlong & Guidikova, 2001; Younnis et al., 2002; Ilišin et al., 2012). However, in Croatia (mirroring other contexts) youth policies for the social integration of youth have mainly failed in strengthening the individual and group role and integration of youth in social life.

Since 2002, when the first National Youth Action Plan was adopted by the state no significant changes have been established in the everyday life of youth.

Youth unemployment and job insecurity work together with other anxieties brought about by neoliberal polices. In the past 20 years unemployment has risen from about 30% of youth to around 55%.[2] This is the third highest rate of youth unemployment in Europe (behind Spain and Greece).[3] Every seventh young person lives in a family on the verge of poverty, one third of them live in families facing daily difficulties in covering bare necessities of life. About 20% live in families, which have difficulties in financing most of the needs of family members. Young people in many families are exposed to limited perspective in life and are at risk of poverty (Ilišin et al., 2012). In this situation most of young choose to continue their education. Around 80% of young people would choose or have chosen the type of education, which would fit with their aspiration of finding a secure job and ensuring a livelihood. More than 40% of them hope to work in public administration (Ilišin et al., 2012) reflecting aspiration for secure job with steady wages.

But despite huge political campaigns on education reform, the system has suffered from enormous financial cuts. There is also widespread dissatisfaction with the system that has failed to adequately respond to policy reform (known as the 'Bologna Process'). The national secondary school leaving exam (in Croatian *Matura*) has also given rise to protests. Introducing of *matura* has, for the first time in Croatian history, brought secondary school pupils on to streets, articulating their demands of the Ministry of Education. Students have also protested against the neo-liberal concept of education that results in high admission and enrolment fees, while supplying an unsatisfactory standard of education. Students have blockaded and occupied universities throughout Croatia for several months,[4] while many students and civic activists have publicly spoken against corruption in higher education.[5] Huge controversy has been shaking the Croatian educational system in past decade around the introduction of sexual education, pitting conservative Catholic groups against proactive civic groups. This has resulted in Croatian youth having little or no education about sexually responsible behaviour, despite figures indicate that early sexual activity, insufficient use of birth control, early pregnancies and STD's are on the rise.[6]

Many current discussions in Croatian society mourn the loss of the role of education in raising the social awareness of young people. It seems that much of the resulting vacuum has been filled by celebrity/fashion culture. However, attitudes of pupils, teachers and principles show deep dissatisfaction with the contribution of education in terms of developing democratic citizenship.[7] Insights into social and political participation of youth have shown poor representation of young in political structures. Figures show that only about 4% of youth have any interest in local legal and executive politics (DIM, 2004). Less than 1% take any significant notice of the activity of the Croatian Parliament,[8] the weak position of youth branches of political parties and youth in party governing, etc. All of the research undertaken in the past twenty years on youth views expose extremely low trust in political institutions and, related to that, low participation. Inclination to volunteering and other forms of civic participation is not of interest to the majority of young people. It is noted in a study relating to the political socialisation of Croatian secondary students[9] that young people have:

- low political literacy
- low understanding of basic political terms and processes
- deep disappointment with the competence of politicians.

At the same time there is a growing non-democratic presence among young people, often encompassing authoritarian political views. 'Youth in time of crisis' points out 'retraditionalisation' of youth views and intolerance towards Serbs and Roma is expressed twice as often than it was during times of conflict by their parents. There is also growing intolerance towards sexual minorities. Existence of certain antidemocratic attitudes, values and patterns among youth is confirmed by the part some youth are taking in violence focused on minority groups (Šalaj, 2005).

Youth in Croatia are rarely introduced to mechanisms and ways of contribution to social change. However, education on human rights, non-violence and democracy is not part of Croatian curricula. Therefore, youth groups and civic organisations generally advocate introducing civic education into schools. The first experimental programme in schools was concluded this year[10] and recommendations have been given to help ensure some long-term changes in field of youth participation in general.

Croatia is challenged with healing the scars resulting from the marginalisation of youth and removing the devastating results of pushing youth into pockets of social exclusion. Current discussions on priorities of a new National Youth Action Plan (NYAP), place the building of trust in political institutions and their capability of implementing and placing youth policies to the fore. However, considering previous experiences, not much is expected in terms of results. The NYAP is expressing concerns about the level of trust and support given to Youth Organisations by state institutions in terms of affirming youth values, their proactive change making and their role in integration actors of disengaged and marginalised youth. The given of such trust would actually mean giving a chance to the youth sector to overcome their marginal position and become one of the solution makers.

NOTES

[1] Analysis of media coverage used at youth training of Croatian Youth Network since 2006. Croatian Youth Network (Cro. Mreža Mladih Hrvatske, www.mmh.hr) is a national youth council and umbrella organization advocating for youth rights and better socio-political representation. It comprises of over 60 youth organizations and has operated since 2002.

[2] Data of EUROSTAT and Croatian Employment Agency for 2013.

[3]   According to EUROSTAT data for 2013 and back.
[4]   www.slobodnifilozofski.hr, www.nvurh.hr
[5]   In 2010 State Attorneys Office has together with Police revealed one of the biggest corruption scandals in Croatian society discovering buying exams and final diplomas at Faculty of Economics.
[6]   The number of early pregnancies or STDs is rather low, according to comparative researches, but still growing. Source: www.cesi.hr.
[7]   Research 'Human Rights in Primary Schools', Human Rights Centre, 2009.
[8]   The latest parliamentary elections in 2011 have introduced a new structure with only two MPs under 30 (www.sabor.hr).
[9]   The study was prepared by GONG and Faculty of Political Science in 2011.
[10] Croatian Youth Network, Centre for Peace Studies and GONG have proposed experimental educational programme in 6 Croatian schools based on previously adopted curricula. The programme was implemented within project 'New era of democracy and human rights into Croatian schools' financed under IPA of the European Commission. Ministry of Education has supported implementation of the programme in additional 6 schools.

PRACTICE

INDRA KHERA

DEMANDING LIVES, DIFFICULT PATHS

INTRODUCTION

This chapter relates to my role as a housing support and development officer in 2010, but it also looks at several practices relevant to youth work more generally.

At that time I was working closely with three young mothers in a hostel in central London. The young women would often informally drop into the office, but structured monthly support and development sessions were also carried out.

According to hostel policy, as a support and development worker, my role was to 'support young people to help them turn their lives around, and develop to their potential'. It would have been easy to fall into a missionary role as a 'helper' in such a situation, but I judged that would neither be appropriate or helpful, given how I saw my function as a practitioner.

The young women with whom I worked, in my judgment (and I think from their own perspective) did not need to 'turn their lives around'. I witnessed them being proactive, determined mothers who were focused on finding paths to goals which *they* had established with little help from myself, or others. There is often an assumption that if a young person is in a hostel they require a relatively high level of professional support, resources and time. Although this can be the case, and the fundamental purpose of the hostel was to provide young people with shelter – one of the most fundamental human needs.

THE AMBITION TO CHANGE

A basic aim of the work of the hostel was for residents to change. This is mirrored in a great deal of the literature relating to youth work; youth workers are not uncommonly referred to (and refer to themselves) as 'change makers' or 'agents of change'. I do not believe we give young people enough credit for being able to make change possible for themselves. I often feel that it suits the 'professional' to dissect a young person's personality and in turn find faults, which they can 'work' on (or 'treat'). This response is set in being convinced that the young person concerned is in some way lacking (in deficit) and is essentially colonizing the individual, robbing them of themselves by undermining their ability to define their own direction (see Fanon, 1952). This in turn fulfils both the workers' and organisation's need to be needed. However, due to the subjective nature of practice, if a significant amount of time is spent examining a human beings' personality, a wide range of varying 'faults' appear, depending on the examiner, their training, background/experience, personality, expertise, etc.

B. Belton (ed.), 'Cadjan – Kiduhu': Global Perspectives on Youth Work, 179–185.
© *2014 Sense Publishers. All rights reserved.*

Rogers wrote extensively about 'empathy'. He explains a means, "… of being with people that locates the power in the person, not the expert" (Rogers, 1975: 140). Although the word 'empathy' is over used, frequently in an inaccurate context, this statement resonates with me. I believe there is an art in simply being with young people and accepting them for who they are, without desperately scrambling to locate a need, which may not even exist. This type of behaviour leaves a lingering tang of colonial times and contexts; people are 'worked on' in order to make them fit in with the oppressor's regime.

If the young mothers were to 'turn their lives around' for some of them, for some of the time at least, it would result in them neglecting their children and themselves. At the same time, tasked with this purpose, the practitioner (in this case me) would effectively be obliged to take on the role of a saviour/missionary.

However, there is little way to measure if anything I did or said would have made a direct impact on making the group or any particular individual change. These young women were fiercely dedicated mothers, with goals and aspirations and extra force driving them: their child. For me, to try to change them would be unprofessional and morally wrong, especially as they did not ask me to change them. 'Will you change me?' is not a request I have ever been asked – and if one answered 'yes' what would this situation be?

The young mothers often dropped into the office where we engaged in conversation and interacted with their children. These meetings often led to insightful understanding of self, others and situations on the part of the women, helping me to have a better understanding of them, their hopes and anxieties. They also provided adequate time to note if there should be a cause for concern. However, monthly support and development sessions were compulsory. If these appointments were consistently missed, a written warning was issued. Should this absence be repeated after being warned, the women could face eviction. In these meetings a main component was recording 'risks'. I sometimes found myself looking for risks/needs or behaviour that may have not been the 'norm' – that may not have actually existed – simply to fill out space on the form. Laing (1976) writes about acceptance and understanding things that may appear 'different' or 'abnormal'. He gives an example of a woman who stares at walls and how her psychiatric 'treatment' could be further alienating her from society. Instead of accepting her and allowing her to stare at walls, 'even encouraging her' or using it as a 'possible avenue of temporary escape' (ibid.: 76) it is 'regarded as the prime symptom of a schizophrenic illness' (ibid.: 76). This demonstrates the dangers of thinking you know what is best for a person instead of accepting their uniqueness and the intricate complexities of the human mind.

The physical structures of the hostel were in need of modernisation. The office space was very limited and located in the basement with little natural light. As there was no communal space, the office became the central location where interactions took place between residents, their children and staff. There was a side office where one-to-one meetings took place, but the walls were thin, which made the room inadequate for private or confidential conversations to take place. When accompanying my client, 'K' to the clinic, I felt being in the outdoors, in a different physical environment, might have affected the content of the conversation. We were usually confined in a small room and when there were silences in conversation it could often be a trigger, a move on, or wrap things up. When walking in an open space, we were not bound by four walls, which I felt contributed to a more relaxed atmosphere. 'K' talked about some personal experiences and although there is no concrete way of being sure if it was the physical environment that made her do so, it could have been a contributing factor. I do not believe that these past experiences 'K' disclosed to me were signs of her changing, but I do believe it was an indicator in building a positive association with an element of trust.

Although I had only been in the role of support and development worker for four months, I had witnessed a tendency amongst staff to start conversations with, 'the problem with 'X' is ...' or 'what 'X' really needs ...' and to then launch into a list of reasons why 'X' is the way she (supposedly) is and why she should change. I often found myself wondering how we were qualified to make such statements.

There was a huge assumption that because the young person was living in a hostel with a child they were deficient and needed help. Whilst there may be additional obstacles that can stand in the path of a young single mother compared to young people without children, having a child at a young age can also have advantages. However, a 16-year-old, single, homeless mother will not unusually be faced with problems relating to money, education, food, shelter, childcare, and health, which can be experienced as a huge strain. Life may be considerably more demanding for them but we must not assume that these additional potential stress factors will have a totally negative impact on their lives. Some people need/want or just live more demanding lives. The implication is that none of us should choose what might seem to be a more difficult path.

Plans for the much needed re-decoration of the hostel, by way of finance from a national commercial television company, fell through. I felt that we should try to seek alternative funding as the living conditions were far from satisfactory. Whilst I was unsure of how these decorations could take place, I believed that we could be proactive, voice our concerns to senior management and start to think of alternative methods to fundraise.

SKY DIVE

When discussing this with the residents at a house meeting, they decided to start by writing a letter to six key figures within the organization, expressing their disappointment. We discussed different forms of fundraising and three young women decided they wanted to do a sky dive. Although this was met with some sceptical opinions from my co-worker, I saw that that this could be a wonderful opportunity to firstly raise some money for the refurbishment and secondly be used as an opportunity for trying something new and exhilarating. The money we would be able to raise would be a small contribution to the £30,000 that was needed to fund the refurbishment, but I often felt that our work revolved around the young women being mothers and perhaps we could sometimes forget that they were also young people. Being mothers and caring for their children was clearly their priority, but I understood that there was a need for them to be given room in our practice to explore avenues of simply having fun. Although the money had been the starting point for the sky dive, I saw it as a good opportunity I could assist with, working with these young women to make their idea a reality while achieving other positive outcomes.

I saw it as my duty with the group to make sure unrealistic expectations were not encouraged. We arranged for a senior manager to attend the next house meeting as I believed an open dialogue between the hostel and the residents about their concerns and disappointments would be beneficial.

Would the sky dive or making the arrangements to make it happen change these young mothers? I doubt it. I don't doubt their capacity however to change themselves by undertaking such activity together. Equally I don't doubt that the effects might just as likely confirm that they are 'good enough' as they are.

CHANGING ME

What was I able to change and improve to meet the young women's needs in order to be a more useful worker? There are many things about which I can speculate to determine what may or may not have brought about change in these young people's lives. However, I felt that the most useful thing I could do for both the young people and myself was to address the changes I could make in myself in order to become a more helpful and skilled worker.

Although there are personality traits I see in myself, which I would like to change, I sense that the most immediate and practical change I can make is to be better informed. A deeper knowledge of the welfare system and possible future changes to it, education and learning opportunities and funding for childcare would make me wiser and more efficient when assisting the women through daily tasks. These types of practical and resourceful actions could be much more beneficial to the women rather than developing plans which pick out supposed problems they might have, highlighting imaginary risks whilst possibly blocking change.

Freire writes about the importance of understanding why situations arise instead of choosing 'reactionary options' (Freire, 1985: 39). Raising awareness, I believe, is the first step to expanding your consciousness and developing a deeper understanding of the society of which we are a part.

I believe that I need to be acutely aware of my emotions when working with young people. An incident occurred when a client was verbally abused on the bus. A man was trying to humiliate her for being so young and having a child. She got into an argument with him and later talked to me about how it has fuelled her desire to study and succeed for her and her child. The way in which this young woman described the situation and talked about her child left me feeling overwhelmed with respect and admiration towards her, so much so that I could have cried. Laing writes,

... the more aware of our feelings, the more competent we are likely to be in restraining them when necessary, and the more easily will we loosen such restraint when circumstances no longer seem to require it. (Laing, 1976: 75)

This precisely describes how I must be extremely conscious of my feelings, for if I am not, the repercussions could be detrimental. If I had started sobbing and wrapping my arms around the client it would have been patronising, unprofessional, inappropriate and probably not very much use to her. As a professional, I needed to give her time to vent her frustrations, show a level of understanding and ensure that she was aware of the respect I had for her. The last thing she needed was a wailing support worker telling her how proud they were of her. For me to be an effective practitioner, like Laing describes, I must know when my feelings need to be restrained in order to respond in the most useful way for the client. Sometimes adversity makes us strong – and can we really protect our clients 24/7 from such experiences?

REFLECTIONS OF REALITY

My work at the hostel included keeping a journal 'as a means of exploring and deepening your practice'. Progoff describes a journal as 'a means of reflection ... its essence is subtle movement and change ... a collage of life in motion' (Progoff, 1975: 16-21). This might of course be true, but there is no concrete, widespread or robust research/evidence to support such grand claims. If I were able to keep a journal accurately in this way it may be useful, however, as I discovered, I could not.

I wrote down weekly entries over a period of two months. I did not want to set aside time at work to complete my journal, as I was busy, so the majority of my entries were completed over the weekend. I encountered many difficulties in recording 'working with an individual'. There were many factors that affected the quality and mood of what I was documenting. Time constraints played a major factor, but also how I felt at the time of writing affected how I reflected and recalled the previous day's work. All reflections are distortions of reality to some extent, although it seems many of us seem to believe our reflections *on* reality *are* that reality.

I began to recognise that what I was writing in my journal may not have accurately mirrored how I felt at the time. As I had moved into a new flat my physical environment was extremely chaotic and it was therefore difficult to focus. This resulted in often writing rushed journal entries. My 'professional' journal, at times, was more like a personal diary. I found it difficult to keep focused on writing relevant information and not to wander off into gossip. My train of thought would often lead me into unethical and inappropriate writing. For example, at one point I came very close to writing deeply personal information about 'K's' family life that only my manager and relevant professionals needed to know. I was getting into the flow, reflecting on the meeting with a social worker and writing so fast that I was not giving myself enough time to think about what I was writing. I wanted to write quickly, partly because the meeting had occurred the previous day and was relatively fresh in my mind, but also, for the simple and selfish reason that I was in a rush to meet my friend. This demonstrates how something as trivial as wanting to get to my friend's house on time could have led me to disclose information on 'K' that would have been completely insensitive, inappropriate and unprofessional.

I often think through situations and incidents that occur throughout the day. I think through my actions and responses and whether I handled situations appropriately and professionally or if I could have done things differently. I often feel that I could have handled situations in another way and I spend time being critical of my actions. Bearing in mind that these situations on which I am reflecting will never happen again, I am now not so sure how useful this is. These thoughts can metamorphose into a daydream where I manage to say the right thing at exactly the right time and am met with cheers all round! I am beginning to question whether this type of reflection holds any relevance in terms of my development as a professional. I am also beginning to feel that too much reflection can simply act as a trigger to criticize myself to the point of doubting all my actions. I believe I need to try to accept myself instead of re-living a situation as someone perhaps stronger and bolder. Perhaps the most useful people in terms of developing and bettering our practice are those we work with and amongst, Are they a more accurate barometer of our performance than endless fantasizing about what might have been?

PROFESSIONAL JUDGEMENT

I suspect with more legal, local and heath care knowledge I could better assist the young women in their everyday lives than endless introspection. I also hope that in the future I will be able to trust my professional judgment more, instead of looking for reassurance from others. The problem with too much reflection is that it picks at my insecurities and then magnifies them, bringing them to the forefront of my mind. Interrogation and examination of practice by way of a structured, disciplined but supportive quality assurance process, that could include supervision or interacting with colleagues and clients, might be a more useful way to understand and develop our practice. I believe I must try to be thoughtful and aware of my words before I say them and not be 'ignorant to my ignorance'. Thinking about one's actions before a situation, I believe, is more effective than after and is part of what professional judgement is.

When I was working at the hostel I met with my supervisor every three weeks and found that talking through experiences at work with her gave me ample time to discuss my feelings and thoughts regarding my development as a practitioner. Even in supervision I sometimes found it hard to keep focused on discussing relevant information and not to stray into the irrelevant waters of gossip.

Due to the reasons above, I do not believe that writing a journal has helped me to deepen my practice. As a practitioner I think about my role and what I am trying to achieve working with young people. I do not have an agenda to try and 'improve them' and 'turn their lives around'. This may be just as well as I don't believe I can change other people in the course of my work. I hope that I accept the young people I work with and work with them to raise their awareness of issues that may affect them, just as they raise my awareness of their strengths and challenges they face. Unless this does happen what can professional judgement be based on? I must ensure that I am well informed so that I am able to be as useful as possible to the people I work with. In being a patient, caring and committed worker I may be able to assist the young people should they want to change any aspect of their life.

CONCLUSION

This piece was written in 2010. Since then I have been predominantly working in mental health. As a new mother myself, I have an even deeper respect and admiration for the young mothers with whom I have worked, knowing how hard it is to be a parent, let alone one without support from a partner and for some, a family.

The concept of change is ever present in mental health in the form of recovery. For a young person hearing voices, for example, it is easy to assume that the first step to recovery would be eliminating these voices. However, recovery for that young person might entail a wide range of prospects such as a long-term relationship, performing at a gig, a meaningful job or coming off medication. Perhaps when these needs are met, there is the possibility that the voices are kinder, less harrowing and less frequent.

From talking with young people and reading numerous stories from survivors of psychiatry, particularly those associated with the 'Hearing Voices Network', it is evident that psychiatric professionals who impose their ideas of (and their voices about) recovery onto young people can have detrimental effects. It is not uncommon to hear that the biggest mistake young people feel they have made is informing services of their voice hearing as this single 'symptom' can provide grounds for diagnoses as severe as paranoid schizophrenia.

As Longden points out, 'the ownership of psychosis belongs to those who experience it. Psychiatry has to accept that' (Longden in Romme et al., 2009: 146). As those who suffer severe emotional distress must define their own roots/route to recovery, genuine youth work should encourage young people to follow their own path to change.

REFERENCES

Belton, B. (2009). *Developing critical youth work theory*. Rotterdam: Sense Publishers.
Cohen, L. (1975). *Leonard Cohen greatest hits*. Austria: Sony Music Entertainment.
Fanon, F. (1963). *The wretched of the earth*. England: Penguin Books.
Freire, P. (1985). *The politics of education culture, power and liberation*. USA: Bergin & Garvey.
Laing, R. D. (1976). *The facts of life*. USA: Allen Lane.
Progoff (1975). In Holly, M. L. (1989). *Writing to grow*. New Hampshire: Heinmann.
Rogers, R. C. (1980). *A way of being*. USA: Houghton Mifflin Company.
Romme, M., Escher, S., Dillon, J,. Corstens, D., & Morris, M. (2009). *Living with voices, 50 stories of recovery*. UK: PCCS Books.

SOFYA GILEVA

HELLO, EVERYONE! WE ARE GLAD TO WELCOME YOU ON THE SUMMER SESSION OF PILGRIM!

Pilgrim (Barnaul, Russia)

I heard these words, standing in a circle of people of different ages, backgrounds and aspirations. I heard these words, standing in a circle in a blue T-shirt, which told everyone that I am among the leaders. That was one of my first days in Pilgrim. Being a youth worker along the line of other young and inspired people, 80 percent of who have been to the camp thousands of times before, I was scared… scared to do something wrong, scared to fail, scared to stand out. It was my first experience working in the camp. The camp, which afterwards became my home, which empowered me to grow and be still growing, to find friends, to travel and to get to know other YMCAs all over the world.

The camp was started as a linguistic camp, but then was focused on building an atmosphere to enable personal growth, while being in a group and letting everyone in the camp express themselves, their wishes, needs, talents, etc.

The camp, which celebrates its 15th anniversary this year, has had an impact on the lives of a huge amount of young people, including me.

The camp welcomes children six to seven times a year to its sessions, each one is different from another, English or Russian speaking, to have fun, grow and learn things from each other.

THE CAMP THAT CHANGED MY LIFE.

The YMCA Camp

In 1999 we came up with the idea of a linguistic camp. Saying linguistic we mean we tried to work in the 'English speaking' atmosphere morning till evening. We were not a YMCA back then; we joined the movement in 2001.

We hold two to four sessions per summer (10 to 21 days each) and a session every school break. That is one session in spring, winter and fall (fall and spring sessions are 'Russian speaking sessions'). Summer and winter sessions usually have in between 50 and 100 kids. Spring and fall are smaller in number. Our target group is kids in the age range of six to 17.

B. Belton (ed.), 'Cadjan – Kiduhu': Global Perspectives on Youth Work, 187–189.
© *2014 Sense Publishers. All rights reserved.*

What we do is we have some kind of testing procedure on the first day where we put our campers into different groups, according to their level of knowledge of the English language. Some groups have real debates and discussions, whereas others just do the basic steps.

At first we were focusing on the learning outcome for quite some time, but later on we realized that, however important that might have been, it wasn't our goal. Our main goal is creating an atmosphere in which both campers and leaders grow and develop personally whilst being in a group. It is very important for us that every child/teenager feels comfortable expressing themselves, their wishes/needs/talents, etc.

Usually every session has its own theme. For example, 'Mass media session' or 'fairy tale session'. We try to make every day and session different from the ones that happened before. That is probably one of the reasons why a significant number of our campers keep on coming over and over again. (Olga Pronina, October 2013)

Let us try and see what the most interesting points are in a camp day. We have what we call; 'hobby clubs', these are something like interest groups. They are workshops that last for about an hour to an hour and a half and are taken up with different activities; sports (football, basketball, volleyball etc.), table games, arts and crafts. Then comes what we call 'English club'. These sessions, again about an hour to 90 minutes long, are taken up with more focused learning, but definitely informal learning.

In the late afternoon we do the 'fresh air activities'; most of the times this is outdoor games (such as 'capture the flag games'). The evening activity is usually some sort of creative work on the topic of the day. This happens in smaller groups and is presented like a theatre sketch.

We end up every day with a 'candle talk' in small groups. This is where kids share how they felt about the day: things they liked, disliked and perhaps the highlights of the day. Each 'candle talk' is concluded with a short story on the values of importance.

There are a couple of other things that are very important to mention when talking about our camp. First of all 'Flag ups' and 'Flag downs'. We start every day in a camp with a flag up ceremony, which is a tradition of 14 years now, it is held in complete silence – a sign of respect to the camp and its traditions; and every day is finished with a flag down ceremony. The candidates for the ceremony are chosen by the camp leaders and these are usually kids who stood out during the day.

Another thing that needs to be mentioned is the Pilgrims. Pilgrims are campers chosen by the 'Council of the Eldest' (consisting of all the leaders, the camp coordinator and the already existing pilgrims). Pilgrims are kids who are respected by both leaders and other campers, who take the responsibilities and carry the camp values.

This place is simply amazing, but to really understand what we mean by this, one needs to come and experience it. (Maria Pronina, July 2014)

GÜNTER LÜCKING

THE GERMAN YMCA IN TENSION BETWEEN INSTITUTIONALIZATION AND MOVEMENT

When I ask older, as well as younger people in today's YMCA to share what the YMCA means to them and share their experience of the YMCA, they come up with many different stories, relating fellowship, felicitous relationships and experiences of a flourishing life. These experiences touched and moved others so much that they were motivated to help with and take part in developing programmes for youth and children.

However, co-workers also get tired, losing the joy of engagement with others, lamenting that only few people take up a programme they have created or help deliver. The tell how situations have changed, how young people have no time anymore, there being so many other opportunities for youngsters which results in them unfortunately not choosing to take part in what they are offering. Yes, conditions have changed, but the question, which appears essential to me, is whether we are concerned with the situation of young people around us? Even though the number of young people who are engaged in youth work might decrease, even though many youngsters move to universities right after high-school, even though the leisure time facilities are overwhelming, still youth and children live in our district, neighbourhood or area and they have seven days per week and 24 hours every day that are filled with life.

Sociologists tell us very clearly that every group and institution has an underlying mechanism of wanting to maintain the things as they are (Calmback, 2012; Grau, 1980; Münchmeier et al., 2006; Pletzer, 2012; Pletzer et al., 2001; Shell, 2010; von der Oelsnitz, 2009). We want to keep and preserve our own good experiences. We glorify the experiences where we did ground-breaking things, but this nostalgia can prevent us being open to new things.

It is of course more than understandable that a generation that experienced, launched or created something new treasures their achievement, reflecting on these experiences thankfully, feeling and having the right to be joyful about it. However, perhaps the next generation will not design and influence to the same extent. Instead of starting new actions they experience stagnation or decreasing numbers of participants, instead of designing something new they administer the things that were passed on to them. The appeal of a beginning and the challenges of a creative designing are missing.

Some local associations preserve a 'one-branch-programme'. Youth clubs are our traditional programme formats. 'Something else never existed here'. But some youth have more sporting ambitions, while some are interested in music and the third group wants to be engaged in projects, another is 'just' looking for an open

B. Belton (ed.), 'Cadjan – Kiduhu': Global Perspectives on Youth Work, 191–193.

gathering to hang around, play and chat. Children and young people are diverse. With a topical and widely spread programme offer, we meet the variety of youth. However, if we do not look for young people in manifold ways some will simply 'lose their way' to us. Too often I experience youngsters, new volunteers and co-workers with innovative ideas, who become disappointed and leave. There was no space for their propositions in the existing YMCAs and they were thwarted.

During my work with TEN SING[1] I found that it is more likely that three highly motivated youngsters initiate a new programme, so expanding the YMCA offer. Established organizations put a lot of effort into their own persistence, preserving 'customary' ways of doing things. The power of the established and feeling the need to stick to the traditions that are acknowledged as valuable, can create fear and distrust of the unknown as the owned past is glorified. All too often this hinders the connection with the new.

There is always the creation of new programme offers in the YMCA, because young initiative sees and embraces the challenges of our time, everything was once new. Drop-in activities, sports groups, open gatherings, and TEN SING were originally contested, but the time for something new had come.

The continuous change of societal and youth-cultural conditions demands a continuous change and openness for new forms of youth work. Existing structures can open up to original thinking and thus may lead to new offers or other initiatives that are able to fill gaps that appear in provision. For this process we need a widely spread contention and debate, which leads to the development for novel ideas and forms of youth work. This discussion is inevitable, as we need to convince whole organizations, often with steering committees, co-workers, members, parents and friends.

New initiatives naturally emanate from individuals or small groups of like-minded people. Someone discovered, saw, heard or experienced something in other places and wishes for such a programme in his own place. Soon allies are found and the question of a new programme offer enters the steering committee, or the co-workers council. The people who are responsible for the existing programme are naturally first of all engaged in maintaining the existing programme offer. Often this leaves little scope for fresh activity and so stifles development; one question can lead to such a result; "Why should we start something new when the capacities are seemingly insufficient for the existing programme offers?" On the other side, every person lives with multiple reference points and every new programme offer increases the potential of co-workers, volunteers and young people.

We need innovative forces and to support them, bringing like-minded people together. Otherwise our programme offer risks becoming impoverished, lacking the enrichment of new challenges. They stop being relevant to young people.

Management needs diversity and a means for sensing what forms of renewal are possible and be able to make sense in the existing conditions. The diversity of different personalities, talents and interests is the basis for a wider horizon. Therefore we are well advised to consider how new youth cultures and personalities can be addressed.

I experience the foundation of a new hockey group in one place, while in the neighbouring town young Christians start their meeting with conversations, praise and prayer, at the same time a district YMCA tests a trainee-course and young adults meet for a 'running dinner'. This creates a range of appeal, why does it not make sense to offer this diversity of involvement?

As a background for renewal I encountered the question whether the new programme offers and the new co-workers are still grounded on the principles of the 'Paris Basis' (a guiding instrument of the YMCA)? Naturally every new proposal and every new co-worker brings in his or her form of piety, his or her questions, doubts and peculiarities. However, that was not much different during the teens of the persons who are currently responsible. Faith and experience only grew in the course of time and some shortcomings hopefully fell by the wayside.

Accordingly, I wish for more openness for new movements in the YMCA, even though the new generation might only give new shape to the things that we regard as proven and tested.

NOTE

[1] Ten Sing is an international Christian youth programme within the YMCA, which focuses on getting young people to express themselves by using their own culture and abilities through performing arts.

REFERENCES

Calmbach, M. (2012). *Wie ticken Jugendliche? Lebenswelten von Jugendlichen im Alter von 14 bis 17 Jahren in Deutschland.* Odenthal. Available at: http://www.dkjs.de/fileadmin/bilder/Aktuell/pdfs/2012_03_28_Ergebnisse.pdf

Grau, H. (1980). *Einführung in die Soziologie.* 6. Auflage, Bad Homburg.

Lange, M., & Wehmeyer, K. (2014). *Jugendarbeit im Takt einer beschleunigten Gesellschaft. Veränderte Bedingungen des Heranwachsens als Herausforderung.* Weinheim and München. Summary available at: http://www.forschungsverbund.tu-dortmund.de/fileadmin/Files/Kinder-_und_Jugendarbeit/13-03-12_Keine_Zeit_Befunde_Download.pdf

Münchmeier, R., Fauser, K., & Fischer, A. (2006). *Jugend im Verband.* Leverkusen-Opladen. Summary available at: http://www.evangelische-jugend.de/fileadmin/user_upload/aej/Kinder-_und_Jugendsoziologie/Downloads/11_02_02_Jugendliche_als_Akteure_im_Verband.pdf

Pletzer, W., Lohmann, G. & Ludwig, P. (2001). *Beteiligung von Kindern und Jugendlichen.* Stuttgart: Boorberg-Verlag.

Pletzer, W. (2012). *Herausforderungen für die Jugendarbeit in einem entscheidenden Jahrzehnt.* Höchst. Available at: http://www.ev-jugendarbeit-ekhn.de/fileadmin/jugendarbeit/downloads/Winfried_Pletzer_Herausforderungen_fuer_die_Jugendarbeit_201X_S.pdf

Shell Deutschland. (2010). *Shell Jugendstudie.* 2. Auflage, Frankfurt: FISCHER Taschenbuch. Available at: http://www.shell.de/aboutshell/our-commitment/shell-youth-study/downloads.html

von der Oelsnitz, D. (2009). *Die innovative Organisation.* 2. Auflage, Stuttgart.

ANNA MIRGA

YOUTH ENGAGEMENT IN THE GITANO ASSOCIATIVE MOVEMENT IN CATALONIA[1]

Emerging "Youthscapes"

INTRODUCTION

Ethnic mobilisation is a process in which 'groups organise around some feature of ethnic identity (for example, skin colour, language, customs), in pursuit of collective ends' (Olzak, 1983). Ethnic mobilisation differs from political mobilisation in that it invokes elements of ethnic identity, based on the existing ethnic boundaries (Barth, 1969) but shares the same process in which 'a group goes from being a passive collection of individuals to an active participant in public life' (Tilly, 1978). Ethnic mobilisation, similar to political mobilisation or social movements, aims at strategic representation of collective interests in attempt to bring about a political change (Vermeersch, 2006). Such process can be based on diverse mobilising structures (McAdam, McCarthy, & Zald, 1996), which become vehicles conveying representation and collective action, like formal political structures (political parties) or civil society entities.

In case of Roma/Gitano[2] communities' ethnic mobilisation, the organisations of civil society (especially as NGOs) became the principal organisational structures which represent collective interests and claims (Vermeersch, 2006; Rostas, 2012; Trehan & Sigona, 2010; Marushiakova & Popov, 2005). This 'NGOization of Roma rights' can be seen as a failure of political integration of Roma/Gitano representatives in formal politics (McGarry, 2012; Rostas, 2012) but can also be understood through the deliberative democracy discourse (Carrasco, 2007), in which public institutions promote 'networks of civic engagement' (Putnam, Leonardi, & Nanetti, 1994) as a means for strengthening the democratic functioning of the State.

These trends of political representation through NGOs rather than through mainstream politics can be observed among Gitano community in Spain, and particularly in Catalonia. The proliferation of this form of civic participation has become common not only among the Gitano population but among the Spanish citizens in general (Pérez Díaz & López Novo, 2003), a phenomenon referred to as the 'global solidarity boom' (Salamon, 1994). As of the 90s, the Gitano organisations begun to grow considerably in number, leading to an 'associative boom' – it is estimated, that the number of Gitano associations between 1997 and 2004 grew from 200 to around 400 (Méndez López, 2005). A similar process can be seen in Spain among the general population where a considerable growth in number of associations can be traced – in 1990, 113,065 associations were

B. Belton (ed.), 'Cadjan – Kiduhu': Global Perspectives on Youth Work, 195–210.

registered, and five years later that number has doubled to reach 206,363 (Fundación Encuentro, 1996). This dynamic has been especially evident in Catalonia in the following decade, where the tripartite coalition government (2003–2010), embraced 'the participation discourse' approach, following the general European trend (Bereményi & Mirga, 2012).

The role of youth in these developments has been significant. In fact, the increase in the number of associations in Spain in the 90s is attributed to its enhanced popularity among young people (Fundación Encuentro, 1999). This assertion is not surprising – 'the youth activism has always played a central role in the democratic process and continues to forge new grounds for social change' (Ginwright, Noguera, & Cammarota, 2006). Furthermore, the youth has been recognised as a major force in social movements, especially in those which may convey risky action, like protests or revolutions, such as during Colour Revolutions (Kuzio, 2006) and has been at the forefront of the most important European political and social transformations in recent years (Flesher Fominaya, 2014), like the 15-M movement (Calvo, 2013) or the mobilisation following the 11-M bombings (Flesher Fominaya, 2011).

Following these considerations, both across Europe and in Spain specifically, this paper inquiries about how do these developments translate into the reality of the Gitano ethnic mobilisation, and more specifically, what is the role of Gitano young people in the ethnic mobilisation?

METHODOLOGY

This chapter draws from my previous and current investigations and forms part of the doctoral research, which aims at analysing patterns of ethnic mobilisation among Gitano/Roma communities in diverse geopolitical, social, legal and cultural contexts.[3] This comparative investigation (Collier, 1993; Lijphart, 1971) is based on case studies (Yin, 2009) and draws from multi-sited ethnography approach (Marcus, 1995), with research so far conducted in Spain and Colombia. The theoretical, methodological and analytical frames are, *per excellence*, multi-disciplinary, drawing from diverse approaches in social sciences. Elements such as political opportunity, leadership, representation versus representativeness, identity frames and identity formation, mobilising structures, discourses and narratives (self-generated and imposed), adapted strategies are analysed in detail.

Specifically, this chapter is based on fieldwork conducted among Gitano organisations and leaders in Catalonia (between 2008 and 2013) while working with Gitano organization over the course of 5 years.[4] Numerous interviews (both structured in-depth and informal), focus groups and a total of 14 open-question questionnaires have been distributed among the young Gitano leaders and novices of the associative movement (age 18–28, 10 men and four women). Following Yin's approach, I combined a variety of different sources of knowledge (Yin, 2009) such as documents (self-produced by organisations, reports, policy-related, minutes of meetings, press, etc.), archival records, interviews, focus groups (two), questionnaires, participant and non-participant observation (as active member of organisations, as observer during general assemblies, working sessions, formal and informal meetings), in order to contrast the data collected during the study. The direct involvement in daily work of Gitano organisations allowed me to gain insightful information and understand the internal dynamics of these structures, as well as get to know the key players (both old and new) among the Gitano organizations in Catalonia.

When speaking about Gitano youth, it is easy to fall into generalisations. As a means of simplification, this chapter refers to 'Gitano youth' as a specific sector of Gitano population (up to the age of 30), however, the reader should bear in mind that this group is not a homogeneous entity, but one which intersects with many other variables (social class, gender, ethnicity, etc.) The profile of my youth informants, to whom this chapter is dedicated, is very diverse, however, a generalised characterisation can be drawn: a) Youth coming from traditional Gitano families, who grew up in typical 'Gitano districts' (often ghetto-like), in a great majority of cases have completed only the basic level of formal education (or drop-outs), are frequently engage in economic activity of their family (such as selling); b) Young educated, in some cases coming from mixed marriages and relatively comfortable economic background. They maintain strong identification with Gitano culture and the community, and are compromised with living in accordance with standards of Gitano culture (like traditional marriage). They maintain friendship ties with non-Gitano peers and often continue with their education; c) Young educated elite, in most cases coming from mixed marriages and who grew up outside of the community. Greatly influenced by the non-Gitano culture, they identify with their ethnic background but reject some of the conservative elements of Gitano culture. They often have the complex of being 'not enough Gitano'.[5]

Finally, this chapter aims to present emerging trends and tendencies affecting other Gitano communities, or in fact, other youth groups.

In order to answer to the central question of this chapter regarding the role of Gitano young people in ethnic mobilisation, the following variables have been taken into account: direct involvement of young people in Gitano associations (profile, what kind of association, form of engagement), leadership patterns (young vs. old), motivational approaches, objectives and strategy of action, constructed narratives and discourses. These variables are applied comparatively (regarding young and older generations, Gitano vs. non-Gitano), looking into the relationship which these different elements establish mutually. Specifically, I propose to look into the presence of youth (as target groups, beneficiaries or in fact as active agents) in these structures *vis-à-vis* the structures of current leadership.[6]

GITANO YOUTH, ASSOCIATIONS AND ETHNIC MOBILIZATION

Gitano Youth

Roma/Gitano can be considered a relatively young community, especially in comparison to the majority population, which currently is experiencing an important demographic decline. In Spain, almost 60% of the entire Gitano population is aged between one and 29 (for majority population it is approximately 35%) (National Roma Integration Strategy in Spain 2012–2020), and 'around a third are aged below 16 years' (Laparra Navarro, 2007). In many aspects, the situation of the Gitano youth varies greatly from that of their non-Gitano peers. Considering that the majority of Gitano population in Spain are in fact young adults, it is not surprising that the youth plays an important role in the economic activity of their families – many teenagers very early begin to help out in the family business. When their non-Gitano peers dedicate their time to education or leisure, the Gitano youth embraces adult responsibilities. This also implies that the Gitano teenagers begin an adult life much earlier: the average age for Gitano marriage is between 17–18 for girls and 20–21 for boys (Fundació Pere Tarres, 2006) and soon after they have children of their own. These developments also affect their educational trajectories. The Gitano teens abandon school much earlier than their non-Gitano peers. Although in Spain it is anti-constitutional to determine ethnicity of citizens, including in school, there are some estimated data which demonstrates the low level of education among the Gitano youth: 43% of Gitano between 16–24 have completed the obligatory education (until 16 years old) while 43.1% have begun the obligatory secondary school but were not able to complete it (Laparra Navarro, 2007). Also, the number of Gitano university graduates are below the Spanish average, but also well below these estimates for Roma in majority of EU countries (European Agency for Fundamental Rights, 2012). The generally low level of education makes the Gitano youth a particularly vulnerable group on the labour market. The data from 2002 estimates that 50.28% of girls and 20% of boys between 16 and 30 are unemployed (Fundació Pere Tarres, 2006). While looking into data on Gitano youth, it is impossible to underestimate the intersection of ethnicity and gender variables – in majority of indicators, the Gitano young women are considerably below the statistical results for men (FRA, 2013). Carrasco and Abajo demonstrate that with regards to educational trajectories, the gender inequality is an evident and transversal variable:

> Roma families are at a crossroads situation: with regards to the role of men and women (to opt for equality between both genders, or, on the contrary, herald as 'cultural' and idiosyncratic and 'reason for pride' for women to play a role limited to taking care of the household and children); with regards to school enrolment (take an active stance in schooling their children and their educational continuity, or, instead, conform with a brief schooling period, arguing that they are not well accepted, that they will be equally discriminated against in the labour market with or without academic credentials, or that 'it's not their thing'), and with regards to cultural change (go for additive inclusion, or, conversely, understand that – given the labelling which they are subject of – the only viable option is seclusion in the proper group). (Abajo & Carrasco, 2004)

These considerations are relevant when speaking about Gitano youth and their engagement in ethnic mobilisation too – as in most European societies, for the

Roma/Gitano communities the main variables which organise status and inequality, are in fact age and gender (Carrasco & Bereményi, 2011). This gender variable inevitably affects patterns of civic engagement among Gitano youth, likewise to the intersection of age variables with social class.

Disregarding of different personal trajectories of individual young Gitano people, they all share a common characteristic, which differentiates them from the older generation. Although the statistics on schooling of Gitano pupils are lower than the average for non-Gitano students, it also demonstrate an important difference with the previous generation of Gitano adults, which in their great majority have not completed any level of education at all (Fundació Pere Tarres, 2006). The fact that majority of Gitano up to the age of 12 and almost half of Gitano teenagers up to the age of 16 have been schooled creates a new dimension for development of the Gitano community as such. This essential difference between the contemporary youth and the older generation leads to inter-generational conflicts (as in the case of majority societies too). For Bourdieu, the inter-generational relationships are potentially conflicting as each generation is developed in its own *habitus* 'which have been produced by different modes of generation, that is, by conditions of existence which, in imposing different definitions of the impossible, the possible and the probable, cause one group to experience as natural or reasonable practices or aspirations which another group finds unthinkable or scandalous, and vice versa' (Bourdieu, 1977). The context of today's world, marked by rapid social, cultural and technological changes creates even greater discrepancies between each generation's *habitus*. According to Beck (Beck & Beck-Gernsheim, 2007) the process of globalisation has contributed to a change in the scale of values and 'has opened a deep fissure which affects also and precisely the generational relationships' (Beck & Beck-Gernsheim, 2007). Nonetheless, the youth condition is inherently transitory (Rossi, 2009). The shape of future societies, and in fact of Gitano community, lie on the shoulders of those who currently represent the youth. The process of redefinition of cultural values, the hybridization of Gitano identity (Tremlett, 2009) and transformation of lifestyles of Gitano youngsters may be seen as a major threat by the older generation, as the very continuity of Gitano culture are potentially 'at risk'. This perceived 'threat', however, constitutes a major transformative force, marking new pathways for future development of Gitano community as such, thanks to increased competencies and resources that the Gitano young people possess.

Given the existence of the Gitano ethnic mobilisation based on NGO structures and the 'youthfulness' of Gitano population, this chapter aims to answer to explore the role of Gitano young people in Gitano associative movement,[7] based on my research conducted in Catalonia.

Gitano Associations and Youth

Federation of Roma Association in Catalonia (FAGIC), founded in 1991, congregates 74 Gitano associations and is the biggest Gitano umbrella organisation in the region. Out of these organisations, 12 are Gitano womens organisations and nine are registered as Gitano youth organisations (ome of these is a young Gitano womens association) and are relatively new as the majority of them have been created in the past several years. The reader should note, however, that the federated Gitano youth associations are lead by Gitano individuals of between 30 and 40 years old, so their condition as 'youth' is arguable. For this reason, they are not youth leaders *per se*, but rather adults who target the youth explicitly in their activities and thus are excluded from referring to them as young Gitano leaders. The remaining 54 federated associations are lead by Gitano men over 50 years old. The composition of the Executive Boards is diverse and may include women or youth; however, the presidency and ultimate leadership are given to older men.[8]

Gitano youth remains, however, a major target for FAGIC as beneficiaries of various activities run by the federated organizations (capacity-building, professional training, education and leisure activities, etc.). Paradoxically, however, the direct participation of youth in defining the activities offered by Gitano associations is very limited, as they are involved only in the decision-making process of their own organisations, if at all. Apart from the service-provision aspect of Gitano NGO's work, Gitano youth are invisible in other areas of activity of FAGIC and their federated associations (such as advocacy or political participation and consultation). No activities or project aiming at shaping youth leadership skills and capacities have been established to-date. The youth, in a way, serves to justify the very existence of Gitano associations (funding often goes for youth-targeted projects)[9] but the shift towards active and direct participation of young Gitano people still hasn't been produced within FAGIC. The youth is *instrumentalised* by associations – as *raison d'être* of Gitano NGOs – but at the same time the youth *instrumentalises* the associations too – they participate directly (as beneficiaries) only pragmatically in order to learn new skills or receive certification of completed courses. Beyond that, their direct participation is ostentatiously insignificant (or non-existent). It can be, therefore, concluded that in Catalonia, participation of young Gitano in the social and civic activity of their local NGOs, not only as active agents but also as volunteers or beneficiaries of projects implemented by associations, is strikingly low. Why is it then, that despite the fact that the Gitano youth is identified as an interests group (both by the Gitano organisations as well as by public administration), their direct involvement as active agents is so limited? Why the agency of Gitano youngsters, some of whom are educated, hasn't transformed into a resource of the existing Gitano associative movement? Following Ginwright we may ask, "What happens, however, when young people are silenced and restricted from participation in important civic affairs? What stands in young people's way in their relentless pursuit of social change?" (Ginwright, Noguera, & Cammarota, 2006).

Possibilities and Limits of Gitano Youth Participation

The limited engagement of Gitano youth is not necessarily evidence of their 'apathy' but rather may point to obstacles, which impede their active engagement.

My investigation points to a number of possible reasons that may explain this status quo.

Camino and Zeldin (2002) demonstrate that one of the obstacles to youth active engagement is the predominance of negative beliefs that the adults hold about adolescents. From adult's perspective, the common beliefs about youth, 'convey the implicit message of youth as a source of worry or threat, not potential' (Camino & Zeldin, 2002) and the youth, 'personify a given society's deepest anxieties' (Maira & Soep, 2004). This perception is often translated into 'deficit discourse' regarding the youth (Colley & Hodkinson, 2001; Belton, 2009). Elements of such discourses have been identified in the interviews conducted with Gitano leaders – some of them complained about the lack of implication of the youth, and pointed to the excessive negative impact of mainstream non-Gitano culture on young people. These comments appeared especially with regards to educated Gitano individuals – often, rather than speaking about these youngsters as potential role models and capable future leaders, they are described as excessively integrated and 'less-Gitano'. On the other hand, the youth has also expressed negative views about the Gitano association, although in majority of cases they regarded their leaders with a dose of respect. In this context it is seen, that both the youth and the adults hold negative stereotypes about each other. Galais (2012) describes a similar dynamic when speaking about participation in formal politics of Spanish young people. This finding can be explained from a standpoint of generational conflict (among Gitano and non-Gitano youth) described in the previous section, although it does not explain the overall reluctance of youth to joining the already existing organisations.

Another element that recurred throughout my research regards the status of Gitano youth within their communities. The concept of community, 'is based on the idea of members complying with a particular, sometimes quite rigid, set of norms' (Belton, 2009), which determines the context in which individuals act. Gitano community, as many other European societies, is based on hierarchical relations, organised, among other factors, around age and gender, in which the elder men are traditionally power holders and the highest (Fraser, 1995). In fact, my youth informants when asked to define key elements of their Gitano identity, always mentioned the rule of respect towards the elders (known as Phuriphen) as essential. The pressure of the community to behave according to some determined models of conduct and the outlook for the family's reputation often guide the decisions made by the young Gitano. In the words of one young Gitano leader:

the Gitano youth, in great, majority, is rather influenced by what elders can say about them, be it parents, grandparents or uncles, and this influences a lot the real freedom of thought or action of the proper youth. (questionnaire)

Consequently, the obedience to the elders imposed upon young Gitano often creates an obstacle to youth participation on equal terms. The authority of elders determines the relationship between youth and adults as hierarchical rather than based on equal power-sharing (and this holds true not only for Gitano communities but also as general condition of adult-youth relationships). Scholars identify this aspect as among the biggest obstacles to youth community engagement (Jennings et al., 2006; Camino & Zeldin, 2002). This unequal relationship is even more evident when considered the gender dimension – the status of a young person who is also a woman is at a considerable disadvantaged position of power in comparison to the elder men's authority (Abajo & Carrasco, 2004).

Furthermore, passivity is always a behavioral choice (Crozier & Friedberg, 1982), leading to suppose that the youth consciously rejects the existing Gitano associations. In fact, the majority of my interlocutors confirmed this supposition, arguing that they do not feel identified or represented by their local organizations or the vast part of their leaders.[10] They do, however, identify with the cause. Contrary to the common and oversimplified perceptions about the increased 'apathy' of contemporary youth,[11] young people (both Gitano and non-Gitano) are often passionate about politics, social affairs and their local communities (Bermudez, 2012; Galais, 2012; García-Albacete, 2008; Forbig, 2005). The interviews with Gitano youngsters revealed that they are indeed conscious of their role as agents of social change and bare on their shoulders the responsibility of cultural continuity and their transmission to future generations.

ALTERNATIVE GITANO YOUTH ENGAGEMENT: EMERGING "YOUTHSCAPES"

Some scholars point to the changes in political and social youth engagement, which requires the re-assessment of theoretical approaches to youth socio-political participation (Flesher Fominaya, 2014; Rossi, 2009). The youth 'are agents of change, not simple subjects to change' (Ginwright, Noguera, & Cammarota, 2006) and search for ways to get involved, but often on their own terms. The results of my research in Catalonia brings evidence to confirm this supposition. Despite the internal diversity of Gitano 'subjects in a youth condition' (Rossi, 2009), the existing obstacles which block pathways to their direct involvement in the existing structures of Gitano associative movement and despite their own reluctance towards these 'power-structures', the Gitano youth increasingly becomes actively engaged, in majority of cases through forging their own spaces for collective action. In the past years, an increasing number of Gitano young activists, leaders and youth organisations have been emerging throughout Spain and in Catalonia specifically.

One emerging pattern of Gitano youth participation demonstrates that rather than joining the already establishing Gitano NGOs (as members, volunteers or members of the board), the youngsters prefer to establish their own, new youth organisations. In such structures the youth possess the ownership of their own organisative process, sharing decision-making power among members of the Executive Boards, in most cases composed of only young Gitano people. The objectives, scope of activities and level of engagement in public policies may vary, however, all of these newly funded organisations share a common characteristic, namely the will of the youth to transform from passive subjects to becoming active agents who play important roles in their communities. These new organisations face the challenge of positioning themselves *vis-à-vis* the already existing structures of power, mostly concentrated around bigger federations, such as

FAGIC in Catalonia, between 'obeying' and 'rebelling'. In the way the new young leaders relate to the current leadership, two different possibilities are available. On the one hand, these youth-lead organisations may choose to adapt to already existing associative structures, by joining the umbrella organisations, such as FAGIC, a step that the new young leaders seldom take. On the other hand, the vast number of youngsters who are reluctant to join the mainstream Gitano associative movement, prefer being independent from their predecessors and engage in activities autonomously. At the moment, to my knowledge, there are five such organisations operating in metropolitan area of Barcelona (one of those is a young women's organisation).

These organisations rarely federate under larger umbrella organisations, and if so, they seek support from international Roma youth organisations, like TernYpe international Roma Youth Network. These entities often search for council in non-Gitano institutions (such as the regional Youth Council) or gain experience aboard, from other Roma youth organisations. In those cases, they adapt new, innovative strategies of collaboration (greater international participation, openness to collaborate with non-Gitano youth organisations) and determine a modern philosophy of Gitano lifestyle and values. Such organisations are generally funded by young Gitano with higher education and establish new, innovative strategies of collective action and are under strong influence of other European Roma youth leaders. However, two of five youth organisations in Catalonia are funded by non-educated young Gitano men, pointing to initial evidence that these developments are not limited to educated youth only. The young leaders frequently come back to their grassroots communities and try to engage others, although the depth and sustainability of their commitment varies greatly. They often possess a greater mobilising potential to recruit new members – on the one hand, these young leaders are seen as role models who can be looked up to, and on the other hand, their youth methodology and international optic creates new opportunities which older Gitano organisations seldom offer, such as international training courses, travels, photographic or film courses, etc.

These new organizations share a number of characteristic elements, which differentiate them from the already existing ones (note that not all of these elements have to be present in each organisation).

The Youth 'Frame'

Numerous young Roma/Gitano leaders search for a new 'frame' for their social and civic participation, shifting away from the victimist discourse towards a more positive approach. Some part of Roma/Gitano youth activists seek an identity that builds around 'affirmative' elements like ethnic pride rather than negative ones like victimisation perspective. In view of a young non-Roma activist:

> The question remains open how a movement can offer an identity and interest frame, which can overcome a 'stigmatised' identity and 'self-stigmatisation', in order to empower Roma and non-Roma to recognise the root causes of

social exclusion; thus, to establish an empowering mind-set that not Roma are the problem, but their marginalisation and stigmatisation in society. (Mack, 2012)

In some cases the youth perceives itself as more progressive and better prepared in terms of how they frame their struggle in comparison to the older generation:

(…) the young Gitano men and women have an idea about politics much more in tune with the spirit of democracy and human rights than the older generation, at least in Spain. (questionnaire)

The young Gitano leaders share the objective of their struggle with the older generations, but not so much the tone of discourse set by their predecessors. Building on positive, affirmative elements of identity, as well as based on frequently greater *de facto* knowledge, these youngsters construct a sophisticated discourse, which is appealing both to their peers as well as to general public.

How They Do It

The influence of the non-Gitano environment as well as their contact with other Roma youth throughout Europe contribute to the new ways in which Gitano youth participate and mobilises others to actively engage. Especially those Gitano youth organisations who decided to 'do it their own way', seek inspiration from a variety of places. These organisations differ not only in discourse but also in action from the older generation. The youth approach is more inclusive or intercultural – the increased contacts with the non-Gitano world, provided by school and professional environments, result in friendships and a constant dialogue between the minority and the majority. This dialogue is translated into the work of the Gitano youth organisations – today an increased number of non-Gitano activists is invited to take a stand for the Gitano rights along with the Gitano community.

Many of these organisations draw from other youth movements, adapting some of the youth methods such as energisers, informal learning methods or strategies to mobilised others (through sports, artistic trainings or social networks). They also adapt new methods of making their claims visible (through arts, self-generated media, flash mobs etc.) and often join forces and support common youth-related issues.

Additionally, Gitano/Roma youth activists are innovative and open to modern technologies: the Internet and social media work to reach out far beyond their own backyard but also draw inspiration from other youth movements, becoming a tool to increase youth participation. The importance of the Internet has revolutionised the way in which the Gitano youth communicate and organise – a dynamic which has become an important tool for active youth engagement across the globe (Kuzio, 2006; Rossi, 2009; Heredia Trucharte, 2005).

All of these elements contribute to creating a welcoming environment 'where youth feels valued, respected, encouragers and supported' (Jennings et al., 2006) which enhances youth empowerment. The youth engage collectively based on peer-to-peer relationships and the sense of ownership of their work is emplaced, an element important to developing pathways for youth engagement (Camino & Zeldin, 2002).

In Search of Elderly and Community Recognition

Although the youth often decides to engage in their organisations independently from the already existing Gitano organisations, they do so not in spite or against the organisations run by elders. Rather, they engage in their own work because they do not see opportunities for their participation and fulfilment of their ambition within the already existing establishment, but the recognition of their efforts by the rest of the community is essential. In fact, in numerous interviews the youth described that they didn't feel represented or identified by their local organisations which is why they created their own, but they see that they work should be 'supervised by' or recognised by the elders of their communities. In the view of many of young Gitano leaders, '*the youth should participate, it is important to make the way for the youth and raise awareness among people under the approval of the elders*' (questionnaire). Therefore, what the youth seeks is not to compete with the older generation but to be recognised as players in the same part of the field, seeking partnership with the elders. Camino and Zeldin (2002) define youth-adult partnership as one of the key elements to developing the youth potential and engaging them actively. Jennings also defines the 'equitable power-sharing between youth and adults as one of the key dimension for critical youth empowerment' (Jenninngs et al., 2006). The Gitano youth feels that the hostility towards their independent engagement, which at times they encounter is due to the fear the older posses about losing their leadership position:

> The only problem that exists is the distrust between the new associative Roma movements and the economic crisis to receive grants, and not to mention the critics we receive from the elders, which won't be helping us too much because the youth is robbing them of their leadership … (questionnaire)

It seems that counter-balancing such perceptions may involve a type of youth-adult partnership, which will bring mutual benefits to both parties, as well as the Gitano associative movement as a whole.

Finally, the life-span of newly established organisations is difficult to evaluate, considering their relative novelty. However, a number of these new and promising organisations, who have accomplished relative success and recognition, die out as quickly as they have emerged. Further research is necessary to evaluate the reasons behind this short life cycle. Some assumptions may point to the frustration related with such work, disappointment with achieved results, economic and structural difficulties or disenchantment with the process altogether.

CONCLUSIONS

The youth often face numerous obstacles, which block their potential pathways to active engagement. The traditional conservatism of the Gitano community where the elders are power holders, the mutual negative perceptions of youth and elders, generational divide and arising conflicts, lack of identification of youth with their local entities and frustration arising from feeling under-estimated and under-valued by their elders, are some of the factors which often stand in the way to Gitano youth engagement. Despite these difficulties, however, the Gitano youth create their own spaces for participation, where they become protagonists as agents of change in their own communities. In this context, the Gitano youth engagement can be framed in the general developments of youth participation – the Gitano youth too creates their own spaces for active engagement, building their corresponding 'youthscapes' (Maira & Soep, 2004). These spaces of youth engagement differ in strategic 'frames' and discourses established, in methodology and type of activities from the older generation. The Gitano youth also feeds from the developments of contemporary world, eager to use the Internet and social media as a tool for working and engaging others. Some positive trends can be witnessed – the Gitano youth is increasingly aware of the importance of their active engagement, however, rather than yielding to the traditional power of senior leadership, the youth establish their own entities, creating a welcoming environment (Jennings et al., 2006) for other youngsters to mobilise around. These new emerging trends of youth mobilisation – more inclusive, affirmative, technology-friendly and based on networks, may change the paradigm of Gitano participation, reaching far beyond the 'older' ethnic-based movement searching for alternative means of participation, other than the already existing forms of representing collective interests and claims. This process is taking place two-directionally: as internal mobilisation and external mobilisation. In this, the Gitano youth resembles the 'global generation' described by Beck, where rapid changes brought by the process of globalisation are incorporated in the mindset of contemporary youth. Given the existence of the generational gap, separating the older Gitano generations from contemporary Gitano youth, it is necessary to promote spaces of intergenerational dialogue, where adults and youngsters can confront the mutual misconceptions they may hold about each other.

It is important, however, to bear in mind that being young is a temporary condition (Rossi, 2009) and that the notion of youth 'has become an accepted political category rather than just a biological age group' (Belton, 2009). The Gitano youth may choose to raise claims based on their ethnic condition or based on biological or social condition of 'being young' (or both). The majority of Gitano young leaders do not necessarily seek to become recognised only as 'youth activists' but rather obtain a status of integral part of the associative movement. This aligns closely to Rossi's work on youth participation too: 'political participation by young people is not structured by their youth condition, instead activists immerse themselves as much as possible in the same institutional and/or social web they wish to become part of. Thus they do not seek recognition as young people, but rather as activists, facilitators etc'. (Rossi, 2009).

These emerging trends described in this chapter focus on Gitano youth in Catalonia but can also be evidenced across Europe (Mack, 2012). The emergence of a new Roma/Gitano youth leadership scheme locally and across Europe still hasn't been well researched by scholars. However, the demand of the young Roma/Gitano people to be recognised as stakeholders has already brought significant fruits – across Europe, the attention of big institutions such as the EU, the Council of Europe or the OSCE shifts to include Roma youth not only as specific target group but also as partners in consultations and policy-making processes. In Catalonia too, the Gitano young organisations are increasingly present in consultative meetings regarding Gitano-politics (a youth working group has been created in 2010 in the Generalitat de Catalunya).

The phenomenon of increased Gitano youth engagement and the appearance of new patterns of mobilisation of action among youth signals a change in the existing strategy of ethnic mobilisation not only locally, but also throughout Europe. These new leaders face the challenge of defining their role in the existing Gitano/Roma associative movement, and choosing strategic frames, building narratives and undertaking action which will both be appealing to the targeted institutions of power, but also and most importantly, will seek engagement and support of their own communities. These developments should be explored in further research in other regions or countries, from a comparative, and possibly inter-ethnic perspective. The intersection of age, ethnicity, social class and gender indicators should be further explored by scholars in order to understand better the dynamics that underlie this process.

NOTES

[1] The term is borrowed from (Maira & Soep, 2004).

[2] "Roma" is an all-encompassing term used by the majority of international organizations (such as the Council of Europe, the EU or the OSCE) to refer to the diverse panorama of Roma, Gypsy, Traveller, Sinti, *Caló* communities. This generic term, considered politically correct, is used in academic literature and policy-making as a means of simplification (Bereményi & Mirga, 2012). However, the term Gitano is used in this article to refer to Spanish Roma communities (also known as *Caló*) in order to contextualize the described group. Where the comments or literature refer to the plethora of Roma communities, the term Roma or Roma/Gitano is used.

[3] The dissertation project "Roma in Europe and beyond: Comparative study of Roma associative movements in Latin America and Europe" is conducted under the supervision of dra. Silvia Carrasco Pons and dr. Bálint-Ábel Bereményi, at the Department of Social and Cultural Anthropology of the Autonomous University in Barcelona.

[4] As a staff member of FAGIC and as founding member of one Gitano youth association.

[5] Nonetheless, the reader should note, that the vast majority of young Gitano who are engaged in one way or another in ethnic mobilization, tend to fall under the last two groups, rather than the first one. Furthermore, the vast majority of my interlocutors are concentrated in Barcelona metropolitan area, which is also an additional, relevant factor.

[6] The reader should note that I have excluded from the sample the assessment of Gitano youth participation in non-Gitano organizations. Throughout my research, this theme has not appeared – the only moments in which Gitano youth claimed to have participated in non-Gitano entities was

strictly instrumental, as beneficiaries of training courses or scholarships. However, I have no knowledge if my informants have voluntarily joined other causes, un-related to the Gitano movement. This aspect requires further research in order to assess the cross-ethnic participation of Gitano youth.

[7] There has been an extensive debate among scholars and activists whether the global Roma/Gitano-rights struggle can in fact be regarded as a social movement (Vermeersch, 2006; McGarry, 2012; Mirga & Gheorghe, 2001). In this article, rather than the Roma movement, I use the term "Roma/ Gitano associative movement(s)". The term "associative movement" draws from the Spanish nomenclature (*movimiento associativo*) which refers to the activity of civil society sector of the population, organized principally around local associations (Marbán Gallego). Roma/ Gitano associative movement refers then to the agglomeration of the diverse Gitano organizations, which although are varied in character and scope of activity, share the commitment to work with Gitano population and are lead (completely or in part) by Gitano leaders. From a theoretical standpoint, the definition and characterization of the "associative movement" can be searched for at the intersection of civil society considerations and theories of social movements.

[8] It is important to acknowledge that due to the lower life expectancy among the Gitano population, individuals over 50 can be considered as "elders", especially in terms of their social role within the communities. According to studies, only 19% of the Roma population is over 45 years old (compared to 39% among the general non-Roma population) (Laparra Navarro, 2007). Other data demonstrates that only 9% of the Roma population is over 54 years old (for non-Roma population 27% of the population is over 54 years old) (National Roma Integration Strategy in Spain 2012-2020).

[9] This reflects a major shift in Roma-related policies in Catalonia and throughout Europe, where the youth has become the principal target group of international institution such as the EU institutions, the Council of Europe or the OSCE.

[10] Among the reasons for not feeling identified with the existing Gitano organizations, the youth pointed to: limited representativeness, relatively small success and efficiency, divided leadership, incompetent organizations, lack of clear strategic objectives, lack of mass support, unclear motivation for getting engaged. It is interesting to note that these elements, enumerated by the youth (but also some adult Gitano leaders) have also been identified by scholars (Barany, 2002; Trehan & Sigona 2010; van Baar, 2011; McGarry, 2012).

[11] In recent years, both academics and policy-makers have been alarmed by the perceived lack of political or community engagement among young people (Flesher Fominaya, 2014; Forbig, 2005; Galais, 2012). Numerous studies demonstrate that the youth are more reluctant to participate in formal politics, through political parties or through casting votes. According to Bermudez, "the resulting 'diagnosis' for youth worldwide, when compared to previous generations, is that they exhibit growing apathy, a loss of interest in civic and political affairs, an avoidance of electoral and other democratic responsibilities and little investment in community wellbeing" (Bermudez, 2012). This hypothesis of "growing apathy" has been re-assessed by scholars, arguing that the relatively lower level of involvement of contemporary youth doesn't necessarily demonstrate their apathy, but rather point to changes in ways the youth mobilize around social and political issues, on the one hand, and to the existing obstacles to youth engagement, on the other.

REFERENCES

Abajo, E., & Carrasco, S. (2004). *Experiencias y trayectorias de éxito escolar de Gitanas y Gitanos en España. Encrucijadas sobre educación, género y cambio cultural.* Madrid.

Barany, Z. (2002). Ethnic mobilisation without prerequisites: The East European gypsies. *World Politics, 54*(3), 277-307.

Barth, F. (1969). *Ethnic groups and boundaries: The social organization of culture difference.* Little, Brown and Company.

Beck, U., & Beck-Gernsheim, E. (2007). *Generacion global*. Paidos.

Belton, B. (2009). *Developing critical youth work theory. Building professional judgment in the community context*. Rotterdam: Sense Publishers.

Bereményi, B. Á., & Mirga, A. (2012). *Lost in action? Evaluating the 6 years of the comprehensive plan for the Gitano population in Catalonia*. FAGiC and EMIGRA/CER-M.

Bermudez, A. (2012). Youth civic engagement: Decline or transformation? A critical review. *Journal of Moral Education, 41*(4), 529-542.

Bourdieu, P. (1977). *Outline of a theory of practice*. Cambridge University Press.

Calvo, K. (2013). Fighting for a voice: The Spanish 15-M movement. In C. Flesher Fominaya & L. Cox (Eds.), *Understanding European movements: New social movements, global justice struggles, anti-austerity protest* (p. 288). London: Routledge.

Camino, L., & Zeldin, S. (2002). From periphery to center: Pathways for youth civic engagement in the day-to-day life of communities. *Applied Developmental Science, 6*(4), October, 213-220.

Carrasco, S., & Beremenyi, B. A. (2011). The cultures of Roma and language. *Green Perspectives on Roma and Traveller Inclusion*.

Carrasco, S. (2007). *Informe sobre inmigració i participació social a Catalunya des de les práctiques locals*. Barcelona.

Colley, H., & Hodkinson, P. (2001). Problems with bridging the gap: The reversal of structure and agency in addressing social exclusion. *Critical Social Policy, 21*(3), August, 335-359.

Collier, D. (1993). The comparative method. *Political Science: The State of Discipline II*.

Crozier, M., & Friedberg., E. (1982). *Człowiek i system. Organiczenia działania zespołowego*. Warszawa: Panstwowe Wydawnictwo Ekonomiczne.

Encuentro Fundación. (1996). *España 1995. Una interpretación de su realidad social*. Madrid.

Encuentro Fundación. (1999). *Informe España 1998. Una interpretación de su realidad social*. Madrid.

Flesher Fominaya, C. (2014). Youth participation in contemporary European social movements. http://youth-partnership-eu.coe.int/youth-partnership/ekcyp/BGKNGE/Youth_and_social_mouvements.html. Accessed January 20, 2014.

Flesher Fominaya, C. (2011). The Madrid bombings and popular protest: misinformation, counter-information, mobilisation and elections after "11-M". *Contemporary Social Sciences, 6*(3), 289-307.

Forbig, J. (Ed.). (2005). *Revisiting youth political participation*. Council of Europe.

Fraser, A. (1995). *The gypsies*. Wiley.

Fundació Pere Tarrés. (2006). *Estudi sobre la població Gitana a Catalunya. Informe final*.

Fundalmental Rights Agency. (2012). *The situation of Roma in 11 EU member states. Survey results at a glance*.

Fundalmental Rights Agency. (2013). *Analysis of FRA Roma survey results by gender*.

Galais, C. (2012). ¿Cada vez más apáticos? El desinterés político juvenil en España en perspectiva comparada. *Revista Internacional de Sociología, 70*(1), February, 107-127.

García-Albacete, G. (2008). ¿Apatía política? Evolución de la implicación de la juventud Española desde los años 80'. *Revista de Estudios de Juventud, 81*, 133-159.

Ginwright, S., Noguera P., & Cammarota, J. (2006). *Beyond resistance! Youth activism and community change. New democratic possibilities for practice and policy for America's youth*. New York: Routledge. Taylor & Francis Group.

Heredia Trucharte, M. (2005). "Entrar y salir, entrar y mirar, entrar y quedarse". Fases metodológicas a una aproximación etnográfica virtual Gitana. *Periferia, 3*, 1-19.

Jennings, L., Deborah, B., Parra-Medina, M., Hilfinger Messias, D., & Mcloughlin, K. (2006). Toward a critical social theory of youth empowerment. *Journal of Community Practice, 14*(1/2), 31-55.

Kuzio, T. (2006). Civil society, youth and societal mobilization in democratic revolutions. *Communist and Post-Communist Studies, 39*(3), September, 365-386.

Laparra Navarro, M. (2007). *Informe sobre la situación social y tendencias de cambio en la comunidad Gitana. Una primera aproximación*. Madrid.

Lijphart, A. (1971). Comparative politics and the comparative method. *The American Political Science Review, 65*(3), 682-693.

Mack, J. (2012). The *social movement of Roma in Europe. Chance and problems of transnational social movement coalitions for empowerment and grassroots mobilization: The case study of ternYpe international Roma youth network*. Freie Universität Berlin.

Maira, S., & Soep, E. (Eds.). (2004). *Youthscapes. The popular, the national, the global*. University of Pennsylvania Press.

Marbán Gallego, V. (2004). Una fotografía actual del movimiento asociativo. In *Congreso 'Nuevos Retos y una Causa Común'. Agencia para el Voluntariado y las Asociaciones de Bizkaia*. Bilbao.

Marcus, G. E. (1995). Ethnography in/of the world system: The emergence of multi-sited ethnography. *Annual Review of Anthropology, 24*(1), October, 95-117.

Marushiakova, E., & Vesselin P. (2005). The Roma – A nation without a state? Historical background and contemporary tendencies. In W. Burszta, T. Kamusella, & S. Wojciechowski (Eds.), *Nationalismus across the globe: An overview of the nationalism of state-endowed and stateless nations* (pp. 433-455). Poznan: School of Humanities and Journalism.

McAdam, D., McCarthy, J. D., & Zald, M. (1996). *Comparative perspectives on social movements. Political opportunities, mobilizing structures, and cultural framings*. Cambridge University Press.

McGarry, A. (2012). *Who speaks for Roma?: Political representation of a transnational minority community*. Blumsbury Academic.

Méndez López, C. (2005). *Por el camino de la participación. Una aproximación contrastada a los procesos de integración social y política de los Gitanos y las Gitanas*. Universitat Autonoma de Barcelona.

Mirga, A., & Gheorghe, N. (2001). *The Roma in the twenty-first century: A policy paper*.

National Roma Integration Strategy in Spain 2012-2020.

Olzak, S. (1983). Contemporary ethnic mobilization. *Annual Review of Sociology, 9*(1), August, 355-374.

Pérez Díaz, V., & López Novo, J. P. (2003). *El tercer sector social en España*. Madrid.

Putnam, R. D., Leonardi R., & Nanetti, R. Y. (1994). *Making democracy work: Civic traditions in modern Italy*. Princeton University Press.

Rossi, F. M. (2009). Youth political participation: Is this the end of generational cleavage? *International Sociology, 24*(4), June, 467-497.

Rostas, I. (2012). Roma participation: From manipulation to citizen control. *Roma Rights. Journal of the European Roma Rights Center*.

Salamon, L. (1994). The rise of the nonprofit sector. *Foreign Affairs, 74*(3).

Tilly, C. (1978). *From mobilization to revolution*. Addison-Wesley Pub. Co.

Trehan, N., & Sigona, N. (Eds.). (2010). *Romani politics in contemporary Europe*. Palgrave Macmillan.

Tremlett, A. (2009). Bringing hybridity to heterogeneity in Romani studies. *Romani Studies, 19*(1), December, 65-86.

Van Baar, H. (2011). *The European Roma. Minority representation, memory and the limits of transnational governmentality*. University of Amsterdam.

Vermeersch, P. (2006). *The Romani movement: Minority politics and ethnic mobilization in contemporary Central Europe*. New York: Berghahn.

Yin, R. K. (2009). *Case study research: Design and methods*. Edited by L. Bickman & D. J. Rog, *Essential Guide to Qualitative Methods in Organizational Research*. Applied Social Research Methods Series, Vol. 5. Sage Publications.

BRIAN BELTON

CONCLUSION

The hoped for joint effect of this clutch of chapters, this little world of words, is that you will have seen demonstrated something of the diversity of practice, its motivation, aims and how it is understood or justified. This has shown, thankfully, that while youth work 'is', it is no one thing, despite the efforts of many 'experts' to corral it under one designation or another (using quite ugly terms such as 'informal education' and 'social pedagogy').

As you might have concluded after reading this book, youth work remains confoundingly (and for me pleasingly) diverse, both in terms of delivery and ideology. It is undertaken within an ongoing process of piecemeal change and reassessment, often manifested by small scale operations and actions, by a mobile (hard to find and harder to hit) mostly volunteer, part-time workforce and a relatively few full-time paid practitioners. Many of the latter and not a few of the former are intent on improving delivery and response generally (creating and maintaining professional standards).

Within the various modes of operation, the ranges of tasks, expectations and duties of youth workers have maintained a learning purpose. While this function moves from a central aim to part of a repertoire or a suite of operations, consistently young people have used youth work to learn about themselves, others and the world, while youth workers have been able to be educated by their clients that they might be of maximum utility to them.

But the youth worker, just as they are not a social worker, is not a teacher; youth work is not essentially didactic in character and although anyone having spent any time in youth work will recognise it a conduit of learning, increasingly throughout my own career I have become more and more doubtful if youth work is, in some sort of fundamental manner, educational. Learning in youth work, if it is true to itself, is not mediated via a systematic (formulaic) structure or any definite structure at all. To this extent youth work is not educational in any way that is meaningful in terms of the way that concept is generally understood; an organised, planned and largely regimented, mostly externally defined procedure, delivered via a curriculum, set in the frameworks of schools, colleges and universities

YOUTH WORK AND EDUCATION

When thinking about this, it is important to keep in mind that education and learning are not necessarily synonymous. Learning is the result of the internal processes and interactions of mind and brain; education refers to structures, practices and techniques that, in terms of the mind and brain, are external. For

B. Belton (ed.), 'Cadjan – Kiduhu': Global Perspectives on Youth Work, 211–218.
© 2014 Sense Publishers. All rights reserved.

many of us, the experience of these structures, procedures and method (treatment) was less about learning and more about forms of management and memorisation; we experienced education as the imposition of an essentially external system that we recognised, at first unconsciously perhaps, as being aimed at controlling our behaviour, brain and mind. The likes of me rebelled and initially suffered the physical and mental retribution of the system (random and arranged beatings, ritual and casual humiliation). However, on continued resistance, along with my mutinous peers, I graduated to higher institutions for the advancement of conformity, which often deployed more subtle forms of coercion, disguised as 'persuasion' and often called 'choice' and/or 'an opportunity for change'; '*A Clockwork Orange*' lite. However, to quote Neil Tennant and Chris Lowe (and as parts of this book perhaps testify) 'They didn't quite succeed' – but 10 out of 10 for trying!

Many teachers of course also resist the tyranny of educational institutions. Indeed good and useful training will help them to do this, cultivating learning environments rather than merely making the machinery of education 'work' on people. Certainly, the learning that happens as part of youth work can be understood by way of educational thinkers and the experience of teachers who have understood the more oppressive aspects of the will to put people though the vast education apparatus that exists throughout our society. For instance John Holt, a teacher and writer had a pretty controversial take on education – outstanding themes in his thinking include:
- Formal schooling often destroys the natural love of learning.
- Extrinsic rewards are ultimately harmful to learners.
- People learn the best from real-life experiences.
- Education should be driven by the learner.

In the first part of his teaching career Holt endeavoured to reform the educational system. He looked to work with children so that they could become more conscious learners, rather than merely involve them in memorising facts (that are all too easily forgotten). Holt looked to engage young people in their learning (not just follow a teacher). In practice this sometimes means more not helping than helping, allowing a process of curiosity and inventiveness to thrive. But Holt ultimately concluded that efforts to reform would not achieve large-scale changes in schools. He argued that children do poorly in school because they're bored with meaningless work, but at the same time are scared of being punished or humiliated. He also had it that they are confused because most teaching progresses from abstract concepts to concrete examples instead of (as would be more sensible) the other way around. He concluded, after long-term observation and teaching, that school is a place where children learn to be stupid. I, over the last few years, have come to see most educational institutions as being equally calculable in this respect, including a great deal of what is passed off as youth work in the UK.

For Holt the rewards offered for academic achievement and conformist behaviour, not unusually turned students off to learning. According to him people will learn because they want to learn and rewards (things like stickers and stars) encourage an irrational motivation that in the last analysis harms learners. In essence this is because the satisfaction of curiousness for its own sake is not taken as enough reward for learning and that much time is spent trying to teach people about stuff they are not, or have not become, interested in. But Holt argued that if you take somebody who's doing something for her or his own pleasure and offer some kind of extrinsic reward for doing it, and allow the person become accustomed to performing the task for that reward, when that incentive is taken away, the individual will stop that activity. He had it that one can even train nursery school children who love to draw to stop drawing by giving them gold stars, or some other little bonus, for a while and then removing that artificial motivation.

His position seems to chime with that many youth workers come to the practice with, because many of them have been more or less failed or been let down by education.

Holt had it that learning is not the result of teaching, but of the curiosity and activity of the learner. For Holt, teacher intervention into this process should mostly be devoted to providing the learner with access to different kinds of places, people, experiences, tools, and books that will;
– correspond with the student's interests
– answer questions when they're asked
– demonstrate physical skills.
While he campaigned for learner-directed education, Holt didn't idealise childhood or encourage people to take a simple way out. He didn't support 'therapeutic' methods, which involve telling someone, 'You're OK, you're really wonderful'. He believed that tackling a job that seems worth doing, and doing it in a competent way, is the most effective means to build the self-esteem required to build on learning experiences.

According to Holt, people are most capable when they were completely free to learn. Although traditional educators often view his writings as 'over radical', quite a few of Holt's ideas have found their way into mainstream thinking and many adults turn to his books looking to understand their educational experiences.

Nonetheless I have found that it is sometimes hard for educators (sometimes youth workers describe themselves primarily as such – presumably understanding those they work with as relatively ignorant) to accept that folk can 'just learn'; that learning is natural to them, a consequence of human ingenuity and inquisitiveness. At the same time we fail to grasp this is a consequence of our own indoctrination; our ideas about learning are bounded by the extent of our 'false consciousness'. While Marx didn't actually use this phrase (although he wrote a lot about related concepts – ideology, 'mystification' and 'commodity fetishism') the notion is drawn from Marxist theory of social class. This is concerned with the systematised distortion of prevailing social relations in the consciousness of exploited groups. The latter suffer from false consciousness because their understanding, awareness of and education about prevailing social relations are effectively hidden and so obscure the realities of their own oppression via exploitation (and domination of those relations).

While this is not the time or place to write at any length about this subject, it is perhaps useful to reflect on the words of Marcus Garvey, laid out in song by Bob Marley; "...emancipate yourself from mental slavery, none but ourselves can free our mind ...". However Garvey's next line is not used by Marley;

> The man who is not able to develop and use his mind is bound to be the slave of the other man who uses his mind.

We have, sort of, just got to 'snap out of it'. But for one to voice such an expectation or hypothesis to another probably takes a certain amount of courage, bravery and respect for the other person; it is a blunt statement for sure. However, this might be the sort of advice George Dennison might give us in relation to our situation. An educator and writer, Dennison put forward the idea that relationships, not instruction, promoted authentic learning. For him, learning can only flourish in places where freedom of choice gives rise to trust, which in turn can facilitate meaningful associations between learners and those charged with taking responsibility for other people's learning.

Dennison's approach (like Holt's) was considered radical because it questioned enforced attendance of educational establishments and problematised the way educators concentrate on the external behaviour of learners as a means of managing them. For him, making the controlling of learner behaviour the focal point of school/education limits the level of relationship that can exist between learner and teacher. As such, Dennison favoured small learning situations, which implies a critique of large schools, questioning the ability of such institutions to work effectively.

According to Dennison, teaching is an art, not (as often mooted) a science; this being the case, the application of techniques will not promote learning. What for him is required is the understanding and enhancement of the full complexity of individual associations between learners and teachers. He argues that the latter is not reducible to the supposed predictability of technique. Dennison believed that significant learning occurs strictly within the learner's individual motivation and between learning peers, when the teachers are aware enough to step back and give such a situation a chance to happen.

The latter paragraph might be informative to proponents of informal education and social pedagogical approaches, who while manoeuvring to cultivate relationships (a form of subtle manipulation) with young people (using a number of clandestine strategies and tactics; see Belton, 2009) at the same time operate by and initiate a range of techniques to initiate (often covert) means of 'education' (pedagogy).

The above can make for hard reading, especially if much of one's life has been given up to instructing, and yes there are plenty of people that look to be instructed, as it makes for a sort of 'free ride'; you just do as you're told and thinking is kept to a minimum. However, I'm not sure those of us interested in learning should encourage this, although we might well need to cater for it. But I know these last few lines might be way too much for some readers. A classic work relating this area is Adorno, Frenkel-Brunswik, Levinson and Sanford (1950). This proposed that prejudice is a consequence of one's personality type. Adorno et al. (ibid.) developed and piloted a questionnaire, the 'F-scale' and concluded that deep-seated personality characteristics inclined some people to have more authoritarian perspectives.

Those scoring higher on the F-scale were rated as having authoritarian personalities, tending to be relatively rigid in their opinions and beliefs and comparatively conventional (upholding traditional values, etc.). They had more of a propensity to follow and take orders. Adorno et al. (ibid.) argued that authoritarian personalities are also liable to categorise people, dividing others into 'us' and 'them' (children and adults, learners and teachers for instance) seeing their own group ('us') as superior to others ('them') and as such more inclined to show discrimination, prone to stereotyping and prejudice. The self-proclaimed 'educators' (us) can as such comfortably identify a comparatively ignorant group (them) and proceed to do their thing, in the case of many of those supposedly involved in informal education without any attempt at a learning needs assessment beforehand; the need for 'education' is just taken as said. This is stereotyping and prejudicial and an attitude that has clear roots in colonial society.

There are, of course, flaws in the above position. Some bigoted/intolerant people do not conform to the authoritarian personality type. At the same time the findings of Adorno et.al. (ibid.) fail to tell us why people are prejudice against certain groups and not others. Neither does it explain how whole social groups (e.g. Fascists) might be prejudiced; it would mean that all members of a group would have authoritarian personalities, which seems improbable.

Cultural or social norms would appear to offer other explanations of prejudice. For example, Hyman and Sheatsley (1956: 35-39) found that those with lower educational levels tended towards higher F-scale scores. There is some suggestion of circularity here, or a form of Freudian compensation; those who do not do so well in education perhaps having the potential to be amongst the most ardent educators? However, the value of this research might indicate how hard it is to give up prejudice about what we might convince ourselves, for whatever reason, to be the nature of things. There is a possibility of course that such attitudes are not helped by, or might even be the/a source of, the education system and attitudes to learning that arise out of the same. This would be a viscous line of causation:

Authoritarian learning systems – Authoritarian personalities – Authoritarian learning systems

Paul Goodman, an influential anarchist critic of contemporary education, seemed to be on to something like this. For him (in our society), schools and the mass media convince people that our existence is unavoidably depersonalised and mundane and that most of us learn that life is inevitably routine. We are thus alienated as we are convinced that everything has a price.

Goodman argues that the concomitant attitude this produces cause us to believe;
- that we are best served by shutting up and conforming
- that there is no place for spontaneity, open sexuality and free spirit.

According to Goodman, this product of school training (education in our society) is carried into employment, culture and politics. He saw that this education is really 'miseducation', socializing us to follow particular norms and regimenting people to effectively fit into or champion the cause of the capitalist society (ultimately exploitation and continued alienation).

Goodman believed that the most valuable experiences in a person's education happen via experiences that promote learning outside of the school. As such, taking part in the activities of society should be the main means of learning. So instead of obliging learners to submit to the theoretical grind of memorising the content of textbooks, he suggests that the emphasis in terms of learning should be moved from the school into work places, museums, parks, shops and so on, where learners can actively participate in what they are learning about.

In this situation the ideal schools (for Goodman) would take the form of small (under 20 people) discussion groups. These groups would make use of any effective environment that would be appropriate to the interest of the group. This type of learning environment would be non-compulsory (for Goodman, compulsion hinders and obstructs people's capacity to learn – see Chappell, 1978: 357-372), as compulsion to attend passes authority to an external body, detached from the needs and ambitions of the learners. This is pretty much what some might recognise as the optimal youth work environment.

Herbert Kohl (1994) provides forceful reminders that contemporaneously accepted notions of choice in the context of school might be camouflaging deep-seated educational issues.

Kohl (1992) is a passionate advocate for learners, the folk he sees most overlooked in the discourse relating to classroom failure. He argues that 'not-learning' is a deliberate option taken by pupils and students who grasp – often pretty swiftly in their careers in education – that the school, as a system, works to compel them to adhere to a particular and definite set of values and concomitant behaviour. This physical and psychological process is often alien or even repulsive to them. According to Kohl, in one way or another, this leads to them being diagnosed (the process is not unusually medicalised or set in the context of an aberrant psychological disposition) when their resistance and disillusion are far more rational than compromising to what is effectively an oppressive regime. Any combination of labels is consequentially applied, for amateur diagnosis of psychological maladies from 'lack of self-esteem' to suggesting forms 'learning-disability' to (colloquially) stupidity and blatant anti-authoritarian behaviour. Sadly such categorisations have become more and more common in youth work settings over the last couple of decades.

For all this, for Kohl, children who seem unable to learn in institutional contexts may well have essentially opted out of the system, focusing their intelligence and creativity outside school and/or on resisting what they understand as a heartless/pointless/punishing institution.

In *The Tattooed Man* (in Kohl, 1994) Kohl argues that, before anything can be achieved, educators need be aware of the sense hopelessness students can feel/experience in the school setting. Two other chapters (ibid.) look at the 'norming of excellence' and 'political correctness'. The final chapter echoes Martin Luther King's plea that we become, 'maladjusted' to injustice and inequity. For Kohl 'Creative maladjustment' is "… learning to survive with minimal moral and personal compromise in a thoroughly compromised world". As I grow old I am tempted to think that the youth work, and even the higher education of youth workers that I have been involved in for decades, is and has been involved in the facilitation of 'creative maladjustment'.

According to Kohl, the blame for the failure of schools and educators is far too often placed on children. Overall Kohl calls on us to act, to refuse to consign young people to forms of 'special education' (which of course, in the experience of the student, can mean all sorts of coercion). In short Kohl offers an opportunity to build a humanitarian emphasis to discussions that often are premised on statements like 'Jane can't read'.

A WORLD OF RESPONSIVENESS

All useful, ethical or good (pick your own word there) professionals would want their clients to learn by way of their expertise and/or association. The nurse would hope his patient would learn how to keep well by their interaction; the social worker might work so that the help she gives can help her client to help themselves. In the best of possible worlds the banker (even!) would want the saver to invest their money wisely and the police officer, in the course of her duty, might do what she can to make sure those she warns or protects will understand something more about themselves in relation to the law. As such it would not be surprising if in the course of spending time with and alongside a youth worker a young person might learn something, but you can learn something from being chained for years to a radiator (see Keenan, 1991; Keenan & McCarthy, 1999).

This said, the multiplicity of responses and the flexible, fluctuating trajectory of youth work has historically, socially and globally been its strength. Youth workers have been able to turn their collective hand to such a range of social tasks, from responding to unemployment and crime to working to combat sexually transmitted disease, from projects with the homeless to promoting health and fun through sport and play. This plasticity has been part of the survival and preservation of the practice. Youth work has been understood as educative and welfare oriented, a means of facilitating learning and extending care, a conduit of social reform and a function to extend social conformity; at points any combination of these at the same time. That we have been able to react and operate with facility and agility is a remarkable tribute to those who have involved themselves in the work, either as young people or practitioners.

So youth work has been able to change direction according to what societies require of it, but we, the youth workers, keep young people at the centre of this; we task ourselves, our responses and our service to be shaped, at base, by them. 'It's a sin' (maybe) but 'we don't need no education' (or pedagogy) – ours is a guerrilla profession.

REFERENCES

Adorno, T. W., Frenkel-Brunswik, E., Levinson, D. J., & Sanford, R. N. (1950). *The authoritarian personality.* New York: Harper and Row.

Belton, B. (2009). *Radical youth work.* Lyme Regis: Russell House.

Chappell, R. H. (1978). Anarchy revisited: An inquiry into the public education dilemma. *Journal of Libertarian Studies, 2*(4), 357-372.

Davis, H. (24 March 2010). *Emancipate yourselves from mental slavery: The origin and meaning behind Bob Marley's redemption song* and *The work that has been done.* http://henriettavintondavis.wordpress.com/2010/03/24/redemption-song/. Retrieved 1/6/14.

Goodman, P. (1960). *Growing up absurd: Problems of youth in the organized system.* New York: Random House.

Goodman, P. (1961). *Compulsory mis-education.* London: Victor Gollancz.

Holt, J. (1967). *How children learn.* New York: Pitman.

Holt, J. (1969). *The underachieving school.* New York: Pitman.

Holt, J. (1972). *Freedom and beyond.* New York: Dutton.

Holt, J. (1974). *Escape from childhood: The needs and rights of children.* New York.

Holt, J. (1976). *Instead of education: Ways to help people do things better.* New York: Dutton.

Holt, J. (1995). *How children fail.* New York: Perseus.

Hyman, H. H., & Sheatsley, P. N. (1956). Attitudes toward desegregation. *Scientific American, 195,* 35-39.

Keenan, B. (1991). *An evil cradling.* Harmondsworth: Penguin Books.

Keenan, B., & McCarthy, J. (1999). *Between extremes.* London: Bantam Press.

Kohl, H. (1991). *I won't learn from you! The role of assent in learning.* Minneapolis, MN: Milkweed Editions: Thistle Series of Essays.

Kohl, H. (1992). *From archetype to zeitgeist: Powerful ideas for powerful thinking.* Boston: Little, Brown.

Kohl, H. (1994). *I won't learn from you: And other thoughts on creative maladjustment.* New York: New Press.

Lightning Source UK Ltd.
Milton Keynes UK
UKOW07f1512191114

241847UK00001BA/26/P